TRANS-
GENDERED

The Center for Lesbian and Gay Studies in Religion and Ministry

Pacific School of Religion
1798 Scenic Avenue
Berkeley, California 94709
Phone: (800) 999-0528
Fax: (510) 849-8212
www.clgs.org

TRANS-GENDERED

Theology, Ministry, and Communities of Faith

JUSTIN TANIS

THE
PILGRIM
PRESS
Cleveland

The Pilgrim Press
700 Prospect Avenue East
Cleveland, Ohio 44115-1100
pilgrimpress.com

Printed in the United States of America on acid-free paper

08   07   06   05   04   03   5   4   3   2   1

Library of Congress Cataloging-in-Publication Data
Tanis, Justin Edward, 1965-
    Trans-gendered: theology, ministry, and communities of faith / Justin Edward
    Tanis.
        p.   cm.
    Includes bibliographical references (p.).
    ISBN 0-8298-1528-7 (pbk. : alk. paper)
    1. Transsexualism – Religious aspects – Christianity. 2. Christian
transsexuals – Religious life. I. Title: Transgendered. II. Title.
BR115.T76T36 2003
230'.086'6 – dc21
                                                        2003043391

Contents

Foreword

The book that you hold in your hands is a work of love by Rev. Dr. Justin Tanis. It is about God, gender identity, sexual orientation, and Scripture. It is also about faith, community, and Christology, all from the vantage point of transgendered persons. God's creation is filled with incredible diversity, and that includes gender diversity. This work is a reminder that all people of faith have much to learn from our transgendered brothers and sisters.

Over the centuries, the church has struggled with an amazing array of personal, ethical, and societal issues — and today, two thousand years after Christ walked among humankind, the church still struggles with issues of gender diversity.

My formative years were spent in the Pentecostal Church — a church with rigid gender boundaries. I still remember how the Levitical texts of the Hebrew Scriptures, quoted in old King James English without linguistic or historical context, became a pretext for imposing the societal norms of the U.S. South in the 1950s upon the church of my youth. Far too often the church has filtered the biblical texts through the prejudices or misinformation of the day to justify society's biases.

The combination of societal prejudices and poor hermeneutics, for example, led the church of my childhood to teach that it was a sin for a man to wear women's clothes or a woman to wear men's clothes. The church even imposed very specific gender requirements around one's physical appearance: Women's clothing was to be modest, usually defined by the church as long-sleeved dresses cut beneath the knee. Women were not to cut their hair and men were not to have long hair. Gender deviation from the societal norm of that day was threatening to the church.

I had my first awareness of gender diversity in 1953. I ran away from home at the age of thirteen, taking a Greyhound bus from Daytona Beach, Florida, to my uncle's farm in southern Georgia. I still vividly recall that the bus stopped in the last little rural town in northern Florida, just before we crossed the state line. A passenger boarded the bus — a passenger whose appearance shocked my young and naive sensibilities. I wasn't alone. I clearly recall the look of shock on the faces of my fellow passengers. Society still had little knowledge, and even less understanding, of gender variation. The passenger who boarded the bus appeared to be a man; he was wearing men's pants and shoes. But he also wore a woman's blouse and makeup. This passenger only rode with us for five miles, but it was the quietest bus ride I ever witnessed. This person stepped off the bus at the next stop and the doors closed behind him; the bus driver then awkwardly announced loud enough for everyone to hear, "That was a hermaphrodite." For the next hour of my journey, the bus was filled with the sound of passengers whispering about what we had just witnessed. But it would take me many years to begin to understand the price that passenger — and tens of thousands of persons like him — had paid in a society filled with ignorance and misunderstanding. I've often wondered what that passenger, in turn, thought about all of us on that bus, and our palpable lack of understanding and compassion.

One of the spiritual callings for all human beings is to continue to learn and grow throughout the course of our lives. I am so thankful for the lessons I have learned — and continue to learn — from my transgendered brothers and sisters, and thankful for the many ways the lives of transgendered people have touched and enriched my own.

In October 1968, I conducted the first worship service of what was to become a new denomination: Metropolitan Community Churches (MCC). From the earliest days of the MCC movement, our churches were places where people who had experienced misunderstanding and rejection in other faith communities could worship openly, just as God created them. At the outset, MCC churches reached out primarily to gay and lesbian people of faith.

Many gay men and lesbians, I discovered, had been made to feel unwelcome in many faith communities, and so the MCC movement grew quickly. It wasn't long before I discovered that people in the bisexual community also desired to participate in a faith community where they could integrate their God-given sexuality with their Christian spirituality.

During this wave of international growth in the MCC denomination, I insisted that our churches must be open and welcoming and affirming of all people who wished to worship God as the authentic people God had created them to be.

The next step in my own faith journey was a growing understanding of transgendered and intersexed persons.

In the early years of MCC, we held a social hour after worship services. These times were opportunities for our members to meet and interact, and we always invited a wide range of people from our community to speak to our members. One of our earliest speakers was an African American man by the name of Sajie who entertained as a female impersonator. Sajie described with humor and pathos how as a heterosexual man he entertained crowds as a female impersonator. But Sajie did far more than entertain. He also taught us lifelong lessons that have helped free us from the self-imposed limitations of gender stereotypes.

Soon after, Virginia Prince spoke to a gathering of our MCC church members. Virginia was a heterosexual male who lived his life openly in female clothing. Virginia did not do this for entertainment purposes as did Sajie; Virginia felt an innate comfort and connection with female attire and lived his life in authenticity. Virginia's acceptance and comfort with her own transgendered nature was another powerful step in breaking down rigid and unnecessary gender stereotypes in Metropolitan Community Churches.

In 1971 — three years after the founding of Metropolitan Community Churches — I received our first transgendered worshiper into membership in our local congregation in Los Angeles, California. Connie Vaughn was a male-to-female transgendered person. I owe a debt of gratitude to Connie, and to her partner, Pat, a wonderful lesbian. They were deeply in love with each other, and I admired the dedication and commitment they brought to their relationship. Connie was a wonderful addition to Metropolitan Community Churches, serving as editor of our early newsletters and helping to open doors of understanding for many in the trans communities.

The greater church is also blessed by the contributions of the Rev. Dr. Justin Tanis, author of this book and a leader in the growing transgender spirituality movement.

It was my privilege to know Dr. Tanis before his female-to-male transition. In 1990, I met the then Rev. Maggie Tanis, who had recently graduated from Harvard Divinity School and had accepted her first pastorate with Metropolitan Community Churches in Honolulu, Hawaii. I followed Maggie's ministry with interest, and she later served as associate pastor of Metropolitan Community Church of San Francisco, California. In this capacity I saw firsthand her commitment to community-based ministry and to social justice issues.

In 1996, Rev. Tanis joined the denominational headquarters staff of Metropolitan Community Churches as director of clergy development. In this role she advised MCC clergy, supervised our denominational educational programs, and prepared local church resources. She became a trusted colleague in ministry.

One day shortly after Maggie began her duties as MCC's director of clergy development, our chief operating officer advised me that Maggie was beginning her own transition from female to male and that she wanted me to know that she was beginning this process. I assured our COO that we would be fully supportive of Maggie's transition. Thanks to MCC's commitment to sexual and gender variation, many of our churches now had transgendered members and we had transgendered clergy; a transgendered person, Rev. Elder Wilhelmina Hein, had served on the Board of Elders, the spiritual leaders of our MCC churches. I watched Maggie go through her chrysalis and come out on the other side as Justin. Just as Maggie was an intelligent and capable young woman, Justin is an intelligent and capable young man.

A wonderful thing happened at our MCC General Conference in 2001 in Toronto, Canada. Justin's father, Rev. James R. Tanis, a Presbyterian minister, was a guest of our denomination. He was at our conference to receive an award we present at each General Conference to a parent who demonstrates love and care for their gay, lesbian, bisexual, or transgender children.

Rev. Dr. James Tanis made these comments about Justin to our entire General Conference:

> It's almost a contradiction in terms that one should receive an award for loving and supporting one's children. Since our two children were first placed in our arms, their mother and I have been entranced by their responsiveness. Our love has only grown stronger in all the changes that life has brought about. Maggie was always a walker, and each night before she went to bed she would come down to my study and say "Dad, let's go for a walk." And we lived in a hilly woodside that's now been cut through by a big highway. But we would go down there and share what was going on in our lives in the course of that day. As she matured, I came to respect her progress and came to the understanding of her life, which made support of her decisions,

and finally his decision, a natural part of our relationship. My main dis-appointment is that he is not now in the Presbyterian Church where his father and grandfather before that have ministered and where his mother and grandmother have served so faithfully. But that disappointment is not with Justin; it is with the church.

Three years ago I was in Rouen in France and happened to be there the week of the celebrations of the great Joan of Arc and on the feast day of St. Joan. In the afternoon there was a great gathering in the cathedral, and a theologian from Paris gave the address. I thought to myself what a wonderful opportunity, where the church was celebrating the life and contributions of St. Joan, for the church to take a stand on the ordination of women. But you know, they decided to stay in the rear guard and ignore the vanguard. Two days later in the *International Herald Tribune,* there was an article about the Southern Baptists and their denigration of women. And I thought again, the church is in the rear guard and not in the vanguard. When I arrived home I learned that the General Assembly of the Presbyterian Church had voted to ban not only gay and lesbian unions, but the possibility of their taking place in our churches or being participated in by our ordained clergy, elders, or deacons. Again, the church in the rear guard rather than in the vanguard. So I am thankful for the work of Metropolitan Community Churches and its witness over these last years, and that it has brought about more understanding for the issues of gay, lesbian, bisexual, and transgender persons. And so though Justin's not in the church that I grew up in, he is in the church that we are all a part of.

I agree with Justin's father. I, too, "came to respect her progress and came to the understanding of her life, which made support of her decisions, and finally his decision, a natural part of our relationship."

REV. ELDER TROY D. PERRY

Acknowledgments

There are so many people to thank for their belief in me, as well as in this project:

For their endless patience, encouragement, and love, I thank my family and companions on this adventure: Daniel, Masen, Michele, and Nick. I couldn't have done this without their input, editing, discussions, and support.

For Kieth, for reasons he knows.

To my dad, mom, and brother, James, for their unconditional love, and thanks, Dad, for all of your support, from editing to just accepting me.

I also want to thank Guy Baldwin, M.S., and Richard Horowitz, M.D., who were not gatekeepers but healers in every sense of the word.

To the Advanced Pastoral Studies program at San Francisco Theological Seminary who were unfailing in their support, allowing me and other students to follow the direction in which the Spirit led us, even when the topic went in an entirely new direction.

Many thank-you's go to my dissertation advisor, Rev. Dr. Bob Goss, who told me I could make it until I proved him right and who helped me hone my ideas and articulate the things that mattered most to me.

And to the staff of Metropolitan Community Churches who have shared with me everything from brilliant insights to the key to the men's room with great support, humor, integrity, and faith.

Introduction

This work rises out of my personal experience as a transsexual person, from my professional life as a clergyperson, and from the points where those two callings intersect. I write out of a desire to have the voices of transgendered persons lifted above the silence that has too often surrounded us and from the din of talk shows and scandals that drowns out any intelligent conversation. I know that we, as transgendered persons, have discovered amazing spiritual truths that we need to tell one another so that we can thrive and grow. In this book, I break from the conventional tradition of using the third person because the reader needs to know that I am speaking as one of us; when I say "we," I mean myself and other transgendered people. I know and say things in this book that others, who are not a part of this community, will not know; however, I also know I do not see certain things because they are simply too close to home. I do not want to distance myself from people I am describing when the description includes me as well.

I was born female, in 1965, and grew up on the East Coast of the United States and, for shorter periods of time, in the Netherlands. I did not fit the prototype of a gender-dysphoric child, although I knew very clearly that I was not like the other girls. I became a feminist at an early age, perhaps in part because my father worked at a women's college, and I felt that the roles prescribed for women were too limiting for me. I remember wishing as a child that I was a boy, but I also remember feeling very strongly that this desire should remain a secret. I don't really know why I believed that no one should know about these feelings, but they were strong. I would play that I was a boy or a man, in my room with the door shut at times when I felt no one would disturb me.

By the time I was in high school, I was convinced that the sexism of the world made me uncomfortable as a girl and young woman. I also joined the theater program at my high school, looking for a way to overcome my sense of shyness. When the theater teacher cast the school plays, she always put me in masculine roles, with the exception of one tomboy part. I played a priest, a spy, and other male roles. I felt a sense of both delight at this casting and a fear that it might expose to others something that I felt within me. In class, however, my teacher tried hard to help me learn to act feminine. I remember one monologue that explored the artifice of women's routine of putting on makeup in the morning. It felt very accurate to me — that being a woman was somehow putting on a front that others would believe.

I went on to attend a women's college and found it to be a haven from the gender roles of society and a place to grow and develop as a human being. There, people were more interested in my mind than in the characteristics of my body, more taken with who I could be as a friend than whether I fit into the categories of male or female. I took women's studies classes from time to time, trying to understand some of the confusion I felt, because surely that curriculum was the place to explore gender. Yet the classes left me more puzzled than ever when the professor declared definitively that penis envy did not exist and that no woman ever desired to be a man. While I won't digress into a discussion of Freud, something inside of me knew that the professor was wrong. I didn't even have words to articulate a response, and my feelings were that I was doing this thing of being a woman all wrong. Rather than affirming me as a woman celebrating her female existence, the women's studies courses made me feel like a fraud failing at being a liberated woman.

When I was in college, I came out as a lesbian. While it wasn't a complete fit for me, it was the closest thing that I had ever seen that described the feelings that I had. Being a lesbian in Northampton, Massachusetts, in the mid-1980s meant, among other things, permission to digress from stereotypical female dress and pursuits. Flannel shirts, jeans, boots, and a crew cut were the norm for dykes that I knew, which gave me the opportunity to try on clothes and a way of wearing them that had felt off-limits to me before. It was at least a place to start in exploring masculinity.

After college, I went to seminary at Harvard Divinity School. While Harvard has had its struggles with how women are integrated within its walls, I experienced it as an environment in which I felt more valued for what was between my ears than what my gender was. At Harvard I met the first transgendered people that I had ever known, including a transwoman seeking ordination in the Unitarian Universalist Association and a male-identified/female-bodied student. I didn't, at the time, feel particularly like them, but at the same time I felt a kind of fascination about them and was very curious about how they lived their lives. Both were visibly identifiable as transgendered, which now I would affirm as part of the diversity of our community and one of our choices, but which then bothered me as too vulnerable, too readily known, too different.

After graduation, I was ordained in the Metropolitan Community Church and went on to serve in congregations in Boston, Honolulu, and San Francisco. In my ministry, I more frequently encountered trans-gendered people; I noticed too that when I was in a church with multiple staff, the transgendered people went almost exclusively to me for pastoral care. I felt a sense of affinity for them as outsiders even within the MCC context. When talking with some of these folks after I decided to transition, one of them said, "Oh, I knew that you'd figure this out someday. When I told you that I was going to transition, there was just a flicker of hope in your eyes. Maybe you didn't recognize it yet, but I did."

In Hawai'i, I discovered a wonderful history of the diversity of gender among persons within Polynesian and South Pacific cultures. One of the most interesting moments in my ministry there was when I received a phone call from the principal of a local high school who had recently moved to the state from the mainland of the United States. He told me that he was calling us as a gay group because he had a situation in his school that he didn't know how to handle. One of the "boys" from the South Pacific had begun coming to school in skirts, dresses, and other articles of women's clothing. He wanted to know what I thought he should do. I asked him if this young person's family knew that s/he was dressing this way at school. Yes, he told me, he had talked to the teen's mother himself and she seemed quite unconcerned. Well, I went on, was this young person experiencing harassment from other kids in the school? The principal said he was concerned about that, but that didn't seem to be a factor. So I asked him what exactly he perceived as the problem if the teen in question wasn't being harassed at home or at school and was comfortable with the clothes that s/he chose. He said he saw the point I was making. I finished by telling him that I thought he should make sure that this young person was safe and was learning in school and beyond that, leave it alone. While not all residents of Hawai'i are, of course, accepting of gender differences, a cultural base there gave me hope and let me see broader possibilities of what it means to be a man, a woman, or both and neither.

As time went on in ministry, I felt increasing pressure to present myself as a professional and tried very hard for a number of years to conform to an image of what I felt a professional woman should be. I felt that I should attend interfaith and community gatherings in a way that seemed mature and professional, but it never felt right. I struggled with a low self-esteem and a sense of insecurity in both my professional and private life. Again, I felt like a fraud, playacting at being female, despite my best efforts to integrate and accept being a woman.

Finally, I reached a crisis point in my life in which I was forced to deal with my lack of self-esteem, a general sense of depression, and some serious challenges in my professional life. As I worked hard on these issues, I began to heal and grow. I started therapy again to specifically work on whatever ghost that seemed to be looming over me. As I became stronger inside, I came face-to-face with the issue of gender and knew that I had to look seriously at it. That was the beginning of this journey to wholeness. Once I began to accept myself as I was, not as I thought I should be, then I couldn't help but look at what gender I was, rather than the gender I thought that I should be. Finally I felt like I could look this question of gender in the face, without being paralyzed by the fear of what I might find.

What I felt was remarkably familiar to me; it was like my experience of discerning a call to the ministry. I realized that God was calling me to explore parts of myself that I had never been willing to look at before but which now I could not avoid. The deeper I went, the more strongly I felt the presence of God and experienced the sense that God was calling me to go further. Once I had started, I could not stop. This was a journey to authenticity, a deeply spiritual process. It was an experience of transformation, not just from female to male, but to a sense of joy and freedom in God. Once I let myself think concretely about the fact that I was transgendered, the decision to transition seemed obvious to me.

I started by exploring a new name and a new identity with a close circle of friends and with an experienced therapist. The more time went on, the clearer it became to me that I needed and wanted to walk down this path. In the spring of 1997, I told my supervisor and coworkers at the denominational headquarters for Metropolitan Community Churches and finally made the information public at our conference that summer. I began hormone therapy shortly after that and had the first surgery a year later. On the day I got my first shot of testosterone, my male coworkers presented me with a lovely certificate and an official key to the men's rest room. That day felt like a day of rebirth. While things became harder in early transition before they grew easier, I still felt like the path was the right one. I had some doubts, although my therapist wisely pointed out that anyone sane enough to do this would have questions about making these changes to our bodies as well as in our lives. As time went on, the doubts and struggles faded, and the sense of exhilaration and freedom grew.

I knew from the moment that I allowed myself to seriously look at the question of transition that this path was the right one for me. What I did not anticipate fully was the degree to which I would feel that a huge weight had been lifted from my life and that I would experience such a strong sense of relief and happiness. I experienced a divine presence that was deeper and more profound than I had ever known. My process of transition was primarily a spiritual transformation, and I was amazed to hear stories from more and more trans people who experienced it in the same way. I further explore the components of that spiritual transformation in this book.

I wrote this book because I wanted to delve into the spiritual nature of transgendered people, to hear the stories of others like me, and to give a positive voice to our community. The book started as my doctoral dissertation at San Francisco Theological Seminary, not one of the usual topics seen in the Advanced Pastoral Studies program. And yet the seminary instructors and administrators were incredibly supportive of my efforts and challenged me to do the best work that I could do.

I interviewed a number of transgendered people, both in formal interviews and in more informal conversations, as part of my research. The people that I interviewed came from a wide variety of backgrounds, including Jews, Protestants from both gay-identified and mainstream churches, former Roman Catholics, and a practicing Wiccan priest. Their words guided my thoughts and feelings about this book. I also did a search for any literature by transgendered authors that mentioned the spiritual in any way — on the Internet, in self-published works, and in publications from the United States, Britain, and Canada. That research comes together in this document. I am indebted to all who spoke with me, who shared their stories, and who challenged and enlarged my thinking. This work is not simply mine, but a community effort.

In my writing, I have followed the places where I see the holy working among us and in my own faith journey as a Christian. I speak out of my experience as a Christian, in dialogue with people of various faiths and religious practices, believing that value lies in all paths of faith that lead us to life and wholeness. I have always felt drawn to people on the margins of the religious landscape, both from personal conviction and because the Bible clearly tells us that that is where we can locate the divine. Following Jesus has meant, for me as a Christian, a continuing journey to the margins, to spend time with those whom society may ridicule and isolate, to see the beauty and power of God working with them. Transgendered people clearly occupy a marginal space in Western society.[1] I believe that when we go to the margins, we can see God.

Within this community of gender-varied people, I have seen the incredible strength needed and mustered for some of us just to walk down the street exposing ourselves to the violence and ridicule our society aims against people who transgress gender lines. I have seen people reeling from the damage done by year after year after year of abuse or caused by a lifetime of hiding, suppressing, and attempting to ignore the question of gender. I have witnessed people willing to risk everything in order to live the truth of their own identity and able to change the course of their entire lives step by step, day after day. From within this context of struggles and triumphs, I have seen great spiritual power unleashed to transform lives. I want to speak about and to honor this unleashed power in this writing. Our community is daring, gritty, rough, frightened, courageous, zealous, bold, and powerful. I believe there is a spiritual force that has kept us moving forward in the face of all that we encounter, moving forward with joy and hope; that force is worth examining for both transgendered and nontransgendered people.

Speaking about the powers that keep us alive and move us forward is not just something that we should do to record our experiences or as an

---

1. The many cultures around our globe deal with gender in a multitude of ways. My intention is to focus primarily on the experiences of people in the United States, Canada, and Great Britain. A broader focus is beyond the scope of this book. For information about the ways in which gender is viewed in a variety of world religions, see Virginia Ramey Mollenkott, *Omnigender: A Trans-Religious Approach* (Cleveland: Pilgrim Press, 2001).

academic matter; it is not a luxury, but a matter of survival. Too many of us have been lost to suicide and to lifetimes spent hiding in pain. We need to share with each other what we have learned that lets us thrive and live in this world. Riki Ann Wilchins of GenderPAC — a national transgender activist group in the United States — writes in the beginning of her book *Read My Lips: Sexual Subversion and the End of Gender:*

> The regime of gender is an intentional, systemic oppression. As such, it cannot be fought through personal action, but only through an organized, systemic response. It is high time we stopped writing our hard-luck stories, spreading open our legs and our yearbooks for those awful before-and-after pictures, and began thinking clearly about how to fight back. It is time we began producing our own theory, our own narrative. No one volume can hope to achieve all this. At best, this is a rough set of beginnings.
>
> I intend to wage a struggle for my life. I intend to fight for my political survival.[2]

I agree with her that this struggle is for life and survival. Taking seriously her challenge that we not just write our painful stories with before-and-after photos, I intend to write about the ways in which religious communities have contributed to our oppression and, occasionally, to our liberation. I want to speak, too, about the beauty and power of our lives. We need to think about how to fight back religiously and spiritually, as well as politically.

We must speak out about the systemic forces that hold gender oppression in place. We need to look at how we, as a community, can respond in a multiplicity of methods so that we can experience greater freedom. At the same time, communities are made up of individuals. Our collective story is made up of individual voices. The statement that the personal is political — articulated by women who are seeking freedom from the rigidity of gender in our society — is also true for trans people. One of the problems with the academic discussion of gender transgression/gender theory is that it often speaks in abstract terms and is not held accountable to the real lives of those about whom it theorizes. We need to take seriously the systemic issues while holding them in tension with the personal stories that are our witness.

---

2. Riki Ann Wilchins, *Read My Lips: Sexual Subversion and the End of Gender* (Ithaca, N.Y.: Firebrand Books, 1997), 25.

This approach is even more important, I believe, when we are speaking about spirituality. Howard Thurman wrote in *Jesus and the Disinherited,* "Again and again [Jesus] came back to the inner life of the individual. With increasing insight and startling accuracy he placed his finger on the 'inward center' as the crucial arena where the issues would determine the destiny of his people."[3] Transgendered people have learned about the value of the inward center and the ways in which it guides us into our identity. We have to speak from the power of that inward center both as individuals and as communities. That inward center drives us forward on this journey of self-discovery. It is the truth about us that we cannot turn away from and to which we are accountable. As Thurman states, the inward center can determine our destiny and so, we must pay attention to the inward center if we, as individuals and as a community, are to find the freedom for which we long and strive.

The time has arrived for us to speak for ourselves; our freedom depends upon it. That we do so right now is particularly important. We must lift up our voices at this time before the religious communities have said too much about us. We see from the battle within the church over gay, lesbian, and bisexual people the sheer destructive power of religion when it is used for oppression. We can see the energy that has been displaced from ministry to an argument over who is acceptable to the church. Tremendous amounts of time and energy have been used to argue, point fingers, exclude, and judge. Before the religious community lines up to support society's opposition to gender liberation, we need to speak out. Before the Gospel is confused with the status quo, we need to lift up our own voices. Perhaps we can change the conversation before it has really begun. There is no time to lose.

We have the opportunity to try to shift the conversation *about* us to one *with* us. As we see in this book, even the religious right has conflicting messages about us; no consensus has yet formed, although it is beginning to emerge. The liberal church has only just begun to even think that we are in their midst. Ours are the voices that need to set the agenda and be preeminent in speaking about our experiences. We must speak about our own spirituality and the truths we have discovered along the way. We need to talk about the ways in which we really live and make the decisions

---

3. Howard Thurman, *Jesus and the Disinherited* (Boston: Beacon Press, 1976), 21.

that transform our bodies and our lives. Virginia Mollenkott writes this about the church:

> For several decades, transgender diversities have become increasingly obvious in various subcultures all over the planet. Meanwhile, most Christian churches have buried their heads in the sand of endless dialogue about whether or not it is compatible with Christian witness to ordain or provide union ceremonies for those members who happen to be gay or lesbian. While the church was looking the other way, gender issues become much more complex, and as a consequence, much of the debate within church walls is increasingly irrelevant to the realities with which individuals are struggling.[4]

For those of us who are part of the church, we have a responsibility to help the church remove its head from the sand and its heart from denial so that we can speak relevantly and compassionately to this question of gender as it is arising in the lives both of transgendered people and others around us.

The reality of our lives is distinct from much of the theory about us, whether it is academic gender theory, the guidelines that many physicians follow, or the nascent discussions in communities of faith. Most of these conversations and studies do not take into account the challenge of using a driver's license, or starting a new bank account, when one is in the midst of transition and no longer looks like a picture ID. They rarely acknowledge the difficulties that people have retaining or finding employment, much less the sometimes impossible task of finding a rest room one can safely use. They may critique the ways in which people stare at us for ambiguous gender presentation but do not offer anything in the way of advice about how to deal with the feelings such stares evoke. Never have I seen any literature address what it feels like to go to church while you are wrestling with the question of gender and hear every gendered reference to yourself as yet another painful reminder. Receiving communion as a "sister" when you feel like a "brother" is not an uplifting experience of Christ's presence but a reinforcement of what feels wrong.

Viviane Namaste writes, "As transsexual and transgendered people, these are the activities of our day-to-day, the fabric of how our bodies are located in, and move through, the world. Although banal, these events

---

4. Virginia Ramey Mollenkott, "Gender Diversity and Christian Community," *The Other Side* 37, no. 3 (May and June 2001). 25.

merit consideration: anything less produces a knowledge of little practical relevance to our lives, reinforcing a world that treats transsexual and transgendered people as inconsequential."[5] While the theories may be interesting, what is urgently needed is something that is relevant and use-able in our lives and the only way to create such relevant material is to do so in the context of real, lived lives that speak about our own experiences.

The voices of transgendered people have been silenced or discounted in overt ways. Our society fears and punishes people who push the gender boundaries beyond a simple division of male and female. In *Ms.* magazine, Martha Coventry makes the point:

> The strict division between female and male bodies and behavior is our most cherished and comforting truth. Mess with that bedrock belief, and the ground beneath our feet starts to tremble. To begin with, we rely on the notion that the bodies of females and males are distinctly different. We imagine a dividing line with penis, scrotum, testicles, testosterone and XY chromosomes on one side, and clitoris, vagina, uterus, ovaries, estrogen and XX chromosomes on the other. But were we to look between the legs and into the chemical and chromosomal makeup of real people, we would see that nature often refuses to abide by that tidy division.[6]

When people cross those dividing lines or obliterate them entirely, a great deal of fear and hatred can be unleashed upon them.

The church has been a willing participant in this process, perpetuating the transphobia of our society. Medical theologian Oliver O'Donovan writes:

> There is nothing, then, that the believing male-to-female transsexual can really be said to *know* about himself: certainly not that he has a feminine psychology. His soul, no doubt, is feminine by literary convention, as all our souls are, but by no scientific criterion can such a thing be claimed for it. All that can be said of him is that he has "feminine gender identity," which tells us what we already knew, that he feels himself to be a woman.[7]

O'Donovan's attitude is both arrogant and unacceptable, but it unfortu-nately shared by others that transgendered people encounter in the world,

5. Viviane K. Namaste, *Invisible Lives: The Erasure of Transsexual and Transgendered People* (Chicago: University of Chicago Press, 2000), 2.

6. Martha Coventry, "Making the Cut," *Ms.* 10, no. 6 (October–November 2000): 55.

7. Oliver O'Donovan, "Transsexualism and Christian Marriage," *Journal of Religious Ethics* 11 (spring 1983): 146. O'Donovan consistently uses male pronouns to refer to male-to-female transsexuals. His language is used here, but the author recognizes that it is offensive to some.

the church, and among the "helping" professionals who oversee our transitions. I intend to be an explicit counter to O'Donovan's statement to say that indeed we do know many valuable things intuitively and accurately about ourselves, information that guides our lives and our transitions as well as our spiritual journeys. In fact, who can know us better than we do ourselves?

These issues are not important only for us. As James Nelson notes in his introduction to Vanessa Sheridan's recent book, *Crossing Over: Liberating the Transgendered Christian,* "We should care [about transgendered issues] because it is a matter of the soul of the church.... Historically, the church has always endangered its soul when it has capitulated uncritically to its surrounding culture. The inclusion of, affirmation of, and celebration of transgendered people within the church is truly counterculture."[8] In order to be truly faithful to our religious heritage, we must listen to all of the voices through whom God might speak. We must listen to the marginalized and the outcast and we must hear the voice of God that speaks through our community and in other communities as well. Nelson goes on to note that some trans people have chosen to stay within the church, despite its difficulties, "believing that the church might yet be a bigger church. Bigger in its integrity. Larger in its ability to stand in connection with all marginalized people. Bigger in its strength of spirit to enable all of us to realize our destiny to freedom, uniqueness, and worth. Yes, a church larger in the size of its soul."[9]

Community after community has discovered that one key to liberation is the finding, claiming, and proclaiming of their own voices. My hope and prayer are that this work will begin a conversation that will help us move in the direction of liberation.

---

8. James Nelson, introduction to Vanessa Sheridan, *Crossing Over: Liberating the Transgendered Christian* (Cleveland: Pilgrim Press, 2001), ix.
9. Ibid., xi.

Chapter One

Trans Issues

Throughout human history, people have had a vast array of understandings of gender, and human beings have repeatedly crossed and reformed those gender lines. Different cultures have had varying understandings of gender and the role it plays in human society, as well as different interpretations about the number of genders. Some cultures have defined three genders, others six or two. In addition to differences about the number of genders, there are varying understandings of what constitutes gendered behavior. What is viewed as masculine in one culture may be considered feminine in another or the characteristic of a third gender. Anthropological evidence has shown that different cultures display a tremendous diversity of attitudes toward gender. Even Western medical science looks beyond two separate genders.[1]

Leslie Feinberg's *Transgender Warriors* is the seminal text about gender-variant people throughout history and cultures. Through photographs and text from cultures as varied as ancient Rome and modern Africa, sie[2] documents examples of the ways in which people have lived that are broader than the current Western culture's bigendered system. Feinberg concludes:

> The more I dig, the more I find that although what we think of as gender today has been expressed differently in diverse historical periods, cultures, regions, nationalities, and classes, there appears to have always been gender diversity in the human population. And there is just as much evidence that

---

1. For more information, see Anne Fausto-Sterling, *Sexing the Body: Gender Politics and the Construction of Sexuality* (New York: Basic Books, 2000).

2. Leslie Feinberg writes, "I am a human being who would rather not be addressed as Ms. or Mr., ma'am or sir. I prefer to use gender-neutral pronouns like sie (pronounced like 'see') and hir (pronounced like 'here') to describe myself. I am a person who faces almost insurmountable difficulty when instructed to check off an 'F' or an 'M' box on identification papers." From Leslie Feinberg, *TransLiberation: Beyond Pink or Blue* (Boston: Beacon Press, 1998), 1.

sexes have not always been arbitrarily squeezed into hard-and-fast categories of woman and man, and that fluidity between sexes is an ancient path.[3]

Human societies have conceptualized sex and gender in many different ways, with more options than exist in our current culture. Reading Feinberg's book and seeing page after page of examples of people living out cross-gendered or intersexual identities is a powerful experience.

Virginia Ramey Mollenkott's recent work, *Omnigender*, also chronicles well the cultural variations on gender. I do not intend to repeat here the work that has been done exploring gender through history but commend these books to you. We should have a broader perspective on gender than just a white, Western, male-dominated view. We should also take great care before deriving meaning from other cultures or times; often, we do not have enough information to fully understand the context in which those lives were or are lived. Kathy Gainor, in her outstanding article on transgendered issues in psychology, notes that often these examples come from non-Western cultures or have been appropriated by lesbians, gay men, and bisexuals.[4] Jason Cromwell documents well the ways in which these analogies have worked better for male-to-female transgendered people than for female-to-male.[5] Yet for us to want to see others like us in different cultures and in various times is normal, as is deriving a sense of strength from people who were our gender ancestors.

For much of history, gender variation has been seen through the lens of religion or society. People have asked about the appropriate roles of women and men (and of other categories, in some societies) and how someone might cross those, and the answers have come either through the social organization of the people, as a religious belief, or both. In some societies, of course, those answers were indistinguishable from one another. We can see the religious nature of the response in the Christian church's response to Joan of Arc, which has varied over the centuries from burning her at

---

3. Leslie Feinberg, *Transgender Warriors: Making History from Joan of Arc to Dennis Rodman* (Boston: Beacon Press, 1996), 121.

4. Kathy A. Gainor, "Including Transgender Issues in Lesbian, Gay, and Bisexual Psychology: Implications for Clinical Practice and Training," in *Education, Research, and Practice in Lesbian, Gay, Bisexual, and Transgendered Psychology: A Resource Manual*, ed. Beverly Green and Gladys L. Croom (Thousand Oaks, Calif.: Sage, 2000), 133.

5. Jason Cromwell, "Traditions of Gender Diversity and Sexualities: A Female to Male Transgendered Perspective," in *Two-Spirit People: Native American Gender Identity, Sexuality and Spirituality*, ed. Sue-Ellen Jacobs, Wesley Thomas, and Sabine Lang (Urbana: University of Illinois Press, 1997), 119.

the stake to her later beatification, as well as in societies like the Dakota people of North America who identified the two-spirited *winkte* people as healers and visionaries.

In many societies, gender and spirituality have been linked. In some cultures, this association has meant particular spiritual roles for those of a particular gender, such as the embodiment of the Goddess in female ceremonial leaders or the ancient Israelite dictate for unblemished male priests. In others, a particular role applies for people occupying a third gender, such as the Indian *hijras,* who are born male, castrated, and who then live as an alternative gender, performing specific ritual functions. Some of the practitioners of modern Judaism, Christianity, Islam, and other religions maintain separate spheres of religious activity for men and for women.

What is relatively recent is the shift to a medical model to address gender and a vast increase in our ability to modify bodies medically to reflect a variety of gender presentations. The creation of synthetic hormones and the ability to deliver them into the human body greatly increases our capacity to develop the secondary sex characteristics of another gender that outwardly and socially mark us as male or female. The ability to alter bodies through surgery has also advanced tremendously. This development has been pivotal to the emergence of a transgender identity, according to some theorists. Bernice Hausman writes:

> The advent and public acceptance of cosmetic surgery thus introduced specific circumstances into medical culture that were central to the emergence of transsexualism in the twentieth century. These developments include the technical procedures involved in genital conversion surgeries, surgeons' willingness to respond positively to demands for surgical treatment that had no physiological basis, and the practice of surgical therapy for psychological problems focused on the body. Most significant, however, was the growth of a medical specialty that enjoyed the prestige and security of membership in the American Medical Association, yet had only a loose and contingent relation to the established therapeutic discourses of medicine.[6]

Because of the advances in medical technique and ability, our understandings of gender and how we might cross from one gender to another are different today than they have been in history. Our ability to pass

---

6. Bernice Hausman, *Changing Sex: Transsexualism, Technology, and the Idea of Gender* (Durham: Duke University Press, 1995), 50.

as another gender has been greatly increased because of medical technologies. As Max Wolf Valerio writes, "My life is one of the extravagant experiments of the 20th century."[7]

For the purposes of this work, I focus on the modern community of transgendered people who live in ways that are different from the sex that they were assigned at birth. I believe that, because of the changes in medical technology, we cannot adequately compare the experiences of people who lived before or live outside of these changes in medical knowledge and technique to those who have access to them. Many trans folk, but certainly not all, have accessed medical technology. Some see themselves as living outside of a bigendered system, but many believe firmly that the only categories for humanity are male and female.

This difference in perspectives highlights one of the challenges that presently face the transgendered community. Much of the recently published literature that addresses gender issues does so from a gender-queer position that encourages us to abandon the gender norms that oppress and constrict us. The key to transgender liberation, they posit, is our ability to transcend and remove the strictures of a highly gendered system. Virginia Mollenkott's book *Omnigender: A Trans-Religious Approach,* the first work on transgendered people and religion from a major religious publisher, argues for a change to a society in which gender is not the deciding factor and where we will have a unified, or omnigender, approach to life. She says, "contemporary transgender people have no desire to reinforce the binary gender construct and would not appreciate being socially scheduled or regulated."[8]

Kate Bornstein, one of the community's most outspoken and influential activists, argues in her books and performances that she is neither a woman nor a man, but perhaps a girl (sometimes spelled grrl) and perhaps something altogether different. She strives for a dismantling of the gender system as well. One of the currently debated issues in the transgendered community is the work of GenderPAC, which strives for gender liberation, not just for transgendered people but for all.

---

7. Max Wolf Valerio, "The Joker Is Wild: Changing Sex and Other Crimes of Passion," *Anything That Moves* 17 (summer 1998): 34.

8. Virginia Ramey Mollenkott, *Omnigender: A Trans-Religious Approach* (Cleveland: Pilgrim Press, 2001), 134.

However, only a relatively small percentage of the transgendered community, based on my observations, adheres to an argument for a non-gendered society. For many transgendered people, the explicit goal is to blend seamlessly into their target gender without any disruption of the gender system. In fact, in my experience, certain trans folk argue more vociferously than others about the necessity of a dual-gendered system and about their desire to be "real men" or "real women." In their opinion, nothing is omnigendered or bigendered about them. Richard Elkins and Dave King note,

> The emphasis today, at least in some parts of the literature, is on transience, fluidity and performance. . . . The experiences and behaviors are made sense of in terms of the deconstructions of postmodernist cultural theory rather than from the standpoint of the experiences of cross-dressers and sex-changers themselves. In consequence, these writings have yet to make a substantial impact on the subjective experience of the vast majority of gender blenders. In that gender fluidity recognizes no borders or "laws" of gender, the claim is to live outside of "gender" as "gender outlaws." Whether this can be sustained remains to be seen.[9]

My intention is to pay attention to this gap between theory and the lives of transgendered people. I am not particularly interested in theories that do not have practical applications for trans lives, particularly if those theories run counter to or ignore the voices of those who cross-dress, cross-live, or cross lines of gender. I believe that our theories must be grounded in the expressed lives of those who are theorized about in order to be both accurate and relevant.

But, of course, no approach can be so simply binary in its thinking. Room exists both for those who move outside of gender and those who uphold gender norms. Both parties can be right. In *Sex Changes: The Politics of Transgenderism*, Patrick Califia concludes,

> Although it would seem that the goals of these two aspects of trans-activism are mutually exclusive, in fact, both are important components of the struggle for a gender-sane society. If the concept of gender freedom is to have any meaning, it must be possible for some of us to cling to our biological sex and the gender we were assigned at birth while others wish

---

9. Richard Elkins and Dave King, "Contributions to the Emerging Field of Transgender Studies," *International Journal of Transgenderism* 1, no. 1 (July–September 1997); *www.symposion.com/ijt*.

to adapt the body to their gender of preference, and still others choose to question the very concept of polarized sexes.[10]

He goes on to note that it will be difficult to have the community see all of these aspects as critical to our liberation, since we often tend to see our own position as right and beneficial to the movement and other positions as backward steps to our progress. I agree with Califia that success will benefit more than one group and will require more than one approach. A society that is free will allow us to make our own choices and to craft our own lives and bodies in ways that are right for us, even if those ways are different from the choices of others. My goal is to listen to and bring forward the voices of those from any side of this debate.

The voices of transgendered people are most important to me. They are more compelling to me than the words of theoreticians and more sacred than the writings of theologians on this topic. My hope is to bring these voices forward for you to hear, to understand, and perhaps to broaden the way you see gender.

I begin my exploration of transgendered spirituality by defining the terms that we use to describe the transgendered experience.

Defining Transgender

Transgendered people are those individuals who do not fit comfortably into society's traditional understandings of sex and gender. We occupy a space beyond and/or between the standard categories of female and male. Some do so knowingly, deliberately, and as a statement against a binary gendered system. Others feel that they have no choice in the matter and were born as they are. There is no way to estimate how many people feel themselves to be transgendered in some way or who live in a way that crosses or subverts gender, either in their thoughts, actions, dress, mannerisms, choice of careers, or in other ways.

A variety of terms are used to identify gender-variant people.

Sex refers to our genetic and physical conditions as female or male and is determined by the type of our chromosomes and by observation of our external genitalia. *Gender* refers to the social, behavioral, and psychological

---

10. Pat Califia, *Sex Changes: The Politics of Transgenderism* (San Francisco: Cleis Press, 1997), 275. Since the publication of this book, Califia has identified as an FTM (female-to-male) and added his partner's last name to his. I will refer to him by his chosen name, Patrick Califia-Rice.

characteristics that we interpret to determine whether a person is a man or a woman. The particularities of these characteristics vary by culture. For example, a strong level of empathy may be viewed as either a feminine trait or a masculine trait, depending on the culture.

Transgender is commonly used as a broad term to encompass a whole range of people who transgress the commonly understood definitions of gender all or part of the time. Sometimes, the short hand "trans" is used, and may be combined with a variety of other words (e.g., transman, transfolk, transart) to designate transgender. Transgendered people come from every race, ethnicity, class, age, and sexual orientation and are identified at birth as girls, boys, and intersexed infants. Generalized statements about this group of people are difficult because the group includes such a broad range of people. How gender variation is presented and lived out varies vastly from culture to culture and is also affected by factors such as age, culture, and economic status. "Transgender" mostly refers to those people who are knowingly crossing gender lines. The word "transgenderist" typically refers to someone who lives or dresses as the opposite sex but does not intend to transition medically.

The terms that follow here can be thought of as subsets of transgender.

"Transsexuals" (sometimes written "transexuals") experience a desire to change our bodies to appear differently than the sex that was assigned to us at birth and generally access, or desire to access, medical technology in order to accomplish this. This desire results from a sense of incongruity between how we understand ourselves and what we see in the mirror. Some transsexuals have, from early childhood, a strong sense of gender dysphoria and discomfort with the gender assigned to them at birth[11] while others may experience a sense of incongruity but are unable to define it until later in life. The process of medical change is commonly referred to as "transition." Some transsexuals continue to identify as transsexual following transition while others then see themselves as fully male or fully female and no longer transsexual. Some refer to themselves as women, or men, of transsexual experience. Modern transsexuals rarely use the concept of being a "woman trapped in a man's body" or a "man trapped in a woman's body" any longer, although this description is still very meaningful to some people.

---

11. Physical gender may have been ambiguous at birth and been assigned by a physician. See the definition of "intersex" for more details.

Estimating the number of transsexual people is difficult because of the paucity of studies and little tracking of this kind of data. Kathy Gainor states, "It is estimated that transsexuals constitute .01% of the population. By 1988, an estimated 6,000–10,000 transsexuals had undergone genital reassignment surgery."[12] While Gainor's numbers show the incidence at approximately 1:1,000, others speculate a range of incidence at between 1:20,000 to 1:50,000 persons. The majority of studies have been conducted outside of the United States and with individuals who have accessed traditional gender clinics for treatments. Some studies have shown a higher rate of male-to-female transsexuals while others have shown approximately equal numbers of transsexual men and women. The majority of people think of male-to-female transsexuals when they hear the term; however, "transsexual" applies to female-to-male transsexuals as well.

"Gender dysphoria" refers to individuals' discomfort and sense of dissonance with the gender assigned to them. The feeling is persistent, continuing over a long period of time, and is not alleviated by other treatments, such as counseling. Gender dysphoria is an internal feeling of incongruity between our physical, external selves and our internal identifications. This feeling of dissonance can exist in varying degrees between vague discomfort and a crisis so profound that it may push a person to suicide.

"MTF" and "FTM" are terms that refer to male-to-female and female-to-male, respectively. These terms are commonly used by transgendered people to describe ourselves and other members of the community. The first letter designates the gender assigned at birth and the last letter notes the target gender. Within the trans community, "transman" refers to an FTM and "transwoman" to an MTF. In some clinical literature, FTMs are called "transsexual women" and MTFs as "transsexual men"; this use of terminology is definitely not endorsed within the transgendered community and is usually used by writers who are not supportive of trans issues.

"SRS" and "GRS" are abbreviations for sex reassignment surgery and genital reassignment surgery. GRS refers to the changes brought about through surgical intervention to remove the organs of one sex and/or replace them with those resembling that of the target gender. While many people are focused on "the sex change operation," the reality is that for most transsexuals, we do not go through only one surgery. MTFs may

---

12. Gainor, "Including Transgender Issues in Lesbian, Gay, and Bisexual Psychology," 135.

have surgery to enhance breast size, reduce the prominence of the Adam's apple, and shape the face and body to a more feminine presentation, in addition to having genital reconstructive surgeries of vaginoplasty and labiaplasty. FTMs generally have mastectomies; may also have the ovaries, uterus, and vagina removed; and may opt for surgeries to lengthen the clitoris and shape the labia to resemble a penis and testicles or may have phalloplasty surgery where the surgeon creates a penis, generally from tissue from the forearm. "Pre-op" (for pre-operative) refers to individuals who have not yet had genital surgery, while "post-op" (post-operative) refers to individuals who have undergone surgery. Our self-identity as a man or a woman is not dependent on our genital status.

"The HBIGDA (Harry Benjamin International Gender Dysphoria Association) Standards of Care" are the guidelines used by clinicians in treating transsexual patients. Named for Dr. Harry Benjamin, an early advocate for the right of transsexual individuals to change gender, the Standards of Care outline a path for a person, and his or her therapist and physicians, to take to transition. While initially set up as guidelines that should be varied to meet an individual's needs, they are now often used as hard and fast rules by clinicians and are controversial within the trans community.

The basic outline suggests a period of time in therapy prior to the onset of medical treatment plus a "real-life test," generally a year of living in the opposite gender to determine if the patient truly wants to pursue this course of action. Depending on the individual's body and appearance, cross-gendered living may well be impossible without hormone treatments and/or surgery. Following the real life test, the patient obtains from her/his therapist, who is licensed and has at least a master-level education (or its equivalent outside of the United States), a letter that is given to a physician to initiate hormone treatments. Estrogen treatments for MTF patients leads to the development of breasts, the softening of the skin, a thinning of body hair (although not facial hair, which must be removed by electrolysis or laser treatments), a reduction in muscle strength, and a redistribution of body fat to more female proportions (thinner waist, broader hips, and thighs). Testosterone treatments for FTMs causes the voice to permanently drop, body and facial hair to grow, the clitoris to increase in size, faster development of muscle tissue, and a redistribution of body fat to more male proportions (larger waist, smaller hips and thighs).

After a period of time on hormones (often at least a year), the patient can obtain two letters, one from a therapist with a master's-level education and another from a psychologist or psychiatrist, to obtain approval for genital reassignment surgery or mastectomy. Transsexuals can usually obtain a driver's license reflecting their new gender after hormone treatment and can change their passports following irreversible surgery. Some states and countries allow an individual to amend her/his birth certificates while others do not. A legal name change can occur through court order or by usage. In some places, a court-ordered change of gender is also possible.

"Transvestites" are individuals who have no desire to permanently change their gender but do receive satisfaction and pleasure from dressing as the opposite gender. The gratification of dressing may be sexual, but also can fulfill other emotional needs. The term generally is used for heterosexual men who dress as women, usually in their own homes, although also at events set up for this purpose. "Cross-dresser" is another term for people who wear the clothing of the other gender.

"Female impersonators," "drag queens," and "drag kings" cross-dress in order to perform on stage. They generally do not have a desire to permanently alter their gender, but when they perform, they do have a gender presentation usually associated with the opposite sex. Traditionally, drag has been thought of as the domain of men who dress as women; the number of women who take the stage dressed as men have been increasing over the past few years. Female impersonators are generally men who earn money by performing as women. Some drag queens are gay men who simply prefer to dress as women in nonperformance venues for their own personal satisfaction or who may have aspects of their dress, appearance, or mannerisms traditionally designated as feminine.

"Gender benders" are people who blend various aspects of gender to challenge assumptions about gender or to shock the viewer. Examples of this would be a man with a beard wearing a skirt and high heels or a woman with a crew cut, a revealing blouse, and a tuxedo jacket. A number of performers in popular culture fit this category, including Madonna, Boy George, and Eddy Izzard.

"Intersexed" persons are born with physical, hormonal, or chromosomal aspects of more than one sex. This condition may or may not be readily apparent at birth. Estimates of the prevalence of intersexuality list it as potentially as common as one in every five hundred births. The Intersex Society of North America estimates that five infants are operated on each day in an attempt to correct genital variations; these surgeries only change the appearance of the infant's genitals and are not necessary for the child's health. The surgery may leave the child with severely scarred or nonfunctioning genitals and the inability to feel sexual pleasure. Intersexed people were formally referred to as "hermaphrodites"; this term has fallen out of use with "intersex" being used by intersexed people themselves. Some intersexed people see themselves as part of the transgendered community, while others do not. I have included some voices of intersexed people but make no attempt to speak for that community or paint a complete picture of those issues. For more information about the issues of the intersexed community, contact the Intersex Society of North America.

"Gender identity" refers to a person's own understanding of him/herself as male or female, or both or neither. Gender identity speaks about how an individual sees her/himself and should not be confused with sexual orientation. "Sexual orientation" refers to the gender of persons to whom we are attracted. Gender identity describes who we are while sexual orientation tells us who we are attracted to. Transgendered people can be any sexual orientation: gay, bisexual, lesbian, heterosexual, asexual, etc.

Gender variation is, however, a significant factor for the lesbian, gay, and bisexual communities. Little boys are not harassed in school because they are holding other little boys' hands on the playground; they are harassed and called "faggot" for appearing effeminate. Similarly, little girls who do not grow out of a "tomboy phase" may be sent to therapists in the hopes of "preventing lesbianism." Phyllis Burke's book *Gender Shock: Exploding the Myths of Male and Female* provides a multitude of examples where gender-variant children were treated with invasive and punitive treatments specifically to prevent homosexuality. In addition, some people in the gay, lesbian, and bisexual communities make deliberate attempts to subvert and play with gender, such as the use of the term "Mary" to refer to gay men and the prevalence in the lesbian community of female "bois" and their also female Daddies. So, while we should not conflate gender identity and sexual orientation, we should understand that in some areas the two categories operate simultaneously.

Chapter Two

A Search for Our Selves

The search for an authentic sense of self is a primary feature in the journey of the transgendered. We are, by our nature, seekers; if we were not, we would never have discovered this aspect of ourselves. We must search more deeply within ourselves beyond what most people think of as obvious and normal. Our bodies are not seen as the final word defining us as girls and boys, women and men. Even without a clear sense of what aspect of ourselves we might want to be different, we find ourselves searching for another way to be, a way that feels more right for us. So many of my colleagues have commented to me that I am so much more peaceful and calm in the years since I transitioned. They say I always seemed angry, driven, and unhappy before. Some of that attitude was the gender dysphoria, but I believe that it was also a sense of anger that I hadn't yet found a place of peace, a place to be that felt right to me. The behavior grew, too, from a sense of spiritual restlessness because I had not found a home within myself where I could be genuinely myself. So we set out to find ourselves.

The search is not always easy or clear to us. A great deal of denial often accompanies it. Robyn Shanor writes:

> From an early age, we are told that we are not who we perceive ourselves to be, who we know we are. In many ways, our very existence seems in conflict with "reality" itself. Since one's gender role is so relentlessly defined and reinforced by others, it may take years for us to even realize what we are experiencing. Like many who are gay or lesbian, transgendered people often spend years in self-denial and suppression, struggling to fit in and be "normal."[1]

We may believe what others tell us about ourselves, convincing ourselves that we are wrong in seeing what it is that we perceive about ourselves.

---

1. Robyn Shanor, "Finding Common Ground," *The Other Side* 37, no. 3 (May and June 2001): 36.

We may suppress our feelings in order to obey what we believe is God's will or to keep peace within our families. We may do this consciously or subconsciously.

The gender roles dictated for us by society feel unnatural and restrictive. For many years, I believed that the discomfort that I felt in my own skin was a symptom of the sexism of society. Sexism is a very real force in our world, and I do not want to dismiss the reality and impact that it has particularly on women's lives. However, on my own search for self, I discovered that sexism wasn't the only cause of my feelings of dis-ease. I wanted to be proud to have been born female; yet I continually had a sense that I was not doing it right and that if I could figure out how to be a woman properly, things would all fall into place. I invested a great deal into the journey of trying to discover how to be a woman and ultimately found that was not a place where I could be; "woman" was not an identity that I could make fit for me. So, I continued in my search for who I was, who I am, and who I want to be.

For people who have struggled with gender, a healthier and more authentic way of living can seem so close and yet so far away on the other side of the gender divide. I asked many times, always in the secretness of my own heart, why I couldn't have been born a boy. I asked this long before I had any idea that I could one day do something about this struggle and cross gender lines. Many transgendered people also have a sense of having lost the boyhood or girlhood that they longed for; childhood was so wrapped up in trying (and often failing) to meet the gender expectations of others that we did not enjoy the time that we had as children. Some people feel that they were robbed of the experience of growing up in the gender to which they knew they belonged but from which they were excluded. Having a childhood as a girl and a childhood as a boy in this society are very different experiences, regardless of one's gender identity.

Most of us simply did not have access as children (and even as adults) to information to tell us that transitioning is medically possible. Yet still we dreamt and searched for a way. For some people, the answer has been obvious to them since early childhood, and for others a lifetime of cumulative knowledge has been required to reach the point of understanding ourselves as being different from the gender assigned to us at birth.

Once we begin to sense that we are not like others, that in our hearts we understand ourselves differently, then we must learn to believe and affirm what it is that we have found if we are to survive and thrive. Many voices cast doubt and derision above and beyond our own hesitancies. Doctors diagnose us with disorders, clinicians require us to "prove" what we know about ourselves, loved ones may react with shock and attempt to dissuade us, and friends question whether we are still the same people they knew. Yet, we manage to discover and uncover the truth within us and move forward on our journeys.

The strength of the truth we discover about ourselves is so profound to us that we are willing to endure the harassment of an intolerant society as well as the shock, and often disapproval, of our families. Once seen, this truth is very difficult to ignore. Transman Cody Wiley writes:

> Human identity is more than just our skin; it is a powerful force. Call it spirit, psychological construct, whatever. Identity has the gravitational pull of a black hole. All the power of the surrounding universe, from your name and image in the mirror, to other people's conceptions of who you are combined, can't pull you away. But should you get caught between your soul gender and your social gender based on body sex, the two can rip you to shreds eventually. To try to live two lives is to walk barefoot on a razor edge between two abysses.[2]

The attempt to live two lives, one known only to us and one that is seen and affirmed by the outside world, is dangerous and even deadly. The Spirit comes to lead us away from that danger and back to the search for authenticity. I believe that the pull of this identity is a sacred process, calling us to be more and more fully ourselves, as we were created to be. The quest is to discover who we were created to be and how we see ourselves in this world.

The search for our selves begins in childhood.

Childhood

For most of us, I suspect childhood is quite different from the idyllic image of play and growth that our culture seems to maintain about that time of life. For those of us who sensed strongly that we were something other

2. Cody Wiley, "I'm a Tomboy Who Grew into a Transman," *Sojourner: The Women's Forum* 26, no. 3 (November 2000): 15.

than what people believed us to be, childhood was a time that included secrets, fear, and attempts to find a place where we could be ourselves. I remember longing quite deeply to play Little League with the boys and having an absolute sense that I should tell *no one* about that desire. I do not know exactly what told me not to reveal that, but I remember the feeling clearly. While it may not seem so cataclysmic from an adult perspective, as a child that desire was very important to me. Veteran community leader Jeff S. said in our interview, "I can't remember a time when I didn't wish I was a boy, even as a little kid. It was the first thing I would pray, or I would put money in wishing wells or blow out candles on cakes, stuff like that, and I can't remember a time when I didn't think I should have been a boy."[3]

For children to feel that they must keep such a secret from the adults around them is a difficult, and even traumatic, experience. Those adults are ones who have the responsibility of caring for us, helping us grow, and loving us, but most of us learn, overtly or intuitively, not to trust them with this information, whether or not our fears are justified. Even with the burden of secret keeping, we learn something about who we are as our childhoods unfold. A deep isolation surrounds children who are different and who know themselves to be different. Often we feel estranged from other children, who also sense our differences, and we are subject to taunting, harassment, and even violence in school and on the playground. One of the reasons given for treating children who are gender nonconforming is the desire to spare them this negative attention from other children, although such treatment does not usually include a focus on changing the behavior of the children responsible for the harassment.

I want to share two stories, written by adult transgendered people, about their experiences dealing with their genders as children. Narrative is the best way to hear and understand what these experiences were like and what they meant to gender-dysphoric young people. In both of these accounts, I hear the strength of self-affirmation even while adult voices are countering it. I see children knowing something critical about who they were, even when no one else wants to believe it about them. Early on in life, these children knew who they were and who they were becoming. Both examples come from a book called *Boys Like Her,* written by a group of

---

3. Interview with Jeff S., August 1, 2001.

young, female-born performance artists crossing the boundaries of gender. The first example comes from Kate Bornstein's forward to the book and the other from the text itself.

Kate Bornstein

There was this one time when I was ten years old — maybe eleven or twelve, but not yet thirteen. I was sitting in a restaurant with my parents. My older brother was off at boarding school. My parents and I had just finished a big Italian meal, and I was feeling comfortably full. It took a lot in those days to make me feel comfortably full. My mother used to buy my clothes in the Husky Boy department of the discount clothing store across the tracks in Asbury Park, New Jersey. This was 1958 or '59, maybe 1960.

My father peered intently at my face. I felt the blush beginning to rise in my cheeks. Was he gonna see anything? My father, a big man, a rude man, a rough doctor of the community, my father turned to my mother, the lady, his beloved, and he said, "Mildred, your son has eyelashes like a girl."

This was one of the big forks in the road of my life. This was where I went to my deep-inside place and wished as hard as I could that my mother would say something like, "You know, Paul, you're right. He does." And then she'd turn to me and say, "Honey, have you thought that maybe you'd like to be a girl?" And me, I'd breathe a sigh of relief, I would. The kind of sigh that only a pre-teen who's been laughed at and left out for his weight and his brains and his clumsiness and his Jewishness, this little me can breathe, really breathe, and I'd say, "Yes, Oh, yes . . . that makes the most sense to me, Mom. Thanks, Dad, for noticing." And my father would smile and say, "Think nothing of it, son — whoops! Better make that 'daughter'."

And the three of us would have laughed, just like families on television laughed together. And the pounds would have dropped off my body, and the rest of my features would have fallen into the conga line of my girly-girl eyelashes, and the next day my mother-the-lady and I would have gone shopping (not in the Husky Boy department) and my name would probably have been Alice or Allison, not Albert, and yes, that would have been that.

I wouldn't have gone through another twenty-five years of silence. I wouldn't have spent hour after hour of every waking day wondering why I was a boy instead of a girl. I would have simply reached an amicable agreement with my parents, and that would have been that.

No more hiding clothes in nooks.

I wouldn't have finally gone through with my gender change only to spend the next twelve years still looking in silence for some gender to belong to, some gender the culture approved of that would somehow include me.

No more teachers' dirty looks.

But this was not yet the freewheeling sixties. This was the if-you-don't-have-something-nice-to-say-don't-say-anything-at-all fifties. So, what really happened was my mother turned to my father there in the restaurant and she said, "Don't talk like that, Paul, please. It's difficult enough with his weight problem."
Don't talk like that.
Lots more silence, lots more fears.
Don't talk like that.
Lots more wishing, lots more tears.[4]

This story is an incredibly poignant look inside a young child, not even yet a teenager, who knows something profound and true about herself. This truth is recognized, in a way, even by her father, and yet it is driven underground, not even to be talked about. This secret is a powerful one to keep inside. This story tells about a child left alone to struggle with something huge, something serious and deep about herself with no one present to really help.

She describes turning to a deep-inside place where she wishes that her parents, who are supposed to love and protect her, would actually notice the truth of who she is and acknowledge it as good and genuine. What makes this story so profound for me is the depth of longing for acknowledgment and compassion that comes through it. To be known and understood, to be cared for and loved, is a common human desire. It becomes even more powerful when we believe that the truth about who we are cannot be named and when it can even put in jeopardy the relationships we have with those we love. What do we do when the truth of who we are cannot be mentioned?

Kate conveys eloquently the sheer force of silence and the way that it is imposed upon us and upon our lives. When the topic finally breaks to the surface, when a moment comes at which they might talk about it, her mother says, "Don't talk like that." I hear in those words a mother's desire to protect her child from more harsh words, more teasing, more difficulty. The silence that surrounds us is often well meant and even compassionate, but silence nonetheless keeps us from speaking our own truths.

Yet even with this silence, and the moment gone and covered over, Kate Bornstein still knew a truth about herself that remained to be uncovered

---

4. Kate Bornstein, introduction to Taste This (Anna Camilleri, Ivan E. Coyote, Zoë Eakle, and Lyndell Montgomery), *Boys Like Her: Transfictions* (Vancouver: Press Gang Publishers, 1998), 9–10.

and named aloud years later. The protection of this truth within a person so that it survives the years, the silence, and the denial is, I believe, a spiritual issue. Something continued to sustain her even in the face of a world that denied her reality.

The next story, a couple of decades after Kate Bornstein's childhood, tells of a slip across gender lines during summer swim lessons and shows the power of a child living his own truth. This story is a child born with a girl's body and a strong spirit.

No Bikini, by Ivan E. Coyote

I had a sex change once, when I was six years old.

The Lions pool where I grew up smelled like every other swimming pool everywhere, that's the thing about pools. Same smell. Doesn't matter where you are.

It was summer swimming lessons, there was a little red badge with white trim that we were all after. Beginners, ages five to seven. My mom had bought me a bikini.

It was one of those little girl bikinis, a two-piece, I guess you would call it. The top part fit like a tight cut-off T-shirt, red with blue squares on it; the bottoms were longer than panties but shorter than shorts, blue with red squares. I had tried it on the night before when my mom got home from work, and I found that if I raised both my arms completely over my head too quickly, the top would slide up over my flat chest and people could see my you-know-whats.

"You'll have to watch out for that," my mother had stated, concern making lines on her forehead. "Maybe I should have got the one-piece, but all they had left were yellow and pink. You don't like yellow either, do you?"

Pink was out of the question, we had already established this.

So the blue-and-red two-piece it was going to have to be. I was an accomplished tomboy by this time, so I was used to hating my clothes.

It was so easy, the first time I did it, that it didn't even feel like a crime. I just didn't wear the top part. There were lots of little boys still getting changed with their mothers, and nobody noticed me slipping out of my brown cords and striped T-shirt and padding, bare chested, out to the side of the pool.

Our swimming instructor was broad shouldered and walked with her toes pointing out. She was a human bullhorn, bellowing all instructions to us and punctuating each sentence with sharp blasts on a silver whistle that hung about her bulging neck on a leather bootlace.

"All right, Beginners, everyone line up at the shallow end, boys here, girls here, come on come on come on, boys on the left, girls on the right."

It was that simple, and it only got easier after that first day. I wore my trunks under my pants and changed in the boys' room after that first day. The short form of the birth name my parents bestowed on me was androgynous enough to allow my charade to proceed through the entire six weeks of swimming lessons, six weeks of boyhood, six weeks of bliss.

It was easier not to be afraid of things, like diving boards and cannonballs, and backstrokes, when nobody expected you to be afraid. It was easier to jump into the deep end when you didn't have to worry about your top sliding up over your ears. I didn't have to be ashamed of my naked nipples, because I had not covered them up in the first place. The water running over my shoulders and back felt simple and natural and good.

Six weeks lasts a long time when you are six years old. In the beginning I thought the summer would never really end, that grade two was still an age away. I guess I thought that swimming lessons would continue far enough into the future that I didn't need to worry about report card day.

Or maybe I didn't think at all.

" 'He is not afraid of water over his head'?" my mom read aloud in the car on the way home, her voice rising at the end of the sentence. My dad was driving, eyes straight ahead on the road. " 'He can tread water without a flotation device'?" Her eyes were narrow, and hard, and kept trying to catch mine in the rearview mirror. " 'Your son has successfully completed his Beginner's and Intermediate badges and is ready for his Level One'?"

I stared at the toes of my sneakers and said nothing.

"Now excuse me, young lady, but would you like to explain to me just exactly what you have done here? How many people have you lied to? Have you been parading about all summer half-naked?"

How could I explain to her that it wasn't what I had done, but what I didn't do? That I hadn't lied, because no one had asked. And that I had never, not once, felt naked.

"I can't believe you. You can't be trusted with a two-piece."

I said nothing all the way home. There was nothing to say. She was right. I couldn't be trusted with a two-piece. Not then, and not now.[5]

Among other things, this story demonstrates clearly the different experiences that boys and girls have in our society. By crossing that line, Ivan entered a world in which he wasn't expected to be afraid, and so gained courage. At the same time, he encountered the disapproval and anger of his mother for attempting to address the issues he was encountering within himself. By finding a way to feel "simple and natural and good," he

---

5. Taste This, *Boys Like Her: Transfictions*, 21–24.

invoked his mother's anger and she accused him of deception. Children who transgress gender face punishment while they try to find a place that feels right for them.

Transgendered people often have to deal with this clash between our inner sense of truth and other people's sense that they are somehow being lied to or deceived. We see this theme again and again in this book. Ivan's testimony that it was not a lie and that he was never naked is very much his own truth and yet his mother sees deception in it because he successfully convinced others to affirm the truth he knew about himself rather than her understanding that her child was a girl. What felt authentic to him was seen by his mother as lying.

I find in this story a wonderful, stubborn refusal to play along with the gender system and the roles it enforced for boys and girls. The reminiscence has a profoundly hopeful and defiant air to it. I find myself wishing that I had had the nerve to do such a thing as a first-grader. Stories of defiance and liberation sustain spiritually people who are oppressed. The Exodus story tells us of a people who refused to see themselves definitively as slaves without hope for freedom. The journey to liberation would not have been possible had the Hebrew people not had a sense of themselves as something other than how the Egyptians defined them. In the same way, I see this story as one in which a child saw more ways of being than those articulated and defined by our society. By refusing to play along with the limited roles, s/he stakes out new territory, opening the doors to a more liberating option. We come out of slavery to externally defined gender roles only when we are able to see ourselves not as slaves unable to break loose of oppressive categories but as free people.

A number of transgendered children know who they are and refuse to lie about it, or they are obviously gender different and cannot hide it. In his article on social work practice with transgendered children, Gerald P. Mallon quotes an eight-year-old client called Mark, who was self-named Monique. The child said simply, "I can't be what I am not, and I am not a boy."[6] Such knowledge carries a high price tag. Mark/Monique's great-grandmother, who is her primary care provider, states that she does not want this child to live with her anymore. Only after other possibilities

---

6. Gerald P. Mallon, *Social Services with Transgendered Youth* (New York: Harrington Park Press, 1999), 56.

were ruled out did she agree that her great-grandchild could remain in her home. Mallon goes on to say:

> Although some transgendered children are healthy and resilient, many gender variant children are at great risk within their family system and within institutional structures. Gender variant children, because they are told that they do not fit in, are in a constant search for an affirming environment, where they can be themselves. In the search for this situation, many transgendered youth are at risk for depression, anxiety, self-abuse, substance abuse, suicide and family violence.[7]

The isolation that transgendered children feel puts them at a high risk for abuse from others and from themselves, draining resources from other developmental tasks and forcing many children to retreat inward.

Phyllis Burke, in her 1996 book *Gender Shock: Exploding the Myths of Male and Female*, effectively chronicles the many "treatments" forced upon young children who are deemed to be effeminate boys or masculine girls. She describes in detail a number of children who became models for teaching physicians about dealing with gender differences; the children were coached to behave in stereotypical mannerisms and play patterns deemed appropriate for their sex. The children faced both extreme positive reinforcement for compliance and punishment, including spanking, for failing to abide within those stereotypes.

Transgendered children face a horrifying dilemma of hiding what they know about themselves until they reach adulthood or being honest and facing the risks of being thrown out of the family home or being punished at home or school with repeated violence. Profound spiritual violence is wrought on an individual for hiding the truth of him- or herself or for facing human hostility year after year.

Adult transgendered people need to think of these children as our children. Drawing on our own experiences, we know what these children experience as they face school and family day after day. We know their struggles in a way that even their parents do not understand and often, unfortunately, do not seek to understand. These children need protection from the psychological, spiritual, and physical harm that is visited on those who are gender different, and we can offer that, at least to some of them. I believe Christians have a mandate to do so. Jesus blessed the children

---

7. Ibid., 57.

and reminded his listeners that whatever they did to "the least of these" they did to him. He did not judge the children or single out the acceptable children, but blessed all of them and reminded people who listened to him that how we treat children is of great importance to God. In the same way, intersexed children need to be protected from invasive surgery that is not medically necessary and that can damage their bodies in irreparable ways.

After describing two gender-variant children, Liza and Hector, Mallon says:

> Although some may view the conditions of Liza and Hector through a lens of pathology, others who approach practice from a trans-affirming perspective may ask, Why can't Liza construct her identity to be male as she sees it, and how can it be so terrible if Hector envisions himself as a girl? The larger question is: Why are gender variant children so disturbing to people, especially to parents?[8]

Why, indeed, is allowing an individual to construct an identity as it feels right to that person so shocking? From a spiritual perspective, what is threatened when some people say that their souls are of a gender different from the gender assigned to them at birth? What is so threatening when people come to a different conclusion about who they are?

Adolescence

All adolescents struggle with a search for identity and with the need to define themselves as individuals, separate from their parents, siblings, and peers. Transgendered adolescents face additional challenges, including the all-too-frequent occurrence of violence and rejection at home, school, and church. Puberty brings about changes in mood and body that are difficult to address. Adolescence brings physical changes that can heighten the sense of being betrayed by a body that is developing the "wrong" way for what the teen feels inside. In addition to the dangers we've noted already for transgendered children, Christian Burgess writes, in an article about the development of transgendered teens, "Because of the internalization of negative attitudes toward gender non-conformity, transgender youth are at an increased risk for low self-esteem, which may manifest itself through depression, substance abuse, self-mutilation and/or suicide."[9]

8. Ibid., 58.
9. Christian Burgess, in Mallon, *Social Services with Transgendered Youth*, 41.

Transgendered teens face the same challenges of finding themselves that other young people face, plus the issue of their gender identity. Alexis Belinda Dinno writes about her experiences as a transgendered youth, noting:

> Beginning the expression of one's transgender identity at the age when one is beginning the expression of one's entire identity is bad. Sucks, bites, lags, wanks. I remarked to my therapist recently that the thing that makes transition so frustrating (go on, read *dysphoric* if you must), is that what really amounts to a small part of a person's overall identity (gender) colors every other aspect of life and interferes with it. If you called me transsexual and expected to get a good understanding of me because the label fits, you would miss so much of what is important about me.[10]

She has a sense of herself as a transsexual and also as someone whose identity is broader than that. Like most teens, she wants people to see not just their stereotypes about her, but who she really is.

Rebecca Klein, a social worker who provides services to male-to-female youth, identifies a number of major issues that threaten the well-being of transgendered teens. In addition to being vulnerable to higher rates of suicide, transgendered youth face higher rates of homelessness and institutionalization as a result of being thrown out of their parents' homes; violence and harassment in school that make completing an education very difficult; difficulty in obtaining employment (other than on the streets) because of gender nonconformity, victimization, and trauma; and high rates of drug and alcohol abuse.[11]

A young FTM named Jeffrey began a support group for other transgendered youth when he was unable to find other support. He says of his own experience:

> During my coming out to my father, he became very angry. He then kicked me out of his apartment and I was homeless. That fight with my Dad catalyzed my move to complete financial independence from my family of origin, and also was my first taste of rejection by those I love. I was eighteen. I had to geographically relocate in order to discover my own self.[12]

---

10. Alexis Belinda Dinno, "From the Perspective of a Young Transsexual," in *Transgender Care: Recommended Guidelines, Practical Information, and Personal Accounts*, ed. Gianna E. Israel and Donald E. Tarver II, M.D. (Philadelphia: Temple University Press, 1997), 205.

11. Rebecca Klein, in Mallon, *Social Services with Transgendered Youth*, 98–100.

12. Leanne McCall Tigert and Timothy J. Brown, *Coming Out Young and Faithful* (Cleveland: Pilgrim Press, 2001), 79.

Sometimes, the only way for a transgendered teen to continue the process of self-discovery is to leave her/his parents' home, either by choice or by necessity. Jeffrey goes on to say, "the transgender experience is often misrepresented in the media, stigmatized by the queer community, pathologized by the medical institution, demonized by communities of faith, and targeted for the most violent of hate crimes throughout the world."[13] In the midst of all this, Jeffrey proclaims his pride in who he is and states that his career goal is to become an ordained minister.

In an article entitled "The Boy Who Grew Up to Be a Woman," Jody Norton describes an adolescence filled with anxiety and nonconformity, self-medicated with drugs and alcohol to get through the days. She has this recollection: "The sexual moments that stick with me most from my adolescence tend to be ones in which another boy modeled femininity for me, and in doing so, made me want both him and the elusive, sexy female identity he freely and beautifully took on. I saw 'he' become 'she' in a crystalline moment, like the sun shining down through a split in the clouds."[14] In the midst of the turmoil of adolescence, she has these moments of clarity, when the sun comes shining down, despite the confusion and difficulties she encounters. She sees beauty in herself and in other feminine boys. This insight offers a moment of self-recognition and acceptance of identity, both her own and what she sees reflected in another youth. She concludes saying:

> My narrative doesn't have an ending, because my gender journey is not complete. I understand my life to this point (insofar as it has a living meaning, rather than a dying one) as having been a struggle to allow myself to claim the right to love, the right to desire, and the right to be. Living for me now is an ongoing series of transformations — yet composed through greater patience, and adhering with more continuity, than ever before. That paradox — that one can stay, moving — stands for me as a metaphor for transgender. May we all stay where we love to be, moving as much as we need to.[15]

Our spiritual challenge is to be able to claim our right to love and our right to be who we are. One of the spiritual forces that transgendered

---

13. Ibid., 80.

14. Jody Norton in Matthew Rottnek, ed., *Sissies and Tomboys: Gender Nonconformity and Homosexual Childhood* (New York: New York University Press, 1999), 266.

15. Ibid., 273.

people recognize and learn about is the sacredness of transformations and the way in which we can change to become more and more ourselves.

In *Coming Out Young and Faithful,* the authors include this prayer for a teen dealing with issues of gender identity:

> Creator God, I am learning things all the time. It is a gift to be young and to get to know you and your world, your beautiful creation.
>
> I am also getting to know myself, and I'm discovering that sometimes I feel as if I were the other gender. Sometimes I feel scared about these feelings. Sometimes I feel wonderful about them.
>
> I know that I am your creation, and you have given me a wonderful gift in my gender identity. I pray for your supporting presence as I become more comfortable with my feelings. I pray for your guidance, that I may know when it is the right time for me to let other people know about this part of me.
>
> I pray for your supporting presence if I should be rejected, knowing that you, God who created me, will not reject me, that you will affirm me as part of your beautiful creation. In you I trust. Amen.[16]

Adulthood

Many of us may have had clues about our difference as children and adolescents, but we do not begin to deal with the issue of our transgendered identity until adulthood. Transgendered people have a unique perspective on the world. We see things through different lenses because of experiences that are uncommon to most people. We encounter different spiritual issues and challenges. Of course, the particular spiritual path varies from individual to individual, but it is often marked by some similar elements. Many of us encounter common elements and go through similar stages.

As we explore questions of identity and transcendence, we encounter profoundly spiritual questions. We cannot separate our spirits from our minds and bodies; all are impacted by the ways in which we explore who we are, how we are to live in the world, and our relationship with that which is Holy. We go through nothing in a vacuum; everything exists within a context and sequence of experiences and ideas. No single list of spiritual issues for transgendered people exists because we come from many backgrounds and are at different places in our journeys. Nevertheless, we look here at some common themes.

---

16. Tigert and Brown, *Coming Out Young and Faithful,* 128.

Finding Ourselves

One of the primary spiritual tasks for us is discovering a sense of self that feels integral and true for us. Before this discovery often comes a period of denial and struggle, with a number of spiritual elements that are common for many, although not all, transgendered people. We are taught so constantly in so many subtle and overt ways that gender is an unchangeable aspect of our being, that we must be wrong to see ourselves as a different gender, and that gender dysphoria is a sign of sickness. Of course, we do not want to identify with those assessments. Many years may pass before a transgendered person is even aware that changing gender is an option.

I was active in the gay and lesbian community for my entire adult life (and part of my teen years) and worked with and knew MTFs all that time, yet not until I was thirty years old did I know that transitioning from female to male was possible. For people living quiet lives in the suburbs or rural areas, with even less access to gender-variant people than I had, a lifetime may transpire before even discovering language for what one feels inside, much less engaging the possibility of changing gender, and even less learning to access the medical and psychological resources necessary to transition. Of course, the Internet is bringing changes to that situation, connecting people who have never before been connected and providing a level of information that was previously impossible. Online communication is certainly not, however, a panacea. Many people still struggle with a lack of language and knowledge about gender possibilities.

For some people, the concept of gender transition seems so enormous and impossible that they remain in denial for many years or even for a lifetime. Others suppress their feelings, choosing not to risk family, career, or other factors, perhaps feeling without options. Many of us believe the stereotypes and think that we cannot be one of "those people." Acknowledging oneself to be transgendered takes an enormous amount of courage. People often encounter a great number of struggles along the way simply to reach that point.

I was able to find quite a bit of documentation from MTFs and cross-dressers about the kind of spiritual and emotional struggle that preceded a sense of self-recognition and some, but not as much, information about a parallel process from FTMs. I would attribute this discrepancy to the fact that effeminate boys are punished more than tomboyish girls and that more stigma is associated with men acting in ways that are usually reserved for women than for women acting in "masculine" ways. While not simple by any means, the process of accepting oneself as male or masculine in a sexist culture may well be easier than identifying as female or feminine. Some of us go through cycles in which we have some knowledge about our identities and begin the process of exploring them, only to "purge" ourselves of the books, clothes, and acceptance that we have struggled to gain.

Depression that may or may not be focused specifically on gender is frequently part of the lives of transgendered. The depression may, instead, come from a vague but still strong sense of disconnection and dissatisfaction in life. I believe that depression is not only a psychological condition, but also a spiritual one, because in the midst of it, many of us feel disconnected from God and from other people. The joy of life is missing, and living becomes more a burden than a joy, more something to be endured than to live abundantly.

I was clinically depressed during high school but genuinely had no clear sense of why or what was wrong. Hours upon hours of therapy did not lift the depression or lead me any closer to understanding its cause. I just knew that something felt wrong with me and I could not name the reason. For others, the inability to resolve questions of gender is clearly the problem. Many of us bury ourselves in work and in denial trying to avoid the question. In describing the time before her decision to transition, Presbyterian minister and therapist Rev. Dr. Erin Swenson writes:

> I struggled with depression, burying myself in work and responsibility in order to hide from the terrible truth within. I applied myself most diligently to the task of living and working as a male, and succeeded for many years. I even convinced myself that I could hold the truth within me for a lifetime, that I would die with my secret still intact. But the depression and denial took their toll on my health. Eventually, I lost my marriage, not because of my "gender problem," but because of my willingness to deny the truth and thereby destroy my self-respect and the respect of my partner. Finally, I decided I could sustain the lie no longer.[17]

For many of us, the failure of our ability to remain in denial forces us to finally address the issues that were genuinely pressing upon us. The

17. Erin Swenson, "Body and Soul United," *The Other Side* 37, no. 3 (May and June 2001): 28.

same path that Swenson outlines here is repeated on literally hundreds of websites, as well as in articles and other writings, by other transgendered people. Unfortunately, such an account is not rare. FTM Jeff S. recounts how he reached the verge of suicide before he made the decision to transition, realizing that confronting the issue was better than dying. Again, unfortunately, this perspective is not uncommon. Trans people can lose many years of life to depression and denial before we are able and willing to look at the issue that lies behind them. Some use drugs or alcohol to numb the pain of the feelings. Karen Kroll reflects:

> Inevitably, like countless others before me, I had to make a change that enabled me to know and experience that peace inside myself.
>   This peace of self was something that I lacked for much of my life. Instead I felt confusion and emotional pain in a major area of my identity. I tried in my early years to understand it, but I was only left with a puzzle that I could not explain. As a teenager I felt like a stranger living in a foreign country and I began to wear a mask to hide my true identity. This mask became an important part of my survival because without it suicide was a real possibility. I began to strike out in anger as an adult, hoping this would relieve the confusion and emotional pain. When this did not work, I tried to kill these feelings by drinking alcohol and by taking drugs to excess.[18]

Not until she was able to acknowledge her struggle with her gender identity was she able to find a way to move forward in an affirming way and put aside that mask.

Some people submerge themselves in work, trying to put their transgendered feelings and conflicts aside in pursuit of a career. Working constantly is one way to avoid having to think about personal issues or to put time and energy into a process of self-discovery that simply feels too painful. I have heard a number of people say that the more successful they felt in worldly terms, the more alienated they felt from God and from themselves. While everything on the outside looked ideal, their inner life was filled with conflicts. Some people become trapped in the mire of perfectionism, thinking that coping mechanism will offset their inner feelings of inadequacy or a sense of being flawed. I also had a strong sense that in order to be taken seriously as a professional, I needed to appear as a

---

18. Karen F. Kroll, "Transsexuality and Religion: A Personal Journey," in *Gender Blending*, ed. Bonnie Bullough, Vern L. Bullough, and James Elias (Amherst, N.Y.: Prometheus Books, 1997), 490.

woman, without shades of gender variance. The tighter I held to this view, the more miserable I became.

For transgendered people who struggle with the thought that being transgendered is sinful, they may strive even harder to find favor with God in other ways, in order to balance out the feelings of unacceptability because of gender. Even in the midst of that, our spirits find ways to shine through. Robin Shanor writes:

> In my case, I sought salvation through a career in Christian ministry. As a late teen, I found that the deepest expressions of Christianity — caring, serving, giving, sharing — connected with the feminine side of me that was breaking through. I was encouraged by those close to me to attend seminary, and I'm grateful now for that experience. But I found that I gradually lost my sense of self and spirituality, even as I strove to become "God's man." I worked for a short time as a pastor, then served for nine years as an active-duty military chaplain where I was quite successful in letting the army "make a man out of me." But I longed for a place where I could be myself as an expressive, creative, spiritual human being. I began to crumble as I struggled in desperation to find the "real me" before God.[19]

Eventually, we may reach a point where our denials, masks, and workaholism fail us, and we must set out on that search for our true selves. I believe that God also calls us to stand before God in our full authenticity.

Once we acknowledge the need for a quest to ourselves, the issues of telling others and of taking action still remain. Some people choose to keep this part of themselves secret for as long as they can. Some are able to do that, and others are simply too obvious to other people. In her article on psychotherapy with transgendered clients, Kathy A. Gainor writes:

> The adult transsexual may be more adept at keeping their gender dysphoria under wraps. They cope by playing a role, but this role playing has a price. The need to hide their feelings can lead to stress-related medical conditions like ulcers, migraines, eating disorders, and anxiety attacks. They may feel as if they are not only betraying themselves but their loved ones as well. In an adaptive response, many transsexuals may postpone pursing the GRS [genital reassignment surgery] until a significant milestone or change in their current life circumstances (e.g., adult children leaving home or death of a spouse). At this point, intense feelings of urgency and hyper-vigilance may be the predominant emotion for the adult transsexual.[20]

---

19. Shanor, "Finding Common Ground," 36.

20. Kathy A. Gainor, "Including Transgender Issues in Lesbian, Gay, and Bisexual Psychology: Implications for Clinical Practice and Training," in *Education, Research, and Practice in Lesbian, Gay,*

She goes on to note, "it should be noted that unresolved transgenderism and the stress related to it (e.g., ongoing abuse by intolerant family members) can result in severe clinical depression or other mental illness."[21]

In addition to the physical and psychological stresses caused by this kind of hiding, a spiritual toll results as well. Having a sense of our own identities and at the same time pretending that this knowledge does not exist leads to a sense of spiritual alienation. What is, then, the authentic person? Who are we? When we are busy playing a role in order to avoid the truth, the temptation arises to maintain that role when encountering God. In fact, if our objections to our own transgendered natures are based on religious grounds, then we may feel as if we must maintain that role in order to be acceptable to God. Maintaining such a stance leads to a sense of spiritual unauthenticity and alienation from God and self. Of course, we cannot hide ourselves from God. Trans people may face a need to find and reconnect with our authentic selves and to learn to honor that connection in the presence of God.

As time moves on, circumstances change, the denial becomes too painful to maintain, or the spirit becomes strong enough to address these issues, we begin to explore the feelings behind them and acknowledge that we are transgendered. The range of circumstances that sets this process in motion is as varied as each individual. For me, the moment of revelation came fairly suddenly; for others, information gathers slowly over the years.

Shortly before my own decision to explore transition, a close friend who I knew had struggled with gender issues for most of life informed me that s/he was joining an e-mail group for female-to-male transsexuals. Immediately, those words touched off a rage inside of me. I knew that I supported this person in the decision to further explore these issues and I could not figure out why they caused such anger in me. After trying to give some words of encouragement, I excused myself, knowing that I needed some time and space to think this through. I drove alone to the beach and sat there looking at the ocean while I sorted it all out. All of a sudden, I realized that the emotion I was feeling was jealousy, something I rarely feel. I realized I was angry that my friend was taking this step and I was not. I went home, called my friend, got the information, and joined

Bisexual, and Transgendered Psychology: A Resource Manual, ed. Beverly Green and Gladys L. Croom (Thousand Oaks, Calif.: Sage, 2000), 148.
    21. Ibid., 152.

the e-mail list myself. Then I knew that I had reached the point where I
could be in denial no longer and that I was now ready to face the issue. I
had had thoughts before that I had wished that I had been born male, but
not until then did I truly acknowledge the degree to which I was unhappy
and the desire to make this change in my life.

For some of us, that moment leads us to go to God and ask for guidance
at this pivotal time. Does God wants us to take this step? Since many of us
have tried for so long to change our feelings, suddenly we approach God
with a different question. Ashley Moore described how she had gone to
see an old documentary about transsexuals; while watching the movie, she
had a sense, finally, of what she is. She left the theater and then describes:

> I knew for the first time in my life what was really going on. As I went
> to my car, I was just driving in my car for a while, and I went home and
> I prayed. I just essentially said, "God, you know that I have been fighting
> against this my whole life, practically. But if this is what's right, then I put
> all of my faith into you to lead me through this transition . . . into this. If
> this is right, then I surrender to your will, so to speak. You need to guide
> me." So immediately, I got on the Web, and I started looking for things. I
> think the first thing I came up with was a letter by someone who had been
> a priest.[22]

Some of us, like Ashley, have a sense that rather than following God's will
all of these years when we've been fighting our transgendered feelings,
we may have been moving away from God. Acknowledging ourselves as
transgendered may be accompanied by a great sense of relief and of affirmation. The point of acknowledgment can be a time of stepping out in
faith to follow God in a new and unexpected direction. This sense of God's
presence and guidance at this point can lead to a renewal of faith and a
stronger sense of connection with God.

The moment we acknowledge what is true about ourselves is powerful
in ways that are both frightening and uplifting. I believe that moment is
one of great spiritual power and importance because it signals the time
when we choose the search for our authentic selves over the other issues
in our lives. The spiritual focus goes inward to discover who we were
created to be and who we are. Acknowledgment is a quest for selfhood.
Some people may charge that this process is selfish, and parts of it may
be. At this time, our own needs may be more important to us than the

---

22. Interview with Ashley Moore, August 2001.

needs of people around us. Living our lives only for ourselves limits us spiritually and emotionally, but so does living only for others and ignoring the callings of our own souls.

Self-discovery may bring about a moment when we spiritually separate the wheat from the chaff of our lives — when we know that we have discovered a truth so profound that nothing in life will look the same after we have seen it. Having seen the truth, we can no longer pretend that we do not know it. Once our eyes have been opened, we cannot shut them again. This event changes our lives. I felt an alternating sense of euphoria and panic, of profound gratitude for what I now saw about myself and a dread of how others might view me if they only knew what I now understood. Questions of "why me?" and "now what?" also emerged.

This process of self-recognition is the start of understanding who we are and what being transgendered means. At this point in the process, the person may experience a strong sense of alienation from her/his body or a sense of a split between body and spirit and may also encounter a strong sense of fear at where or to what this self-revelation will lead. Many of us carefully analyze the cost of transitioning — the potential to lose a job, end a career, tear apart a marriage — and the cost of remaining in the pain of denial.

A very real loss often does occur. Far too many transgendered people experience a profound crisis in their primary relationships or even the ending of the relationship with spouses, children, and parents. In most places, discrimination against transgendered people in housing and employment remains completely legal. While some of us are lucky enough to have supportive workplaces, too many trans people face great difficulty in finding meaningful employment during or after transition. At the same time, some of us suffer more from our fear of those losses than we do from actual loss. The process of coming out and revealing our transgendered identity shows us clearly the people in our lives who are willing to stand beside us, no matter what comes along. We may see strength and compassion from our family members that we did not know existed. Until we take that step to come out to ourselves and to those we love, we will not know all of the resources that may be available to us.

Living with the Information We've Learned

We begin by recognizing and stating what is happening within our own hearts and lives, but then we must learn to come to terms with that self-revelation. In this stage, we ask and answer, at least in part, the question of what we are going to do with the information that we now have about ourselves. This stage also brings to a close the process of self-rejection and prayers for deliverance from the gender dysphoria and a stronger acceptance of who we are. Erin Swenson notes this step, after years of prayer to accept herself as a male:

> I expect my prayers were, indeed, answered. Not by some miraculous change in my gender identity, but by an equally miraculous arrival at self-acceptance. I believe that God does answer prayer, though often the answers we get are not the ones we wanted or expected. My burden has been lifted....It's just that I now am able to accept the identity I have been given, giving up the struggle to seek some other identity that does not belong to me.[23]

With a sense of acceptance, we may find that our spiritual focus shifts from trying to move away from what we perceived about ourselves to a focus now on accepting what we know about ourselves. The purpose of prayer is no longer to relieve a burden, but a search for a path through this experience, going deeper into ourselves.

One of the primary issues that arises with an acceptance of a trans-gendered identity is a sense of discontinuity between the body and the spirit. As we see later, some people in the religious community argue that there can be no such sense of discontinuity or that the "truth" of the body is ultimately more important than the feeling of the spirit, while others note that the truth of humanity is found in both body and spirit. For many of us, a sense of alienation from our bodies has been a feature of our inward lives for as long as we can remember. Claiming a transgendered identity allows us a new way of thinking about our bodies.

For transsexuals, the body becomes not "wrong" but rather part of a process of change, a realization that is incredibly liberating. Our bodies do not have to remain the same, but can be the very agents of liberation as we realize that we can change our bodies. In looking at our bodies in a new way, as changeable, we then embark upon the process of reconciling the inner and the outer parts of our nature. Instead of trying to force ourselves to accept our bodies as they are, we instead can be empowered

---

23. Erin Swenson in "Materials on the Ordination Case of Erin K. Swenson and the Presbytery of Greater Atlanta, Presbyterian Church, USA, 1995–1997," 26.

agents to change our bodies. Instead of having to live as other people view us, we gain control over how we present ourselves in public.

For people who identify in other places along the transgendered spectrum, the body may become a way to express the totality of a person's being, rather than simply one part. Our body can be a way of showing on the outside what is present on the inside. Lauren René Hotchkiss notes:

> I have often wondered whether part of our motivation in crossdressing stems from the fact that we are perhaps subconsciously trying to transform ourselves into the part of our inner being from which we have separated ourselves. We have been so conditioned to believe that we must look outside of ourselves in order to find someone with whom we can become complete, though constantly disappointed in the attempt, that we have lost sight of the fact that wholeness comes from within. Because of this misperception, we have found it necessary to create this second person within ourselves, and manifest them accordingly, in order to fill a self-perceived void.[24]

Part of the process of claiming an identity is the willingness to explore the issues that Hotchkiss raises, including a search for inner wholeness. This task is about embracing a process of no longer attempting to suppress our inner feelings, but seeking to express them in a more holistic and total way. This process may include finding ways to let the inner self be more completely expressed on and in the body itself.

Reconciling the inner and outer natures of ourselves is a key component of and motivation for claiming and continuing to explore a transgendered identity. The Rev. Carol Stone, an Anglican priest who has continued in her parish in England while transitioning from male to female, commented to a reporter:

> "Among my earliest memories are of me wishing that I was other than I am," he [sic] recalled. "Every night I prayed I would wake up as a girl. I thought it was perfectly normal and reasonable at the age of four or five to do that. If there was another way for me, I would not be here today. Nobody does this by choice. The whole thing is full of agony. I am looking forward to that moment when I will consider myself to be a matching head and body and heart."[25]

---

24. Lauren René Hotchkiss, "Is Transgenderism Wrong?" *http://members.tgforum.com/bobbyg/ istranwrong.html*, 11/22/00.

25. PlanetOut, *www.moss-fritch.com/First_TransVicar.htm*, 3/19/01.

Bringing these elements into congruity is a critical task of this stage. Transitioning is not simply about surgery or body modification to bring those pieces into alignment, but also about having a sense of a common self, a self that is expressed in all situations and through all aspects of one's being.

Transitioning is also the time to forge a new identity. Mildred Brown in her book about transsexuals notes, "As transsexuals slough off the outer shell of the male or female persona they have presented to the world, they must create a new identity. Having repressed their instincts about their true gender for such a long time, even though they are finally in a position to demonstrate it outwardly, they are unskilled and awkward at the outward expression of their new role."[26] For transsexuals, the stage of self-acceptance includes a sense of embarking on the revelation of a new identity that more accurately reflects the inward reality. Developing a new sense of identity and integrating the knowledge that we now have about ourselves take time.

Another stage in the process of accepting ourselves as transgender may be the selection of a name that is more compatible with the expression of another gender. This name may become permanent and used at all times, or it may one that is used when the person is dressed in the clothing of the other gender. Our names express a great deal about us, including information about our families of origin, our ethnicity, and how we see ourselves. The selection of a new name is usually undertaken with great seriousness and care because it will signify a new sense of identity. Some people use a gender-neutral nickname, such as Chris or Robin, or a variation of the name given to them by their parents, such as Samuel to Samantha or Nicole to Nicholas, while others choose a name based on its meaning, sound, or just preference. Sometimes, people have the sense of a name being revealed to them from a higher source, either in a dream, in prayer, or during a time of quest. Some transgendered people choose to have the name change ritually celebrated within a community of faith with a prayer of blessing in their new name, a rebaptism or a ceremony of bar or bat mitzvah.

We also may develop a sense of pride in ourselves and in our community for our courage and strength. I remember going to a trans event shortly

---

26. Mildred L. Brown and Chloe Ann Rounsley, *True Selves: Understanding Transsexualism — For Families, Friends, Coworkers, and Helping Professionals* (San Francisco: Jossey-Bass, 1996), 127.

after my decision to transition and looking around the room full of people and thinking how incredible this community was. Here was a room full of people who were following their dreams, even when that dream meant that walking down the street was not always safe. Here were people willing to listen to their hearts, against all odds, and affirm themselves. Riki Ann Wilchins addressed a crowd at the Boston Pride celebration, saying, "Now look around you at the transsexual and transgendered faces here tonight, at the dignity and survival written in these faces. Let me assure you: We are more complex than your theories, more creative than your dogma, and much more stubborn and rude and resourceful than your politics."[27]

Another issue that often emerges during this stage is the question of truth. While a trans person sees this as primarily a discovery of the truth within us, we are frequently accused of perpetuating some kind of deception against the rest of the world. Some people charge that by altering our appearances, we are fundamentally misleading others about our natures. Yet, for us, our approach is about making visible that which has been invisible. Rather than telling others a lie about who we are, we are expressing the elemental truth about ourselves. We are not creating something that has not been present, but revealing that which has always been there. Chris Paige, who identifies as both/neither gender, says this about his/her identity:

> As an adult, when store clerks call me "sir" and then recognize their mistake, I find the intensity of their anxiety confounding. As a child I was often mistaken for a boy, and such negative reactions, experienced regularly, communicated a great deal to me about the impropriety of my identity. In fact, I wore long hair from junior high through college *specifically* to avoid that experience. Such adaptations helped me survive, but they also threatened my integrity.[28]

For many of us, acknowledging our transgendered selves is pivotal to regaining a sense of integrity, and we may even feel the need to confess the fact that we had lived what felt like a lie.

Our desire to live with greater integrity is often the factor that leads us to the conclusion that we must come out and acknowledge to ourselves,

---

27. Riki Ann Wilchins, *Read My Lips: Sexual Subversion and the End of Gender* (Ithaca, N.Y.: Firebrand Books, 1997), 62.

28. Chris Paige, "OtherWise," *The Other Side* 37, no. 3 (May and June 2001): 34.

God, and others that we are transgendered. Quaker Petra Doan describes how her search for a more authentic spirituality lead her to this question:

> It was Wilmer Cooper's *The Testimony of Integrity in the Society of Friends* (Pendle Hill pamphlet #296) that helped me realize how my gender jour-ney and my spirituality were intimately connected. Cooper's analysis of integrity's four parts — truthfulness, authenticity, obedience to God, and wholeness — cast a spotlight on my own lack of integrity. I was comfortable with the basic truthfulness part, but it was in authenticity that I suddenly felt completely hollow. By denying my authentic identity for so many years, I had created a huge roadblock for myself, for my spirituality and for my survival. As I contemplated the illusory life I had created, I felt such distress that for a while it seemed as if I could not continue living. I sought out a therapist who had worked with other transgendered people and he helped me come to terms with myself. I set out to see what steps I needed to take to reclaim integrity and live an authentic life.[29]

This process of self-acceptance and claiming a transgendered identity is, for some, the first time in which they feel that their inner and outer selves are reconciled and that they are living a life of integrity.

This sense of reconciliation can lead to a deeper sense of peace and inward harmony. Spiritual peace results from having the sense of living with integrity. Drawing upon her background in the *Course in Miracles* (and quoting from it at the end), Lauren René Hotchkiss writes:

> Although it's true that the gender presentation that many of us in the transgender community adopt may not be consistent with the accepted role for our anatomical sex, it is equally true that the role that we have been conditioned to accept for ourselves is often not in harmony with our spiritual truth. As paradoxical as it may seem, it is a situation in which one must live a lie, as others would term it, in order to live one's own personal truth. What this suggests to me is that rather than being considered a losing proposition, transgenderism or ambigenderism can be seen in the more positive light of expanding the entire gamut of gender and sexual identity, and opening the door to the forward path of spiritual growth through the integration and balancing of the masculine and feminine within us. "Healing always produces harmony, because it proceeds from integration" (T 112/121).[30]

Rather than being a lie, this stage of development is about revealing the truth and seeking integration and harmony.

---

29. Petra Doan, "The Spiritual Side of Gender Journeying," *Transgender Tapestry* 92 (winter 2000): 41–42.

30. Hotchkiss, "Is Transgenderism Wrong?" 5.

For me, this period of time was one of great spiritual growth as I learned to rely increasingly upon God. I felt able to pray in a way that had not been true before, and I felt like I was more authentic in my prayers than I had ever been. I learned a great deal about relying on God for strength and hope. During the period of time when I did not look like my driver's license photo and when I had changed so much that even friends did not recognize me, I still had a strong, abiding sense that God always knew who I was, which was very comforting.

This early time of transition can be very difficult. As many questions arise as answers, and many more decisions to make about the future come. Some people become afraid of God's anger, worried that what they are doing is not God's will for them. Darin Issac Blue writes, "I had the stomach flu for three days last week and when the fever peaked I hallucinated the voice of an angry god I don't even believe in, and the angry god said he was punishing me because my transition was against his law and his nature."[31] Michelle Dee says in her article on the Internet:

> I can remember feeling continuously at odds with God during that first year, hating God and actually condemning the day I was born because I had been forced to undergo such identity torture. In my prayers to a God I didn't really know I was asking for physical safety, while occasionally screaming epithets against Him for making me a transsexual. . . . I was out of options. I had already given in to my one greatest desire in life, to change sex. There was only one place left to turn, to the very God I was cursing, and I wasn't exactly pleased with the prospect. What's more, I was pretty ambivalent about the very God I sought. I just wanted to make sure I wasn't going to hell for changing sex, that's all. I wanted my cake and to eat it, too. If I could just get square with God, maybe he'd get off my back and just let me be a girl.[32]

This passage clearly illustrates the kind of emotional chaos and uncertainty toward God that some people feel. God is both a help and a source of blame, both cursed and needed.

We must also develop some level of self-acceptance. In this stage, we come to see ourselves more realistically as we are. We explore the options that are available to us to reflect more accurately our inward nature.

31. Darin Issac Blue, "Translations," *Fireweed* 69 (spring 2000): 14.

32. Michelle Dee, "Good News! Jesus Loves Us, T*oo!" *http://members.tripod.com/~michelledee/jesustg.html*, 11/22/00.

What's more, we find ways of accepting the reality of who we are. Something is profoundly spiritual about coming to accept and love that which God has made us to be. This acceptance is a way of letting go of trying to control and change one's own God-given nature and a way of affirming the goodness of the creation as it applies to us.

Gaining a Sense of Balance

Early in our journeys, so much of our attention is focused on ourselves and on our needs to explore and define who we are and where we are going. People around us may think that we never talk about anything except trans issues and our own appearance and experiences. This time takes up so much of our energy, focus, and attention. As we continue to explore, we begin to look more broadly at our lives, our needs, and what is happening around us. We seek to put our trans lives in context and pick up some of the interests and activities that we may have let go of during the early stages of the process. For some of us, this action also leads to a realization that transition did not solve all of our problems or that we might not wish to reintegrate certain parts of our lives.

This dilemma of looking for one particular change in life to change all of the things that cause unhappiness is not limited to transgendered people, of course, but can apply to anyone. Yet even after that change, we may still be looking to see what living faithfully and fully means. We may discover that our lives are still confused and so move on to look for clarity in aspects of our lives other than gender.

Integrating is about seeing ourselves as part of a larger whole, a larger community. Having had the courage to address the question of gender, we may be more willing to look at other parts of our lives that are keeping us from wholeness, or perhaps the healing we have experienced has led us to transition. We may take on a new job or take up an interest that had been dormant while we were dealing with the questions of gender. We may find some activities more pleasurable now that we feel freer to express our gender in a way that feels more authentic. When I identified as a woman, I did not mind cooking, but it was not a particular interest of mine. However, as a man, I feel freer from the gender stereotypes that say that a woman must be in the kitchen preparing the food, and I find that I enjoy cooking a great deal. Aspects of our spirituality may also feel fuller and freer because we feel more at home within ourselves.

At this point, we may also want to explore more about ourselves and who we are becoming. *Under Construction,* a support and information group for female-to-male transsexuals in the Los Angeles area, headed by Jeff S., had a meeting focused on the question, "Okay, now you are a man. What kind of man will you be?" This question is very important — a way of acknowledging that gender does not change everything about us and that we still have choices to make about how we will be and how we will live in the world.

We may also refocus ourselves spiritually on how best to embody the spiritual principles of our faith. Having made steps to resolve an issue that we had struggled with for many years may give us the resolution and the need to look beyond that to see where else we can grow and how much more we can discover in our spirituality.

Reaching Out

At this point in our journeys, we no longer need the same focus on ourselves but look beyond ourselves to the needs of others around us. We may find ways to help others who are living the same journey as we are. I want to share the writing of one person who has set out to do this on her web page. Dr. Jaye Reviere writes:

> What those of us who have walked long upon the road of faith can do, however, is share our thinking and experience with others. In this sharing we can perhaps offer some light, some room for insight, and some reassurance that the constant drumbeat of fundamentalism pounding our ears has not deafened us to the small voice of God, who created us as we are. That's right! It is God's idea for us to be different. We can't know the mind of God. We can only infer it from the revealed word, from the movings of the Holy Spirit within, and from what our pitifully limited human senses can detect. Because we are, it is abundantly evident we are made to be as we are. We are assured of two irrefutable things. God makes no mistakes, and we are created for a purpose. It is, I believe, up to us to search and prayerfully seek to find the purpose God has for us, particularly in having created us to be apart from the common heard [sic] of humanity. Toward this end, may I offer some of the things I've discovered in my life journey? We are taught, and rightly so, as Christians, that we are created in the Image of God. I submit that this is not as so many humans presume, something physical. Rather, this Image of God in which we are created is purely spiritual image. You see, God is SPIRIT and has no one physical being. Thus God has no physical image. Now, God being Spirit sees not what is external in our

physical sense, and in the physical realm which was made merely to support and sustain the spirit beings we are while we are living in the physical. I have come to believe, it is essential for us to be the spirit beings, within the confines of this physical realm in which God has placed us, in just the way God made us to be. For those who find being different an essential element of our being true to our creation, we must be different in order to be as God intends us to be. In this way of understanding, we are an abomination in the sight of God when we work so very hard to be anything other than what God made us to be. When we deny, when we hide, when we repress, and when we go overboard or extremes [sic], we are not being what God made us to be. When we are doing these things, we are an abomination before God. When we go simply, quietly, respectfully, and reverently about being the human being God made us to be, then we are a joy to our Creator.[33]

Many of us begin to ask, and formulate answers to the question, of why we are here, why we are transgendered, and how we should live, as Reviere does here. At this time, we can reach out to people at other places on this journey. We are also led to the broader question of our individual purpose in life that is part of the process of transcending ourselves.

This process involves also seeing ourselves as part of something larger than we are, part of the creation itself. Carol Ochs writes of the Genesis creation story,

> [A] final understanding of our self must take into account that we were called into being. Our meaning, then, will be bound up with the larger Creation with which we were called into being and of which we are a part, and with the Creator who has called us forth. Self-understanding that derives from the larger Creation does not depend on socially constructed definitions. We are more than the many roles we have played in our lives. The self freed from its social moorings may well be a mystery.[34]

While her text is of general focus, these words certainly apply to trans folk. Transcendence involves moving beyond a single label or identity to seeing ourselves as part of the larger whole of creation. We become part of the Creator's plan, rather than an individual person making individual choices. As we move in this process, we may find that we are ultimately a mystery, because while we know ourselves, we always have more of us

---

33. Jaye E. Reviere, "Ethics and Crossdressing," *http://members.aol.com/_ht_a/gnlnews/ethics.html*, 11/22/00.

34. Carol Ochs, *Song of the Self: Biblical Spirituality and Human Holiness* (Valley Forge, Pa.: Trinity Press International, 1994), 6.

to discover and understand. Self-knowledge is not something that we can ever complete.

Transcendence is not, however, about losing a sense of self. Rather, transcendence is a way of gaining perspective and seeing the self as part of a larger whole. Riki Ann Wilchins writes:

> A friend once said to me that all this was about Buddhism, about transcending the self. The problem of my male self would be resolved when I transcended the very ideas of "self" and "gender" and merged with the greater Oneness. This echoes the notion that transpeople should somehow aim to be "genderfree," as if that were a possible or desirable goal.
>
> No doubt, for some it is. For me, it is not. . . .
>
> I want just three things: (1) the right to choose my own meanings — including none at all; (2) a freer marketplace from which to choose; and (3) freedom from the constant threat of punishment for my choices. That's all. Many of us, both trans and nontrans, are not interested in transcending or relinquishing our selves, but in being very particular and specific selves, ones which give meaning and resonance to our lives. It is this search that leads each of us down the varied spiritual paths we travel, hoping to find ourselves at the end, sitting quietly in that primeval playground — happy and alive and waiting.[35]

---

35. Wilchins, *Read My Lips*, 156–57.

Chapter Three

Gender Variance and the Scriptures

Many passages in the Hebrew and Christian Scriptures make explicit reference to gender, and a smaller number can be applied directly to the question of gender variance. These texts are important for us not only as persons of faith seeking guidance from the Scriptures, but also because, when misinterpreted, these texts are used to exclude transgendered people from communities of faith. I have selected eight passages that I feel are most relevant to our community.

Genesis 1:26–28a

Then God said, "Let us make an earth-being in our own image, after our likeness; and let them have dominion over the fish of the sea, and over the birds of the air, and over the cattle, and over all the earth, and over every creeping thing that creeps upon the earth." So God created humanity in God's own image, in the image of God, God created them; male and female God created them. And God blessed them.

The question of gender occurs here, at the very beginning of the story of creation. If we are to examine the understanding of gender in the Bible, we need go no further than the first chapter before we encounter it. This passage has been used both to support a broadened understanding of a range of the gender of humanity and God as well as a way to support the concept of the division of humanity in two distinct and separate genders.

Some people have used this text from the beginning of Genesis to argue that God created the binary divisions of humanity that humans should then observe. Because God created man and woman, they argue, these are the only two categories of humankind. Oliver O'Donovan states:

Human beings come into existence with a dimorphically differentiated sexuality. . . . The story of Adam and Eve, in the literary context in which the whole redaction of Genesis has given it to us, is of the greatest significance

in shaping Christian thought; for there the Yahwist interest in marriage
as relationship ("a man leaves his father and his mother and is united to
his wife") is interpreted by the Priestly interest in sexual differentiation as
creational order ("male and female he created them"). It was not a theologian who first thought that this redactional association of thoughts was
important; it was Jesus of Nazareth (Mark 10:6f. and parallels).[1]

Jesus' citing Genesis in his discussion of marriage is significant; we discuss
more about Jesus and gender later. In my interview with Richard,[2] he
stated that transsexuality falls outside of God's original plan for creation
of man and woman and that the existence of people who are somewhere
between the two genders is the result of original sin.

However, other people argue that the creation story in Genesis supports
the understanding of a broad view of gender. A closer look at the text
reveals nuances in its presentation of gender. We need to look closely at
the ways in which gender is treated within the text, both the gender of
God and the gender of humanity.

While most of us in the Jewish and Christian tradition have been taught
that God is exclusively male, Genesis 1 clearly states that God encompasses
both the female and the male since both women and men are made in
the image of God. *The New Interpreter's Bible* states, "That both male
and female are so created (see also 5:2) means that the female images the
divine as much as the male; both are addressed in the command of v. 28."[3]
The New Interpreter's Bible goes on to state that a theological argument
for God as both female and male could be made from this passage; I think
that point is clear.

God uses plural language to refer to Godself in this passage, stating
that humanity is made "in our image" and "after our likeness." Scholars
debate the reasons for the use of the plural. *The New Interpreter's Bible*
puts forth the idea that God was referring to other heavenly beings or a
"divine council,"[4] although no reference has been made yet in the book
of Genesis to any other heavenly beings, while E. A. Speiser notes that
the word *Elohim* is a plural form and the use of "our" is simply consistent

---

1. Oliver O'Donovan, "Transsexualism and Christian Marriage," *Journal of Religious Ethics* 11
(spring 1983): 141–42.
2. A pseudonym.
3. *The New Interpreter's Bible* (Nashville: Abingdon Press, 1994), 1:345.
4. Ibid.

with the noun form.[5] The use of the plural could refer to the plurality of God's own being — male, female, and beyond — which is broader than what can be understood in a single term or gender. Holly Boswell states in her article "The Spirit of Transgender," "Adam mirrored an androgynous God before the split into Eve."[6]

Biblical commentators Danna Fewell and David Gunn note some interesting characteristics of God that are revealed in the story of creation. In the early part of the story, God is engaged in dividing the world into separate parts. Day and night are differentiated from one another, and the land and the sea become separate entities. As Fewell and Gunn observe:

> On the other hand, when the account reaches a climax with the creation of humankind, that is, the creature in the image of God (Gen. 1:26–30), we see movement against that desire to differentiate. Blurring the binary poles, God desires to create likeness or sameness, to recreate self, a desire impossible to achieve. Equally interesting are the sharp edges of God's naming. The binary impulse is there very clearly. Yet in all this careful defining, separating and opposing there is a curious slippage. God "himself" is unsure whether he is plural or singular.... Significantly the slippage extends from the God(s) to the human(s) created in his/their image. While humankind is one (him/it) it is also plural — male and female (them).

Thus, despite the appearance of a world ordered and sustained by exclusive and fixed definitions, God's own blurred and slipping self-definition suggests that things might be otherwise. This world might in fact be as inherently indeterminable as the identity that creates it.[7]

This understanding of God as creating a being similar to God's self is very important. Rather than differentiation being the primary impulse, God instead creates unity with a being, unity reflective of that being's creator.

I do, however, see earlier in the text than they themselves argue this process of blurring that Fewell and Gunn note. While in the Genesis account, God separates the day from the night, the sea from the land, and the plant from the animal, our own observations of the creation reveal less differentiation than the text seems to imply. Day and night are not fixed entities with clear boundaries where one ends and the other begins;

---

5. E. A. Speiser, *Genesis*, Anchor Bible (New York: Doubleday, 1964), 7.

6. Holly Boswell, "The Spirit of Transgender," *www.homestead.com/transpirits/files/SpiritOfTG.html.*

7. Danna Nolan Fewell and David M. Gunn, *Gender, Promise, and Power: The Subject of the Bible's First Story* (Nashville: Abingdon Press, 1993), 23.

every day contains both dawn and dusk, which create a time in which day and night exist together in the same moment as one moves into the next. The tides make it difficult to see where the division of land ends and sea begins, because the earth continues on under the sea and the sea rises up to cover the shore. Distinguishing plant from animal, as is the case with coral, is not always easy. In the story of Genesis, even while God was creating apparent opposites, God also created liminal spaces in which the elements of creation overlap and merge. Surely the same could be said about the creation of humanity with people occupying many places between the poles of female and male in a way similar to the rest of creation.

The earth-being (*ādām*) created originally is both male and female, created in the image of God. This view is strongly supported by the Hebrew text, which uses the term *ādām*, not as a name as is currently familiar in English, but in description of this being created from the earth.[8] The word *ādām* is a play upon the Hebrew word for earth, *'adamah.* Rather than translating this word as a proper name, a more accurate rendering of the word would be "earthling" or "earth-being." Originally, this earthling was one, without gender differentiation, encompassing both female and male.

This creation in the image of God extends beyond gender to the intangible aspects of humanity. William Reyburn and Euan Fry note, "Scholars have argued whether the comparison is to a physical or spiritual image. No general agreement exists, and there is no clear reason why it should be the one or the other. It is probably both."[9] Nothing in the text suggests that God is drawing a distinction between the physical and the spiritual, and so it implies a more holistic perspective.

God's creative process is also different in regards to humanity. When referring to earlier acts of creation, God says either, "let there be..." or "let the waters/earth...." When speaking of humanity, however, God says, "let us make."[10] The very act of the creation of humanity is different, with God claiming a more active role.

---

8. Nahum M. Sarna, in *The JPS Torah Commentary: Genesis* (Philadelphia: Jewish Publication Society, 1989), notes that *ādām* is a singular noun used with plural verb forms, and includes both male and female, 12.

9. William D. Reyburn and Euan McG. Fry, *A Handbook on Genesis* (New York: United Bible Societies, 1997), 50.

10. Michael E. Williams, *Storyteller's Companion to the Bible*, vol. 1: *Genesis* (Nashville: Abingdon Press, 1991), 27.

God also implies a sense of co-creativity, both with the other beings possibly referenced by the plural language and with humanity itself. After noting that God was probably in dialogue with other divine beings, consulting with them about creation, *The New Interpreter's Bible* states,

> The involvement in the creative process of those created in the divine image takes the form of a command (1:28). These first divine words to human beings are about their relationship, not to God, but to the earth. They constitute a sharing of the exercise of power (dominion). From the beginning God chooses not to be the only one who has or exercises creative power. The initiative has been solely God's but once the invitation has been issued, God establishes a power-sharing relationship with humans.[11]

We can argue, then, that from the beginning humanity has been invited by God to participate in the creation process. The development of our lives, our minds, our bodies, and our spirits, over the course of our lifetimes, has been given to us as a responsibility from God. Therefore, the ways in which we have learned to modify our bodies to reflect our spirits could be part of this creative process that has been ongoing from the origins of humanity. We share, with God, the responsibility for creating our lives; God designed creation in this fashion.

The account of the creation, described in Genesis 1, tells a story that strongly supports a broader view of gender. Not only does God's own being incorporate both the male and the female, but so too does the human creation. The act of creation, even while differentiating between elements of creation, still leaves space for "in between" things: dusk, dawn, intersexed persons. God blesses all of those parts of creation, calling them good.

God also calls upon the first created human beings to participate in the ongoing care of creation as it continues to emerge. Part of the concept of having dominion over the earth signifies an autonomous responsibility to change and care for the created order. As transgendered people, this charge implies the need to care for our selves and to take responsibility for our ongoing creation and development.

Genesis 2:4b–9, 18–24

At the time when God made earth and heaven — no shrub of the field being yet in the earth and no grains of the field having sprouted, for God

---

11. *The New Interpreter's Bible*, 1:345–46.

had not sent rain upon the earth and no human being was there to till the soil; instead a flow would well up from the ground and water the whole surface of the soil — God formed an earth creature[12] from clods in the soil and blew into that one's nostrils the breath of life. Thus the earth creature became a living being.

God planted a garden in Eden, in the east, and placed there the person whom God had formed. And out of the ground God caused to grow various trees that were a delight to the eye and good for eating, with the tree of life in the middle of the garden and the tree of knowledge of good and bad. . . .

God said, "It is not right that the earth creature should be alone. I will make an aid fit for the earth creature." So God formed out of the soil various wild beasts and birds of the sky and brought them to the person to see what that one called them; whatever the person would call a living creature, that was to be its name. The person gave names to all cattle, all birds of the sky, and all wild beasts; yet none proved to be the aid that would be fit for the earth creature.

Then God cast a deep sleep upon the earth creature and, when that one was asleep, God took one of the ribs and closed up the flesh at that spot. And God fashioned into a woman the rib that he had removed from the man, and he brought her to the man. Said the man, "This one at last is bone of my bones and flesh of my flesh. She shall be called Woman,[13] for she was taken from Man."[14] Thus it is that man leaves his father and mother and clings to his wife and they become one flesh.

Probably written earlier than the first story of creation, this second account of creation comes from a different author and provides a different, less utopian, perspective. The first creation story was written by a Priestly source, whom scholars denote as "P," while this second story comes from the "J" source. The term used to denote God changes from the earlier account, as does the language about the created beings.

In this version, the androgynous earth creature, *ādām*, is put into a deep sleep by God, who then takes something from the side of this being and fashions it into a woman, creating the dichotomous genders of male and female. In the traditional understanding of this text, human beings can only have the experience of one of these roles and thus look to the other for a sense of completion and return to the original wholeness of *ādām*, the earth creature. God's breath then makes the being live but should not

---

12. *ādām.*
13. *'iššā.*
14. *'īš.*

be understood to create a soul separate from the body; rather, it creates simultaneously a living being with both body and spirit.

P emphasizes the goodness of the creation throughout the story while the author of J finds a fault — it is not good for *ādām* to live alone. Reading the text as meaning that woman was only to be a subordinate helper is inaccurate. The word used for "helper" here, *'ezer,* is used most commonly to refer to God's assistance to humanity and implies a superior help. The point of this passage is not to set up a hierarchy of humanity but rather to show and correct the problem of loneliness. Commentator Donald Gowan warns against reading too much into this text. He says of *ādām*'s deep sleep,

> "We cannot visualize what happens now. What sort of creature has 'the human' (*ha'adam*) been, that part of him could be built up into a woman and what was left over was then a man? Even to formulate such a question is so difficult that we ought to be warned against trying to make too much of this scene. The author's very choice of vocabulary thwarts every effort at a description of such an event."[15]

Gowan also notes that the emphasis of the passage is on equality of woman and man and does not support earlier sexist readings of the text that add a concept of male primacy to the text.

While this text is traditionally used to support the concept of heterosexual marriage, with the argument that we find our full completion only in a partner of the opposite sex, a sense is also here that from a single, androgynous being come two types of beings. More than one created being can come from the earth creature. The earth creature became a woman and a man when God removed a part of it and fashioned it into a whole. We know now that human fetuses can create either (or both) set of genitals in the womb, depending on hormones as much as on chromosomes. People who are genetically male but who have androgen insensitivity, for example, appear female. From that bit of human tissue, a child of either genital sex will emerge. We could read this passage as opening up the possibilities of gender. If completeness comes from having both male and female, then a person who possessed both is a return to the original completion in the earth creature.

---

15. Donald E. Gowan, *Genesis 1–11: From Eden to Babel* (Grand Rapids, Mich.: William B. Eerdmans, 1988), 47.

As Virginia Mollenkott notes:

Ironically, there is a traditional method of reading Genesis 1–2 that provides a stronger sanction for omnigender than for the binary gender construct. ...When this hermaphroditic earthling is later placed under a deep sleep, he/she is divided into the human male and female. From this perspective, intersexuals are not only part of God's original plan, they are primarily so.... From this angle, hermaphrodites or intersexuals could be viewed as reminders of Original Perfection.[16]

However, the problem that God sees with the earth creature was not that it lacked gender but that it was lonely. Traditionally, the loneliness was linked to gender, but nothing in the passage indicates that interpretation. Our reading of this passage can conclude, then, that gender is not the problem, but our isolation from love, connection, and relationship. Many trans people experience the breakup of primary relationships and isolation from their families of origin. This passage reveals to us that God is more concerned with our loneliness than with our gender and longs for us to have an appropriate companion and helper. Love brings completion, not gender, because a man and a woman who are together without love surely do not correct the problem that God identifies in this section. Rather, people who are appropriate companions and helpers for one another bring the creation back to a sense of goodness and completion.

Deuteronomy 22:5

A woman shall not wear a man's apparel, nor shall a man put on a woman's garment; for whoever does such things is abhorrent to the Sovereign your God.

Deuteronomy 22:5 is the only verse in the Bible that explicitly talks about cross-dressing. While it has not been used as extensively or stridently as biblical passages understood by some to condemn homosexuality, this verse has been troubling to faithful transgendered people who are concerned that they are breaking a biblical injunction and also to some people of faith concerned about the spiritual well-being of transgendered persons.

---

16. Virginia Ramey Mollenkott, *Omnigender: A Trans-Religious Approach* (Cleveland: Pilgrim Press, 2001), 91.

Religious authorities have used this passage to condemn transgendered people. Virginia Mollenkott notes that Kate Bornstein's rabbi used this verse to argue against her transitioning. Bornstein says:

> He quoted me the Old Testament saw that "A woman shall not put on the garments of a man, nor shall a man put on the garments of a woman." I explained to him that I wasn't a man. He said, "In the eyes of the Lord you are and always will be." No empathy, no entering into the lifelong pain of a boy who had always known he was a girl, just legalistic pontificating.[17]

Lee Frances Heller wrote on her "Grace and Lace" website, speaking specifically to male-to-female transgendered people and cross-dressers, "I thought that God put Deu 22:5 in His Bible just for me. It tortured me for years."[18] We need to look closely at this passage because of the way in which it has been used to condemn and ostracize.

First, this verse includes prohibitions against both men and women wearing the clothing deemed to be for the opposite sex. The word translated as "man's apparel" refers to all things relating to men, including weapons, ornamentation, and tools, while the second half of the verse refers only to men wearing women's clothing.

Scholars cite a number of explanations for this section of Deuteronomy and its prohibitions, and no clear consensus exists about the meaning or reason for the prohibition of cross-dressing. Probably the most prominent explanation is that this verse was designed to prevent the Israelites from participating in pagan worship that included elements of cross-dressing and cross-gendered behavior. Samuel Rolles, in 1895, stated,

> No doubt the prohibition is not intended as a mere rule of conventional propriety — though, even as such, it would be an important safeguard against obvious moral dangers — but is directed against the simulated changes of sex which occurred in Canaanite and Syrian heathenism, to the grave moral deterioration of those who adopted them.[19]

Interestingly, both Rolles's reference to "obvious moral dangers" and the passage in Deuteronomy itself tell us that people were, in fact, cross-

---

17. Kate Bornstein, quoted in Mollenkott, *Omnigender,* 81.
18. Lee Frances Heller, "Grace and Lace," *http://members.aol.com/_ht_a/gnlnews/gracelace.html.*
19. Samuel Rolles, *The International Critical Commentary on the Holy Scriptures of the Old and New Testaments* (New York: Charles Scribner's Sons, 1895).

dressing at earlier points in history and that religious people were viewing and judging that behavior.

More recent scholars, including Peter C. Craigie and Ian Cairns, and transgendered authors, such as Danielle Webster and Terri Main, also cite as the impetus for this prohibition a connection with fertility cults connected with Canaanite and Syrian religious practices. They posit that male priests dressed as women as part of their devotion to a goddess, most probably Astarte and later Cybele. Cultic prostitution was forbidden in the Hebrew Scriptures, and cross-dressing was seen as related to that practice. The Torah emphasizes keeping Israel pure and distinct from the religious expressions of neighboring societies, and this prohibition may have functioned as part of that process. Cairns notes, "Deuteronomy 22:5 then has nothing to do with unisex jeans, but aims to preserve the purity of Yahwehistic faith by checking the encroachment of such distortions as the manipulative fertility cults."[20]

Another theory is that cross-dressing could be used as a disguise and is thus forbidden to prevent social disruption. Several speculations have been made about what danger such a disguise could present to society. Jeffrey Tigay, in *The JPS Torah Commentary*, suggests that a disguise could allow a member of one sex to move freely among the opposite sex in a gender-segregated society, and thus increase the opportunities for forbidden sexual contact between women and men.[21] Rev. Lauren René Hotchkiss, in her Internet article on cross-dressing, notes that this passage could be interpreted as an attempt to prevent men, while disguised as women, from gaining access to women's spaces in order to commit rape.[22] Similarly, she notes that this passage would also speak against women gaining access to male sacred spaces, such as the temple, where they were forbidden to go. With a disguise of the opposite sex, women could potentially gain access to those places, and this ban was designed to protect the integrity of gender-segregated space.

Calum Carmichael, in *The Laws of Deuteronomy*, states that the use of such a disguise was forbidden in order to prevent women from entering

---

20. Ian Cairns, *Deuteronomy: Word and Presence* (Grand Rapids, Mich.: William B. Eerdmans, 1992).

21. Jeffrey H. Tigay, *The JPS Torah Commentary: Deuteronomy* (Philadelphia: Jewish Publication Society, 1996), 200.

22. Lauren René Hotchkiss, "Is Transgenderism Wrong?" *http://members.tgforum.com/bobbyg/istranwrong.html*, 11/22/00.

the army disguised as men and to prevent men from dressing as women for homosexual sex. He sees this passage as connected with the practices of war for the Hebrew people. Men could potentially dress as women to avoid conscription while women might pose as men in order to gain access to have sex with men or to serve in the army themselves. Carmichael cites an example from Ugaritic literature in which a heroine, Pughat, dressed as a man and used a sword against her enemies.[23]

Yet another interpretation notes that this section falls in the midst of prohibitions against mixing and blending things of distinct nature. The verses following this section, in the same chapter, state that:

> You shall not sow your vineyard with a second kind of seed, or the whole yield will have to be forfeited, both the crop that you have sown and the yield of the vineyard itself.
>
> You shall not plow with an ox and a donkey yoked together.
>
> You shall not wear clothes made of wool and linen woven together. (Deut. 22:9–11

One speculation is that cross-dressing "blurs the sexual differences God created."[24] Mixing and blending various elements is a serious concern, and keeping these things separate was part of what distinguished Israel from its neighbors. As Patrick Miller states in his commentary on Deuteronomy: "The regulations thus introduce into the life of holiness and purity a concern for the order and structure of things, the recognition of difference and sameness, and a desire to maintain things as God has created them. Nahmanides, a Jewish interpreter of the Middle Ages, saw in these statutes 'an effort to preserve the integrity of creation.'"[25] Thus he supports the Priestly desire to maintain as separate the boundaries between the parts of the created order.

Note, however, that modern Christianity, and many in modern Judaism, no longer follow literally the prohibitions listed in Deuteronomy. We are not concerned about fields with more than one type of crop or with clothing made with fabric blends. We do not see these issues as part of the integrity of creation. We do, though, make many distinctions between

---

23. Calum M. Carmichael, *The Laws of Deuteronomy* (Ithaca, N.Y.: Cornell University Press, 1974), 147.

24. Tigay, *The JPS Torah Commentary*, 200.

25. Patrick D. Miller, *Deuteronomy: Interpretation: A Bible Commentary for Teaching and Preaching* (Louisville: John Knox Press, 1990), 163.

what people view as "feminine" and "masculine," and our society has a great deal of discomfort with individuals who cross those lines. As Cairns states:

> Positively stated, the theological thrust of v. 5 is that Yahweh has created male and female with specific and complementary characteristics so that in their relationship the two constitute the full expression of humanity. To blur the intersexual distinction which Yahweh has established strikes at the natural order and harmony willed by the Creator.[26]

This concept of the natural order of creation is one that links ancient and modern thinkers. Yet, how do we determine what is naturally "feminine" and naturally "masculine"? The type of dress and articles appropriate for men and for women are culturally determined and change with the times. No one is advocating that modern women and men return to the dress of the seventh century B.C.E., when Deuteronomy was written. In fact, the book of Deuteronomy restates the law articulated in Numbers in a way more accessible to the people of that time. Surely we should follow that process, rather than attempting to impose an ancient practice on modern people.

For me, the most compelling argument against this passage as a prohibition against cross-dressing is that we fail to follow any of the other directives around it. No outcry is heard in Christian communities against the eating of shellfish, even though Deuteronomy is clear that the practice is forbidden. The same chapter in Deuteronomy includes a provision to stone to death a woman who has been rejected by her husband and who is not able to prove that she was a virgin at the time the marriage took place. Certainly our society would condemn any church or synagogue that attempted to put this into practice, and we would charge those responsible with murder. No one is preaching about the dangers of mixing two or more types of seed in the garden. Modern communities of faith are unconcerned about any of the blending of things cited in Deuteronomy, other than the blending of male and female. My conclusion is that the concerns are more about gender and very little about the need or desire to follow the dictates of ancient law.

---

26. Cairns, *Deuteronomy*, 47.

Deuteronomy 23:1

No one whose testicles are crushed or whose penis is cut off shall be admitted to the assembly of the Sovereign.

Some cite this passage as a reason to prohibit the participation of trans-sexuals in worshiping communities. As Victoria Kolakowski notes, "There appears to be support in these scriptural passages not merely for the rejection of sex reassignment as a viable treatment for transsexuals, but further, for rejection of post-operative transsexuals from the community of faith."[27]

As we saw in the discussion of Deuteronomy 22:5, this book of Scripture places a great deal of emphasis on preserving the purity of Israel and making clear the distinctions between Israel and its neighbors. As *The New Interpreter's Bible* states,

> It is strongly arguable that the book of Deuteronomy contributed a great deal to strengthen and reinforce the awareness that a marked boundary separated those who were within Israel from those who stood outside of the privileges of the covenant community. The deuteronomic legislation both idealizes the boundaries of Israel by its concepts of membership (lit., "brotherhood") and at the same time seeks in practical terms to regularize and define the status of those who belonged within the community.[28]

Neighboring peoples did have traditions in which priests serving other deities were castrated and where those charged with protecting and serving royal women were castrated as a means to ensure the "safety" of these women from sexual intercourse. In addition, castration was a punishment used in some nearby societies. Whether this practice was used in ancient Israel is not clear.[29]

The Hebrew Scriptures also emphasize the need for procreation, both as a part of God's dictates in Genesis and through the various laws. The nation was small and often embattled, and the need to grow the population was strong. Castration would remove a male from the ability to assist with procreation and was thus discouraged in every way possible. Children were necessary for furthering the family, assisting in tasks necessary for continuing life for the community, caring for elderly parents, and as a

---

27. Victoria S. Kolakowski, "Towards a Christian Ethical Response to Transsexual Persons," *Theology and Sexuality* 6 (March 1997): 20.
28. *The New Interpreter's Bible*, 460.
29. Tigay, *The JPS Torah Commentary*, 210.

way for life to continue. The Hebrew culture had no strong sense of the
afterlife, and continuing the family line was one way to live on after death.

Concerns also existed about both offerings and priests being free from
blemishes or physical deformities. In the culture of the time, only those
who were considered whole should approach God, excluding those who
were injured or deformed.[30]

From reading the surrounding verses, the vast majority of modern
people of faith clearly do not heed the prohibitions from this section
of Deuteronomy. Subsequent verses, for example, give instructions for
cleansing yourself after a nocturnal emission, how to dig a latrine, and
in the appropriate ways to take grapes from a neighbor's vineyard. We
do not teach adherence to these other laws, and pulling one line out of
context and applying only that one does not make sense. In addition, we
shall see that other parts of the Scriptures speak directly counter to this
particular prohibition. Clearly, too, we make no efforts to forbid worship
by men who have lost their genitals because of accidents or illnesses. To
apply this passage only to transsexuals, while ignoring its implications for
others, would be wrong.

Interestingly, Sally Gross notes that we could interpret this passage as
one that prohibits genital surgery for intersexed infants.[31] If permitting
worshipers who have mutilated or altered genitalia is contrary to God's
plan she argues, then subjecting infants to unwanted surgical procedures
surely is inappropriate.

In discussing the impact of this passage on transsexuals, Victoria
Kolakowski states:

> A tension is therefore clearly present.... On the one hand, there are Scrip-
> tures and traditions which arguably prohibit such surgery. On the other
> hand, surgery has been demonstrated to be an effective relief for people
> suffering, through no fault of their own, and with no realistic alternative
> therapy available. Opponents of the traditional approach would use argu-
> ments very similar to those advanced by gays and lesbians for inclusion: that
> the traditions are based upon archaic and incorrect social theory which does
> not contemplate our modern understanding of sexuality and identity, that

30. Michael E. Williams, *Storyteller's Companion to the Bible*, vol. 7: *The Prophets II* (Nashville: Abingdon Press, 1991), 90.
31. Sally Gross, quoted in Mollenkott, *Omnigender*, 120.

the Scriptures were never intended to apply to the present situation, and that compassion is superior to the Law.[32]

This approach seems to me to be the most sensible and faithful response to this passage. We shall see that the Hebrew and Christian biblical traditions contradict this prohibition and argue for a more expansive and inclusive view.

Isaiah 56:1–5

Thus says God: Maintain justice, and do what is right, for soon my salvation will come, and my deliverance be revealed. Happy is the mortal who does this, the one who holds it fast, who keeps the Sabbath, not profaning it, and refrains from doing any evil. Do not let the foreigner joined to God say, "The Sovereign will surely separate me from this people"; and do not let the eunuch say, "I am just a dry tree." For thus says God: To the eunuchs who keep my Sabbaths, who choose the things that please me and hold fast my covenant, I will give, in my house and within my walls, a monument and a name better than sons and daughters; I will give them an everlasting name that shall not be cut off.

In this passage, the prophet emphasizes that justice and faithfulness are the primary things that God wants from humanity. In earlier sections of the Scriptures, as we have seen, both eunuchs and foreigners are very specifically cut out of the covenant that God has with Israel and are forbidden to participate in the community's worship of God. This passage reveals a new commandment from God that directly contradicts earlier law. Part of the justice that God now demands requires that the people practice an acceptance and inclusion of others in their midst, including foreigners and eunuchs. Not only are such people to be included, but the prophet goes on to declare that God will give them a name better than sons and daughters, an everlasting name. This declaration marks a radical change from the views of Deuteronomy.

Eunuchs are the closest biblical analogy we have to transgendered people. Not only were eunuchs subject to physical modification through castration, but they also shifted roles in society from the clearly defined male and female gender roles. Victoria Kolakowski notes, "[T]he eunuch's

---

32. Kolakowski, "Towards a Christian Ethical Response to Transsexual Persons," 22.

sexuality was viewed as marginal, somewhere between male and female."[33] Kolakowski's work is the most complete examination of the connections between biblical eunuchs and modern-day transgendered people. Virginia Mollenkott concurs, stating: "Regarding gender inclusion in Scripture, perhaps the best example is that of the eunuch, a term that refers to castrated men or to people who are unable to have children. By modern understanding, the term includes intersexuals and post-operative transsexuals and symbolically includes homosexuals and celibates."[34]

In this passage, God clearly shifts the focus from the physical perfection and origin of worshipers to an examination of their commitment to observing the Sabbath and perpetuating justice. The emphasis is now not the external characteristics of people who worship Yahweh, but rests upon the faithfulness of the person. Paul Hanson, in his commentary on Isaiah, writes, "Obedience and covenant fidelity, especially in relation to Sabbath observance, are such decisive issues that they are capable of overriding ritual considerations."[35]

For transgendered persons who have a sense of an internal reality that is or may be in conflict with our physical bodies, the prophet speaks a word that focuses us on the faithfulness of our lives, not on the particularities of our bodies. God's emphasis is not on where our bodies came from or how they have been altered, but rather on the ways in which we practice our faith. Justice, inclusion, and faithfulness become the primary indicators of people who are acceptable to God.

In addition to the change toward inclusivity, Edgar Conrad notes that this section of Isaiah represents another shift in thinking for Israel. Earlier in Isaiah, God refers to the community and to the "servant" in the singular form. God is in essence speaking to one community. This passage, however, marks a departure from that stance, and God begins to refer to the people in the plural form. As Conrad notes: "There is a movement toward

---

33. Ibid., 24. I would concur with her analysis here and elsewhere that eunuchs are often subsumed within gay and lesbian history, when, in fact, they are more closely related to modern transgendered people. See also Kolakowski's article, "The Concubine and the Eunuch: Queering Up the Breeder's Bible," in *Our Families, Our Values: Snapshots of Queer Kinship,* ed. Robert E. Goss and Amy Adams Squire Strongheart (New York: Harrington Park Press, 1997), 48, and her article in *Take Back the Word: A Queer Reading of the Bible,* ed. Robert E. Goss and Mona West (Cleveland: Pilgrim Press, 2000).

34. Virginia Ramey Mollenkott, "Gender Diversity and Christian Community," *The Other Side* 37, no. 3 (May and June 2001): 26.

35. Paul D. Hanson, *Isaiah 40–66: Interpretation: A Bible Commentary for Teaching and Preaching* (Louisville: John Knox Press, 1995), 194.

pluralization that represents a movement also toward disintegration and diversity.... That democratization leads to disruption and division is evident in other ways in the book. For example, old boundaries dissolve and are subject to redefinition."[36] God is not speaking simply to one community, but to multiple communities. Here we see this redefinition of the rules regarding who is acceptable to enter the holy presence, a redefinition that would be useful for modern communities of faith to apply.

This recognition of diversity is evident in this first section of Isaiah 56, and it is also important to us as contemporary people of faith. We see in this section of Isaiah that the divine vision of the world is now one that embraces differences and gathers the outcasts, rather than one that limits, distinguishes, and excludes. A little later in the chapter, God promises to bring together on God's holy mountain those who keep the Sabbath and follow the covenant; the passage goes on to say, "Thus says the Sovereign God, who gathers the outcasts of Israel, I will gather others to them besides those already gathered" (Isaiah 56:8). God is the one who gathers the outcasts, and God, not humanity, deems who is worthy to be a part of God's realm. God states clearly that God's holy mountain shall be "called a house of prayer for all people." Differences become an intrinsic, holy part of the divine order, rather than occasions for exclusion.

Yet another change takes place here. In earlier parts of Isaiah, God declares what God will do. Here, God goes on to state what God calls the community to do.[37] Not only does God state what the hallmarks of God's dominion will be, here, by contradicting earlier rules of behavior, God requires a change in human behavior in response. We are called to be like God, creating inclusive communities.

This section of Isaiah has a series of promises for the outcast. Elisabeth Anne Kellogg writes, referencing Isaiah 54 and 56,

> [T]he post-operative transsexual is not just a male eunuch. She has passed over to the female side, but with one important exception. She will never be able to give birth to any children, a burden for any woman whether genetic or neo. Even after SRS when you have ceased to be a man and have become a barren woman, the Lord will still have words of encouragement for you.[38]

---

36. Edgar W. Conrad, *Reading Isaiah* (Minneapolis: Fortress Press, 1991), 147.

37. Hanson, *Isaiah 40–66*, 193.

38. Elisabeth Anne Kellogg, "Transsexualism from the Perspective of the Biblical Eunuch and the Barren Woman." *http://members.tgforum.com/bobbyg/eunuch.html.*

The Bible offers a number of examples of barren women as outcasts, most notably in the story of Sarah. In Genesis 13–20, her barrenness is mentioned a number of times and leads to great conflict within the family until God intervenes and makes it possible for her to bear a child. Isaiah clearly states that barren women are included in the dominion of God as they are, valuable to God whether or not they bear children. The same is true of castrated men who are loved regardless of their ability to impregnate. Thus, God's care and love for humanity is no longer dependent on the ability to produce offspring but is given to people as they are, a free gift of love from a loving God. God's primary concern for us is not whether we bear children, but whether or not we live in a way that upholds God's dominion of justice and righteousness.

God's promises to gather in the outcasts and to bring rejoicing to those brought low in society's judgment are promises to all of us. Here eunuchs and barren women are affirmed as part of God's dominion and clearly included in God's plan.

Matthew 19:11–12

> But Jesus said to the disciples, "Not everyone can accept this teaching, but only those to whom it is given. For there are eunuchs who have been so from birth, and there are eunuchs who have been made eunuchs by others, and there are eunuchs who have made themselves eunuchs for the sake of the dominion of heaven. Let anyone accept this who can."

As we have noted, eunuchs are the closest biblical analogy that we have for transgendered people. Here we see Jesus directly addressing the issue of eunuchs and including them in *his* understanding of the dominion of heaven. Note that he says that not everyone can accept this teaching, not unlike the current situation regarding the acceptance of transgendered people within communities of faith.

This saying of Jesus comes directly after his teaching that forbids divorce. Earlier in this passage, Jesus quotes Genesis, stating that God created humanity male and female and then he goes on to speak about divorce. Yet immediately after he discusses men and women and their relationship to marriage, he goes on to discuss gender variance, speaking about a variety of eunuchs. The inclusion of both of these concepts says to me that Jesus was not prescribing "male and female" as the only options for humanity but specifically spoke of a range of human expression.

Jesus does not make explicit what this teaching on eunuchs has to do with the subject of marriage. In the Anchor Bible, W. F. Albright and C. S. Mann state:

> [I]t is possible that the saying in this verse has been attracted to its present context as being loosely associated with a discussion on marriage. In reality, only two classes of men are being described here — those physically incapable of marriage, either from birth or from being rendered so by others, and those who while at one time physically capable of marriage have renounced that state either by self-mutilation or voluntary celibacy.[39]

Many scholars argue that this passage is not to be taken literally, but refers primarily to those who have forgone marriage and become celibate in order to better serve the church. Jesus' intention was clearly broader than that, because he includes not only people who abstain from marriage but all possible configurations of eunuchs. Limiting Jesus' teaching solely to celibates oversimplifies this passage and does not hold us, as the community of faith, fully accountable to the full extent of Jesus' words.

At least one prominent example survives of a Christian taking the words of Jesus in Matthew 19:12 literally. According to one tradition, the third-century theologian Origen castrated himself out of his conviction that eunuchs could be made so for the dominion of heaven.[40] However, throughout most of church history, self-castration or mutilation has been frowned upon.[41]

In his book on honor and shame in the book of Matthew, Jerome Neyrey comments as follows on this passage:

> Male honor was also thought to be symbolized by the male sexual organs, the penis and testicles.... Jesus comments about those who have lost honor because of their eunuch status (19:10–12). After Jesus proscribes all divorce, some male disciples lament, saying, "It is not expedient to marry" (19:10), that is, no honor can be claimed by enjoying the exclusive sexual rights to a female and the offspring that marriage brings. Jesus says that there are three classes of eunuchs, those born without male honor, those

39. W. F. Albright and C. S. Mann, *Matthew*, Anchor Bible (New York: Doubleday, 1971), 227.
40. James B. Nelson, *Body Theology* (Louisville: Westminster/John Knox Press, 1992), 37.
41. Albright and Mann, *Matthew*, 227.

who have been deprived of this honor by others, and those who voluntarily do this to themselves (19:12).[42]

Neyrey argues that this example is just one of many in which Jesus acts in ways that dishonor the body in conventional Hebrew thought and transforms the concepts of both shame and honor. Some people have argued that transsexuals dishonor their own bodies by transitioning, yet here we see Jesus' acceptance of those whom society has deemed dishonorable.

The important aspect of this passage is that Jesus recognizes and comments upon the lives and situation of gender-variant people in his society. A number of transgendered authors write about Jesus' saying regarding eunuchs. Virginia Mollenkott says the following about Jesus' teaching:

> Jesus' words about eunuchs in Matthew 19:12 reveal an accepting, respectful attitude that ought to be the norm for the modern church: "For there are eunuchs who have been so from birth" includes at the very least all intersexual people; "and there are eunuchs who have been made eunuchs by others" includes post-operative transsexuals; "and there are eunuchs who have made themselves eunuchs for the sake of the kingdom of heaven" includes not only pre-operative and non-operative transsexuals but all other transgenderists, celibates, and homosexuals who do not engage in reproductive sex. The kingdom of heaven is located within us (Luke 17:21); so perhaps what Jesus means by being eunuchs "for the sake of the kingdom of heaven" is the Jewish counsel of being true to one's deepest nature.[43]

Clearly this process of seeking to be true to one's inner nature is crucial in the spiritual lives and development of the transgendered.

In the web article "Jesus and Male and Female," author Michelle Dee writes:

> In Jesus' day, there was no SRS, though there were transgendered people, naturally. (After all, why would crossdressing have been mentioned in Deuteronomy at all if it hadn't existed for thousands of years?) Jesus openly acknowledges that "some are eunuchs because they were born that way," and this naturally opens up the door to consider the intersexed hermaphrodite, whose sex is simultaneously both and neither. Jesus acknowledges sexual diversity and did not judge it.[44]

---

42. Jerome H. Neyrey, *Honor and Shame in the Gospel of Matthew* (Louisville: Westminster John Knox Press, 1998), 66–67.

43. Mollenkott, *Omnigender*, 120.

44. Michelle Dee, "Jesus and Male and Female," *http://members.tripod.com/~michelledee/jesustg.html*, 11/20/00.

This last point is critically important for Christians to consider. Clearly, Jesus knows that some people are born outside of the binary gender system and people whose lives lead them beyond it. He speaks of multiple ways in which someone might have become gender variant, and he does so with compassion and clarity. We are called to do likewise.

Jesus goes on to acknowledge a connection between the dominion of God and eunuchs. We see in the words of Jesus an acceptance and acknowledgment of gender diversity. Modern science and medical knowledge support Jesus' concept that someone can become a eunuch in multiple ways, including being born intersexed and those who choose this status.

Victoria Kolakowski notes that some may have considered Jesus a eunuch because of his unmarried status:

> It is frequently argued by those who hold that Jesus was celibate that Jesus himself had been derisively called a eunuch, and that it was this charge to which Jesus was responding in this statement, placing himself in the third category [of Matthew 19:12]. The notion that Jesus placed himself into the third category makes this passage particularly fascinating for purposes of the present discussion, since it would place Jesus in direct solidarity with the eunuch. It is very important that there is no condemnation of eunuchs implicit in this statement; rather, Jesus is placing himself in an analogous situation with the eunuchs.[45]

This understanding of Jesus seeing himself as analogous to eunuchs also fits with his identification with others on the margins of society. In Matthew 9:11, the Pharisees ask the disciples why Jesus spends his time in the company of people considered disreputable — the tax collectors and sinners. This statement about eunuchs would not be the first time that he placed himself in connection with outcasts. In fact, we could argue that a modern parallel to the tax collectors and sinners might be spending his time with drag queens and bikers, people seen as outside decent society and social norms.

We need to remember Jesus' words of acceptance for eunuchs and his way of allying himself with people outside of accepted norms of society. For way too long, Jesus has been used as a tool of exclusion and self-righteousness, when his own words counter that view and present for us a radical statement of positive inclusion in the dominion of God.

---

45. Kolakowski, "Towards a Christian Ethical Response to Transsexual Persons," 25.

Acts 8:25–39

Now after Peter and John had testified and spoken the word of the Sovereign, they returned to Jerusalem, proclaiming the good news to many villages of the Samaritans.

Then an angel of God said to Philip, "Get up and go toward the south to the road that goes down from Jerusalem to Gaza." (This is a wilderness road.) So he got up and went. Now there was an Ethiopian eunuch, a court official of the Candace, queen of the Ethiopians, in charge of her entire treasury. He had come to Jerusalem to worship and was returning home; seated in his chariot, he was reading the prophet Isaiah. Then the Spirit said to Philip, "Go over to this chariot and join it." So Philip ran up to it and heard him reading the prophet Isaiah. He asked, "Do you understand what you are reading?" He replied, "How can I, unless someone guides me?" And he invited Philip to get in and sit beside him. Now the passage of the scripture that he was reading was this:

> "Like a sheep he was led to the slaughter,
>   and like a lamb silent before its shearer,
>   so he does not open his mouth.
> In his humiliation justice was denied him.
>   Who can describe his generation?
>   For his life is taken away from the earth."

The eunuch asked Philip, "About whom, may I ask, does the prophet say this? About himself or about someone else?" Then Philip began to speak, and starting with this scripture, he proclaimed to him the good news about Jesus. As they were going along the road, they came to some water; and the eunuch said, "Look, here is water! What is to prevent me from being baptized?" He commanded the chariot to stop, and both of them, Philip and the eunuch, went down into the water, and Philip baptized him. When they came up out of the water, the Spirit of God snatched Philip away; the eunuch saw him no more, and went on his way rejoicing.

One of the most powerful stories in the Scriptures for gender-variant people is the conversion and baptism of the Ethiopian eunuch in the book of Acts. The eunuch was a court official of the Candace, a title for the queen of Ethiopia. He was in Jerusalem to worship and was now returning home, reading a section of Scripture filled with words of consolation and inclusion, as well as the description of the Suffering Servant of God from Isaiah 53:7. As a foreigner and eunuch, he was in a spiritual border zone, both included and excluded in Judaism, and between genders. A number of transgendered authors have noted that while the prohibitions of

Deuteronomy would have excluded him as a eunuch and a foreigner from worshiping at the temple, he was in fact reading a passage from Isaiah shortly before the prophecy declares God's inclusion of both eunuchs and those from outside of Israel that we have already discussed.

This story is about faithfulness, both on the part of Philip and the eunuch. Philip hears and follows the word of God that tells him to reach out to the eunuch. The eunuch hears the gospel and responds seeking baptism. In his commentary on Acts, Paul Walaskay writes:

> In his mission to Samaria, Philip had already broken through the ancient barriers of religion and race which bred tremendous hostility between Jews and Samaritans. Now he was prepared to take on a third serious barrier — sexuality.
>
> Philip's heroism and leadership is understated in the New Testament. He was an amazing man of deep faith and great courage. It is not at all difficult to make the leap of two millennia to see the need for just such heroes in our own time. The parallels are all too obvious. He not only baptized those whose race and religion were problems for the guardians of right religion in Jerusalem. Now he gladly received into the Christian sect of Judaism a man whose sexuality was a problem for the temple elite. Perhaps he and the eunuch read a bit further into Isaiah's prophecies, discovering [Is. 56].[46]

Not only the eunuch's sexuality is in question, but also his gender. He did not fit in conventional categories of male and female as a castrated man who served a queen. Philip is a model for an understanding of evangelism that reaches out with Christ's message of inclusion, without the legalism that marks so many of our faith communities.

In his commentary on Acts, F. Scott Spencer points out three ways in which the eunuch occupies a border zone between two realities. First, the eunuch is traveling in midday, an unusual time for travel in desert climates. He says, "Ordinary activity (travelling) at an extraordinary time (midday), out of 'synch' with regular natural and cultural rhythms, opens a window of opportunity for world-shattering knowledge and experience."[47] Second, he is traveling on a wilderness road, separated from community. Spencer notes that he is on a reverse journey from the exodus route: from Jerusalem to Africa. Yet out in this desert, Philip and the eunuch are able to encounter one another outside of the social conventions that might have

---

46. Paul W. Walaskay, *Acts* (Louisville: Westminster John Knox Press, 1998), 86–87.
47. F. Scott Spencer, *Acts* (Sheffield: Sheffield Academic Press, 1997), 90.

prevented their interactions. The eunuch clearly has wealth (the chariot, the servants, and his own scroll) while Philip was an itinerant preacher. Third, the eunuch is somewhere between Jew and Gentile, worshiping in Jerusalem but from Ethiopia.

Spencer goes on to say that the eunuch's status as a eunuch also places him in a liminal space. As Spencer notes:

> First-century Jewish commentators, such as Josephus, . . . regarded eunuchs as unnatural "monstrosities" who must be shunned on account of their gross effeminacy and generative impotence (*Ant* 4.290–91), and Philo, who classified eunuchs as various "worthless persons" banned from the sacred assembly because they "debase the currency of nature and violate it by assuming the passions and the outward form of licentious women." (*Special Laws* 1.324–25).[48]

The very negativity of the commentators' reactions strengthens the argument that eunuchs are analogous to modern transgendered persons since they were considered to have crossed gender lines. Certainly these views sound familiar to us and are ones against which we have had to struggle.

The fact that the eunuch encounters Philip in the midst of all of these "between" spaces affirms the workings of God outside of human boundaries and conventions. In fact, this encounter is made possible in part by the unusualness of the space and time in which they encounter one another.

Spencer argues that the eunuch's questions of Philip ("How can I unless someone shows me?" and "What is to prevent me from being baptized?") speak to a history of the eunuch having been excluded from the community of faith. His question about baptism particularly may show a focus on the forces of religious exclusion; that is, he expects to have to surmount obstacles, rather than simply being included. Philip shows him a way of inclusivity that must have been part of why the eunuch went on his way rejoicing. Philip demonstrates for us the power of one person acting with a single act of inclusion, which clearly makes all the difference.

Philip's ready acceptance of the eunuch as a candidate for baptism proclaims a message of inclusion for the gender variant. As Kolakowski writes about Acts 8:

---

48. Ibid., 93.

The radicalness of this story lies in the fact that the early Christian church appeared to think that baptizing a eunuch was nothing so important as to be even worth discussing. No moral condemnation is applied. There is the appearance of total acceptance because Jesus spoke about and identified himself as a eunuch for God's reign.[49]

Starchild, in *A Transsexual Theology*, writes the following about the conversion of the eunuch:

> Unlike Peter who needed a vision from heaven to cross the boundary of including Gentiles, Philip needed no prodding to know that the Spirit was calling him to include eunuchs in the Kingdom of God. Philip proclaims the Good News, the eunuch believes and is received into the family of faith immediately by Baptism. Thus the first boundary that was broken down in our Baptism in Christ was not one of religious differences or race, but one of unusual gender conditions.[50]

Once again, we see an affirmation in Scripture that neither the gender of the eunuch nor his gender variance is pivotal to his inclusion or exclusion in the community of faith, but rather his *desire* to be baptized and included. Again, we see God's focus on faithfulness rather than physical characteristics. The categories in which society placed the eunuch were not God's categories and did not limit his access to the Divine. His willingness and his enthusiasm were the hallmarks of his conversation, not the external categories that surely controlled many of his other options in life.

At the same time, the fact that this person is a eunuch is not erased or marginalized in the story. He brings the particularity of his gender to his encounter with Philip and ultimately to his relationship with God. The power of this story lies in its specific description of inclusion. He is not baptized in spite of being a eunuch or after a lengthy session of apologetics explaining his gender to Philip, but simply at the point at which they passed a body of water. Bringing our whole selves, just as we are, is part of the integrity of our witness to God. In this story, we see that God does not ask us to put aside who we are in order to be a part of the community of faith, but rather calls us as we are in our specificity.

---

49. Kolakowski, "The Concubine and the Eunuch," 46.
50. Starchild, "A Transsexual Theology," *www.whosoever.org/v2Issue2/starchild.html*, 5/14/01.

Galatians 3:28

> There is no longer Jew or Greek, there is no longer slave or free, there is
> no longer male and female; for all of you are one in Christ Jesus.

This verse of Scripture calls into question, and ultimately into accountability, the human divisions of race, class, and gender. When I first heard
of feminist theology and was encouraged to look at the Scriptures as a
woman, as I identified myself at that time, this text was a radical discovery for me. I had never heard or encountered this passage, as far as I can
remember, until I was in college. At that time, Galatians 3:28 signified for
me a radical shift in my understanding of what it meant to be in Christ; I
was no longer bound to the divisions of gender, or to the roles our society
assigns to women, but was set free by Christ. This verse was part of what
enabled me to choose to identify as a Christian and to claim for myself my
Christian heritage, because I could see this new world opening up before
me, a world in which gender was not the ultimate dividing force in my
life. Williams, in his commentary on Galatians, notes, "The formula thus
envisions a state of affairs such as no one has ever seen, a situation super-
seding even God's original creation!"[51] It was a promise for the world, as
well as a promise that I saw for my own life.

In his commentary on Galatians, Sam Williams describes a powerful
implication of this text: Not only will there not be divisions between Jews
and Greeks, slaves and free, male and female, but the entire process of
distinguishing some as superior and some as inferior is to pass away. In
Christ, we are not to create categories in which some have power, influ-
ence, and privilege while others do not. If those of us who are Christians
would follow this mandate, such a change would have a profound impact
on how we live and are. Among other things, transgendered people would
not be excluded from or just tolerated in communities of faith but welcomed as equals; nor would distinctions be placed on the roles of women
and men in our religious bodies. We would not have categories of acceptable churchgoers and respectable Christians, separate from unacceptable,
disreputable queer folks. Rather, all would be welcome in the body of
Christ.

Mollenkott begins and ends her book *Omnigender: A Trans-Religious
Approach* with a discussion of Galatians 3:28. This vision of a humanity

---

51. Sam K. Williams, *Galatians* (Nashville: Abingdon Press, 1997), 106.

that transcends the categories of human division, including gender, is at the heart of her argument and passion. As she writes in her introduction:

> It's worth noticing that the three statements in Galatians 3:28 about the New Creation's transcendence of race/ethnicity, class and gender are not precisely parallel in the Greek text. This lack of parallelism is reflected in the New Revised Standard Version translation: "There is no longer Jew or Greek, there is no longer slave nor free, there is no longer male and female; for all of you are one in Christ Jesus." If there is any meaning to be found in that grammatical shift from or to and, what might it be? Does it reflect a belief that women and men are so necessary to one another that or cannot be spoken, because without either there could be no human-kind, a fact Paul emphasized in 1 Corinthians 11:11–12? And does it point toward a time when instead of separate gender obligations, both physical maleness-femaleness and masculine-feminine social roles will be recognized as a continuum on which individuals may locate themselves comfortably and without fear of reprisal? At any rate, I concur with Professor Fulkerson[52] that "it is time to read Galatians 3:28 with a new literalness, admitting that we are all performing our sex/gender."[53]

Interestingly, Charles Cousar obliquely references transgendered people in his discussion of this passage in his book on Galatians. He says, "The three sets of polarities Paul mentions are not exactly parallel. One is born either male or female, and that is that (at least for Paul's day)."[54] He goes on to say:

> Being in Christ does not do away with Jew or Greek, male or female, even slave or free, but makes these differences before God irrelevant.
> At the same time, the new unity in Christ has tremendous social impli-cations. The very fact that the differences no longer matter means that Christians must treat people and groups in this light not only in church on Sunday but in the total affairs of life, in the so-called secular arena as well as the sacred.[55]

This point is important. Paul is not simply ignoring or erasing differ-ences here, but rather altering the way in which we relate to those

---

52. She is citing Mary McClintock Fulkerson, "Gender — Being It or Doing It? The Church, Homosexuality, and the Politics of Identity," in *Que(e)rying Religion: A Critical Anthology*, ed. Gary David Comstock and Susan E. Henking (New York: Continuum, 1997), in which Fulkerson argues for the performativity of gender, citing Judith Butler.

53. Mollenkott, *Omnigender*, viii.

54. Charles B. Cousar, *Galatians: Interpretation: A Bible Commentary for Teaching and Preaching* (Atlanta: John Knox Press, 1982), 85.

55. Ibid., 86.

differences. Unity in Christ requires us to treat people as equals and without prejudice.

Of course, the church has a long history of treating men and women very differently. An approach that took Galatians 3:28 seriously would benefit not only trans people but others as well. As Kathy Rudy writes in *Sex and the Church*:

> We could strengthen our faith by the way we transcend gender and sexual classifications, by the way that we correlate sexual activity with spirituality, by the way we embody Paul's prescription of Galatians 3:28: "In Christ there is no male and female." Such communities, I believe, would serve as a beacon of light for those who feel oppressed by the way our churches today correlate gender roles and spirituality.[56]

Such an approach could focus communities of faith on the spirituality of adherents, looking at the gifts that each one brings, rather than assigning value and meaning to people based on their real or perceived gender.

Galatians 3:28 calls the Christian community to accountability for the way in which it has used identity to delineate what is acceptable. As Fulkerson posits:

> Radical love is invoked in the community to support a reality where there is neither slave nor free, male nor female in Christ Jesus, a reality defined by a grammar of justification by faith alone. A contemporary version of this grammar can expand its logic, a logic which refuses to put conditions on access to the gospel, and do that by refusing to require binary gendered identity just as it refuses to require circumcision. This Christian grammar of iconoclasm for the purposes of love is, in short, intrinsically expandable — even to gendered identity itself. It extends our notion of justification by grace through faith in a new way. It confesses that our conceptions of identity are susceptible not only to the located and limited perspectives of the cultures that produce them, but that we are not saved by making of them requirements for full communion.[57]

Failing to apply the broad acceptance of Galatians 3:28 takes a community further from the Christ it seeks; rather than making the church more holy, it adds barriers for those who seek Christ. To find the infinite grace of God, we must be infinite in our grace and embrace. The realm of God is marked not by limitation but by expansiveness. As Fulkerson

---

56. Kathy Rudy, *Sex and the Church: Gender, Homosexuality, and the Transformation of Christian Ethics* (Boston: Beacon Press, 1997), 101.

57. Fulkerson, "Gender — Being It or Doing It?" 199.

notes, this approach applies to gender identity as much as to any other human category.

This passage was most likely an ancient baptismal formula. As such, the verse calls us, through our baptisms, to participate in the dominion of God, a limitless realm open to all. We are baptized into Christ, who calls us to an identity broader and deeper than our human identities of gender, class, and nation. Christ calls us to be co-creators of a dominion where these limitations fall. We come with our particularities and our identities, but these do not prevent any from participating in the dominion of God. As Rudy notes,

> As Christians, we are called by God to identify ourselves as the people of God. We are in this world, but not of this world; we diligently and consciously must challenge those worldly categories that do not help us lead more faithful lives. We are taught to disregard the things that divide us, to include in our midst outcasts, tax collectors, prostitutes, people with whom — under any other set of normal or worldly circumstances — we would hold nothing in common. Through our baptism we become new people, with a new and radically different ontology; everything that we think and see and do in the world should reflect that we are a part of the Body of Christ. What holds Christians together is not wealth or class status or human-made law or ethnic background or race or nationality, but rather God's self, which is revealed to us through our membership in the Christian Church. Our primary identification is and ought to be Christian; any identification that takes precedence over our baptism is to be avoided.[58]

Galatians 3:28 calls us to a unity that extends to all and provides us with a way of seeing one another, not as male or female, Jew or Greek, slave or free, but as Christians and children of God first and foremost. Rudy goes on to argue that if "Christian" is the primary identity to which we are called, are the categories of male and female even useful? In fact, if the Christian community fulfills its mission to embrace all, as Rudy suggests, then she says, "surely 'gender' is not the most interesting thing that can be said about each member [of the community]."[59] This passage paints for us a vision of world beyond gender, in which there is room for infinite variation and infinite grace.

---

58. Rudy, *Sex and the Church*, 97.
59. Ibid., 100.

Conclusion

Scripture can be read in many ways. Transgendered people have as much right as anyone else in the world to look to the Bible or other sacred writings for words of inspiration and hope and to hear good news; the Scriptures are ours as much as they are anyone's. The texts that some religious people use to condemn us show us that even in biblical times gender-variant people were living in communities of faith and striving to find their place within society and before God. We have been a part of the story of the Bible from the earliest days, from the intersexed origins of Adam, to the cross-dressing Israelites in the times that the law was set out in Deuteronomy, to the eunuchs, to a vision of a world and a community beyond the bounds of male and female. To me, seeing the record of our ancestors there at all, is affirming and amazing, but we are there.

When transgendered people hear words of condemnation, rather than simply "taking it," we can take the Bible and talk back. The Bible should never serve as a weapon. Nor should it be taken away from us as a tool for spiritual growth and understanding. Certain passages speak directly to our experiences as gender-variant people and these verses should serve as a resource for people for whom the Bible has spiritual meaning and authority. Do not let people who preach condemnation take that tool away from you.

Throughout the Bible, messages of inclusion, hope, and love are present that transcend all human boundaries. Those messages are there for us and for all people. The biblical stories call us to look toward a time of liberation when all oppression ends and when all of God's people gather together in peace. When we feel besieged by life and the demands of transition, we need that hope. When we are on top of the world and filled with joy, we need to move toward that reality.

Chapter Four

Transgendered People
and Faith Communities

Near the beginning of Jane Anderson's play *Looking for Normal,* a typical Midwestern married couple is sitting in their minister's office for pastoral counseling. Reverend Muncie suspects that the problem is that Roy is experiencing impotence, so he sends Irma to the chapel so that he and Roy can speak man-to-man. Instead, Roy reveals to the pastor that for the past year, Roy has been seeing a gender therapist and is making the decision to transition from male to female. S/he chooses the pastoral counseling session as the place to tell his/her wife about this decision. The pastor is shocked and is clearly uncomfortable with this turn of events, but reassures Roy that he will be welcome in the congregation. The minister is clearly shocked, dismayed, and completely out of his element.

As the play goes on, Reverend Muncie works with Irma, Roy's wife, to develop ways to dissuade Roy, who takes the new name of Ruth, from transitioning. The pastor uses Scripture, consults other pastors, and searches for a way to cope with this completely unforeseen situation. He sees transsexuality as being similar to homosexuality and tries to come up with a cure. All of his actions and clear discomfort drive Ruth further and further from the church that had been one of the mainstays of her life. While she continues to have a relationship with God, it cannot be expressed or experienced in community.[1]

This fictional account comes close to reality for many transgendered people who attempt to remain part of a church or other religious community. Most communities are unprepared to deal with issues of gender transition and have no idea how to respond. In addition, the social prejudice against gender variance remains strong within faith communities;

---

1. Jane Anderson, *Looking for Normal* (New York: Dramatists Play Service, 2002).

in fact, in many instances, such communities are one place where gender conformity is strongly embraced, enforced, and preached as a divine directive. Some communities, though, overcome prejudice and confusion and are fully able to embrace their members and adherents wherever they are on the gender spectrum.

The experiences of transgendered people within faith communities vary widely, from acceptance and affirmation of a trans identity to intolerance and excommunication to humiliation and mockery. Throughout my readings and conversations with other trans people, they articulated a broad range of experiences, some of which differed greatly from one another — even within the same faith tradition or denomination. Many transgendered people that I spoke with were hesitant about participating in a faith community for fear of harassment or ridicule. To avoid that response, a number of them engaged in solitary religious practice, or accessed religious services through the Internet or on television, so that they could see, but not be seen by, the church. Of course, some transgendered people participate regularly in worship services, remain closeted, and are not known to be trans by anyone in the congregation. We focus in this section on trans people who are known to be trans, either because they are visibly gender variant or because they self-disclosed to a religious leader or congregation, and their experiences face-to-face with a community of faith.

Trans people in the midst of a congregation experience a broad range of reactions. Somewhat of a corollary seems to exist between the conservatism of a group and their degree of acceptance; however, conservative groups are not necessarily rejecting and liberal groups are not necessarily accepting of trans people's participation in communities of faith. A great deal seems to hinge on the views of the specific religious leader, the individual transgendered person, and the community in question. We see an increased rejection of trans people from conservative communities of faith as they begin to talk with one another. Recently some conservative voices have emerged that have condemned trans people, and these sentiments are on the rise.

Distinctions are also made based on the degree of gender variance of the individual. A transsexual who passes easily can integrate into a community without great disruption of or knowledge by the group. Some communities accept transsexuals and intersexuals, viewing these conditions as medical, but not cross-dressers, who are seen as pathological or perverted. Some communities allow gender-variant people in groups with adults but not in situations in which children are present.

To assume that a faith community's treatment of gay, lesbian, and bisexual participants would necessarily predict the group's acceptance of transgendered members is a mistake, based on my readings, conversations, and personal experience. I spoke with members of the Assemblies of God who are well accepted within their churches and with pastors who are aware of their background as transsexuals and accept that fact as part of who they are, while condemning homosexuality. I also heard from a Wiccan practitioner who has not been able to find a community to worship and practice with, and from members of Metropolitan Community Churches who have had both strongly positive and negative experiences. Some people within gay and lesbian caucus groups of mainline churches have expressed fears that the presence of transgendered people will erode the hard-won gains those groups have made within their communities, while others have seen the issues of gender identity and sexual orientation as parallel and connected movements.

The lack of conversation on a national or ecclesial level about transgendered issues seems to have left most of the theologizing to individual ministers, rabbis, and other leaders, for better or for worse. These leaders have come up with their own responses to Scripture, tradition, and the individual in their community. In many cases, this occurrence is a positive thing because the religious leader must develop her or his own practice when faced with a transgendered person in the community or congregation. Thus, the conversation is not merely theoretical, as sometimes happens around issues of sexual orientation, but one that takes place in the context of a particular faith community face-to-face with a particular person. However, in such circumstances, individuals are making determinations on their own, often outside of guidance from other religious leaders or a broader context and understanding of the issues at hand. Sometimes these individuals feel very isolated when dealing with a situation not covered at all in their pastoral training, and the experience is both stressful and demanding. Nonetheless, I was encouraged by those who engaged in free thought, made decisions based in faithful compassion, and were willing to take a stand within their own religious communities.

In addition to the relative isolation that religious communities face in
dealing with transgendered persons, other forces within communities of
faith make us unlikely to look very closely at the questions raised by gender
variance. Virginia Ramey Mollenkott argues in her book *Omnigender: A
Trans-Religious Approach* that compelling the church to look clearly at
the issue will be very difficult. She recognizes that shifting the view that
religious communities fundamentally have toward gender will be even
more challenging:

> In all probability, official church policies will be the rear guard on gender,
> being dragged toward gender justice kicking and screaming when the secular
> society will no longer tolerate anything else. History has repeated itself, alas,
> concerning the church and racial issues, women, sexual orientation, peace,
> capital punishment and corporal punishment. Why should gender be any
> different?[2]

She points out that "there are certain interpretations of scripture that
may block otherwise loving people from acting as loving as they might
like to act."[3]

She also argues, correctly I believe, that we tend to create God in our
own image. If we ourselves are uncomfortable with gender variation, then
we say that God is uncomfortable with it. Rather than looking to the
image of Jesus in the Christian Bible and his nonjudgmental approach to
difference, we define our social strictures as God's ordained will. We also
tend to project onto others our own fears and discomforts, and then hate
the other for displaying those characteristics.

These points are all profoundly important points to consider when we
look at the ways in which religious communities approach gender. As
Virginia Mollenkott points out, we are the culture as much as anyone
else is and we see things through the lenses of our own culture. Only
occasionally does the church question that lens at all. By declaring that our
way of doing things is God's way, we take an enormous risk of committing
hubris and taking on the very arrogant position that we can define for God
what is holy or good or natural. Yet such thinking seems to be a common
human tendency.

---

2. Virginia Ramey Mollenkott, *Omnigender: A Trans-Religious Approach* (Cleveland: Pilgrim Press,
2001), 82.
3. Ibid., 84.

When we look at the place of transgendered people within communities of faith, we need to keep in mind the relative rarity of encounters that religious groups have with transgendered people and the factors that make it difficult for congregations to engage these questions. Because of the variation in position about transgendered issues, a useful approach is to look at communities that are similar to one another and examine the different opinions that arise out of similar worldviews and religious beliefs. We begin with some of the more conservative faith communities and then move on to examine mainline churches and alternative communities of faith.

Conservative Communities of Faith

A wider variation takes place in the experiences that transgendered people have had within conservative communities than we might expect. Some communities embrace a movement to encourage transsexuals to return to the sex assigned to them at birth, similar to ex-gay programs. Ministries and outreach to transgendered people take place to assist them in returning to the community of faith. Some religious leaders see trans-sexuality in particular as a medical problem with a medical solution that does not necessarily have spiritual implications, while others cite Scrip-ture that they believe forbids cross-dressing and gender reassignment surgery.

In many communities, of course, the subject is simply not addressed, with people tacitly but firmly expected to follow gender norms. Irene Mon-roe comments about the way this stance is enforced in the black church, particularly as it impacts gender-variant gay men and lesbians:

> But part of the Black church is that the dress code is rigid, and you don't even have to voice it because it's instilled in the practice of each person who goes to church. It's passed on generationally that we have this rigid dress code. So, when I say we cloak our identity, the code says you can be lesbian but you make sure that you wear your dress. You wear dresses to Black churches, if you're female. Even if you are a butch woman who can't wear dresses as well as a real drag queen, the point is that you give the external surface of what is called proper clothing, proper decorum, which is heterosexual, of course. That's explicit as well as implicit. So, in that sense the doors of the church are open to you, but not for you to give voice,

whether as a gay man or a lesbian woman or, God forbid, we won't even dare mention transgender.[4]

This firm sense of gender norms and expectations of dress that reinforce those norms is prevalent both within and outside of the black church. Many religious bodies would never mention the presence of gender-variant people in their midst and have not even contemplated the possibility of such a thing occurring in their place of worship. Gender conformity is stressed as a prerequisite to worship and participation, and thus gender variance is completely alien and unacceptable.

Acceptance in Conservative Communities of Faith

When I interviewed Richard, he told me that the pastor of his Assemblies of God church knew that he was a transsexual and accepted him as a man and as part of the congregation. Richard has told a couple of other members of the congregation who have also responded positively to him. He said that he told one of them specifically for spiritual accountability because he wanted to be sure that he was acting in an appropriate way for a Christian and was willing to let his actions be seen and known as part of that accountability process. He said, "There was one other guy in church I told because...I wanted to be accountable. I want to be minding God, I don't want to get out on my own thinking I'm doing the right thing and find out that I'm not." That these men keep the information about his background confidential is important to Richard because he did not feel it was necessary for other members of the congregation to know that he was transsexual. From talking to Richard, church is clearly an integral and important part of his life, and his acceptance there as a Christian man is central to his identity.

A viewer who said, "I'm forty years old and have had a sex change," contacted Pat Robertson on the *700 Club* program. The letter went on to say, "I've been watching your program and wonder if God forgave me, should I live as I am now or go back to my birth gender?"[5] The viewer's gender identity is not clear from the transcript of the program, so we do not know if this person is an MTF or FTM. Robertson acknowledged variations of hormonal activity in different people and stated that he knows

---

4. Irene Monroe in Gary David Comstock, *A Whosoever Church: Welcoming Lesbians and Gay Men into African American Congregations* (Louisville: Westminster John Knox Press, 2001), 62.

5. *www.emergenceministries.org/resources/pat_Robertson.html*, 7/19/01.

a plastic surgeon who performs such surgeries. He went on to say that sex reassignment surgery is not a sin, although the person could revert to her/his birth gender if that is what s/he wished to do. The dialogue between Robertson and his co-host Terry Meeuwsen continues:

Meeuwsen: But God's interested in his heart, attitude ...

Robertson: His heart and soul.

Meeuwsen: ... and what he's seeking spiritually, right?

Robertson: Not — not what your external organs are, one way or the other, whether it's male or female. The question is, where are you living? Are you living for God and yes, he forgives you and yes, he loves you and yes, he understands what's going on in your body.[6]

Robertson's position here is much closer, I believe, to Jesus' teaching about eunuchs: that people come in a variety of ways, but their way of living is what is important. Rather than focusing on the particulars of someone else's body, he looks instead to the spiritual questions. His affirmation that God loves and understands a transsexual person is very meaningful to a large number of transsexual conservative Christians. They do use male pronouns to refer to the viewer; from the transcript, we cannot tell if this is because the viewer identified himself as male or because they are using male pronouns for someone they are assuming is MTF. Nevertheless, they offer a surprisingly supportive response.

Conservative Churches That Advocate a Return to Birth Gender

The worst example I have seen of a response to a transgendered person within a community of faith is in Jim Cymbala's autobiographical work, *Fresh Wind, Fresh Fire*, about his ministry at the Brooklyn Tabernacle in New York City. Describing the urban nature of the mission, he says, "[T]he roughness of inner-city life has pressed us to pray. When you have alcoholics trying to sleep on the back steps of your building, when your teenagers are getting assaulted and knifed on the way to youth meetings, when you bump into transvestites in the lobby after church, you can't

6. Ibid.

escape your need for God."[7] Here apparently the presence of trans individuals is seen as problematic as assaults, knifings, and alcoholism. He
goes on to describe how the church initiated an outreach program to a
group he calls "a sick subculture"[8] of male and male-to-female prostitutes
working in New York City. One Sunday he had the following encounter:

> Walking down the center aisle, I bumped into an attractive woman in
> a black dress, with blond, shoulder-length hair, nicely done nails, black
> stockings, and high heels. "Excuse me, ma'am," I said.
>
> She turned ... and this low voice with a heavy Spanish accent replied,
> "No, that's okay, man."
>
> My heart skipped a beat. This was not a woman after all. But neither was
> it a sloppy transvestite. This was a knockout of a "woman" — bone-thin,
> no body hair thanks to hormonal treatment. As I took closer notice, the
> only visual giveaway was the Adam's apple.
>
> I edged toward my wife. "Carol, you're not going to believe this," I
> whispered, "but that's a *guy* standing over there."
>
> "Don't fool me," she said.
>
> "I'm not kidding. That *is* a guy — trust me."
>
> His name was Ricardo, known on the street as "Sarah."

Cymbala's harsh view of trans people is so extreme that he even includes
this anecdote in which he and his wife talk together like two young
schoolkids giggling over an outcast schoolmate. He apparently feels his
readers will approve of his shock and his response to Sarah/Ricardo. Note,
too, his use of the word "it" to describe Sarah and his reference to "a sloppy
transvestite." He goes on to call her "a half-and-half person"[9] presumably
meaning half male and half female, although he does not actually clarify
this comment.

He and other pastors in the church go to work with Sarah/Ricardo, giving her/him instruction in how to walk and sit as a man, and they present
him to the congregation as a male. He says, "The congregation couldn't
help but cheer and praise God for this miracle."[10] While the congregation's willingness to accept and cheer for Ricardo is perhaps touching,
the insistence that s/he conform to their wishes about her/his gender in
order to gain that acceptance is troubling. Nowhere does Cymbala talk

---

7. Jim Cymbala with Dean Merrill, *Fresh Wind, Fresh Fire: What Happens When God's Spirit Invades the Heart of His People* (Grand Rapids, Mich.: Zondervan, 1997), 49.

8. Ibid., 75.

9. Ibid., 77.

10. Ibid.

about his rationale for encouraging Sarah/Ricardo to return to a male gender presentation, nor does he ever say what Sarah/Ricardo's wishes were at the point where s/he came to the church. He seems to consider self-evident the concept that Christians should remain in or return to the gender assigned to them at birth and that the church should cheer such an action.

Ricardo eventually moved to Texas, and Cymbala then described him as "every inch a real man."[11] Ricardo married a Christian woman and settled down. He had contracted AIDS, presumably during his work on the streets, and became very sick. Cymbala did call upon his congregation to pray for Ricardo's health, which led to a brief respite in his illness. Ricardo returned to Brooklyn to testify about how he turned his life around with the help of the church. Presumably, at that point in time then, he did agree with the church's desire for him to live as male.

Interestingly, Cymbala goes on to point out the ways in which the early Christian church was the model of a multicultural community, which he sees as God's plan for humanity (and I would concur with him on that point), but in doing so, Cymbala avoids any reference to the Ethiopian eunuch in his list of early converts, although the eunuch's story would bolster his argument. What I find most troublesome about Cymbala's work with gender-variant people, including Sarah/Ricardo, is the lack of any articulated theological concepts that he thought through before setting out to change the course of someone else's life. He makes the broad assumption that his understanding is correct and is thus justified, even though his assumption does not seem to be based on any research or theological underpinning.

A story with a similar outcome, but with considerably more clearly articulated thought and struggle, comes from an anonymous pastor in England whose story is told on the Parakaleo website. Parakaleo describes itself as a ministry designed to help "those seeking to re-establish their God given gender identity and destiny."[12] The group is led by Keith Tiller, an Australian who was once recommended for gender reassignment surgery, who, according to his testimony, has recovered his sense of his own male gender through his following Christ.

---

11. Ibid., 78.
12. *www.parakaleo.co.uk*, 9/4/01.

In "Transsexualism in the Church: A Pastor Responds," the unnamed minister describes how he came to find out that a new convert in his congregation, Mandy (a pseudonym), was a post-operative transsexual. While displaying a little of the titillation that we saw in Cymbala's account, this minister focuses more on pastoral issues and admits that he did not know how to respond appropriately. Again and again, he looks to his conversations with Mandy herself to guide the pastoral counseling he undertakes. He does wrestle with Deuteronomy 22:5 and has an overall bias that Mandy should live as a male; nonetheless, he takes seriously her own wishes and the sense of God working in her. When Mandy requests baptism, he weighs his questions and, after getting her permission, speaks with a colleague about his concerns. Their conclusions:

> Of course we should baptize Mandy, just as she was. Baptism is an initiation, a start of the journey. We bring all our mess into the waters of baptism.... [I]t would be totally unreasonable to expect Mandy to go back to a male lifestyle; after all the operation was irreversible. We must accept her as she is in Christ. We felt that there had already been sufficient evidence of repentance and faith on Mandy's part, together with a peaceful confirmation in our hearts. We felt we could not refuse baptism.[13]

What I found most compelling about this story is that the pastor was willing to accept Mandy as she was and that he is clear about the ways in which he struggled with his own prejudices. This pastor is prepared to accept Mandy into his church, regardless of her gender, and consistently uses female pronouns to describe her, although he wishes for her to live as a male. He notes that he did not expect her to live as a man and was prepared for the fact that she might never do that.

Over time, Mandy, according to the story, becomes increasingly uncomfortable by what is described as "the deception of Mandy's chosen lifestyle and a growing desire on her part to be more honest with others."[14] During the next eighteen months, Mandy begins to move closer to a male gender identity and eventually begins to use the name given to her/him by her/his parents, James (also a pseudonym), and changes to male dress and pronouns. Mandy/James goes on to live as a man and eventually marries a "Christian girl" like Sarah/Ricardo did.

---

13. Ibid.
14. Ibid.

Clearly the pastor thinks that a return to a male gender and name was the right course of action and notes that true repentance is marked by the attitude he describes as, " 'God is right and I am wrong' on the matter of gender."[15] The main theological objections he cites are Deuteronomy 22:5 and a concern that Mandy/James was deceptive in presenting a female image to others.

The Evangelical Alliance, a group that seeks to bring its evangelical principles to bear on policies and practices in Britain, has recently published an eighty-seven-page policy statement about transsexuality. Parakaleo Ministries is their primary point of referral, and Parakaleo's web pages and publications compose the majority of their source material. The only trans voice that I was able to distinguish from their bibliography was Victoria Kolakowski's article "Towards a Christian Ethical Response to Transsexual Persons." While stating that their subject is perhaps obscure, they note that the issue of transsexuality in the church is arising with growing frequency. They go on to say, "To date, the evangelical Christian community has not seriously attempted to respond to the issues raised by transsexuality. Where it has, it has tended to adopt differing approaches to the question: some reject the option of gender reassignment (including surgery), others cautiously approve it."[16] This finding is similar to my own.

The Evangelical Alliance characterizes the trans experience as "living a transsexual lifestyle." Exactly what characterizes a transsexual lifestyle is unclear, and they provide no definition for the term. In reality, a great deal of variation exists in the kinds of lives trans people lead, as is true for the rest of the population. Their characterization seems to me to be a reference to the "homosexual lifestyle" or an attempt to create a similar façade in the readers' minds that people become transsexual out of choice or in order to become part of an interest group. The use of the term "lifestyle" in this context is simply not helpful to their argument or to the transsexual people that they claim they might help. They also raise the specter of a transsexual lobby or political force, much along the same lines as U.S. evangelicals have put forth with the concept of a "gay agenda." Given the numbers of transsexual people and the prejudices that we face in society, crediting us with such a lobbying force seems rather fantastic.

---

15. Ibid.

16. Evangelical Alliance Policy Commission, *Transsexuality* (Carlisle, Cumbria, U.K.: Paternoster, 2000), 10.

A number of themes recur throughout the Evangelical Alliance report. The issues of perceived deception, same-sex marriage, and ability of technology/medical science to genuinely change someone from male to female or vice versa are central in this report. They do speak against using Deuteronomy as a proof-text opposing transsexuality, correctly noting both Isaiah's and Jesus' references to eunuchs, which they confusingly dismiss as being a metaphor for Christian marriage. As we have seen, Jesus' statement is more than simply an affirmation of monogamous, heterosexual marriage. The main scriptural basis for their positions lie in the creation stories and the concept of the fall and redemption of humanity.

They admit several times in the report that gender reassignment is desired by transsexuals, does provide relief of gender dysphoria, and for some people, comes with a sense of support from God. The Evangelical Alliance states: "Most transsexuals who undergo gender reassignment surgery are relatively satisfied and adapt reasonably well (at least in the medium term), frequently presenting a very realistic impersonation of the opposite sex. For many it is 'a dream come true.' "[17] A perplexing aspect of this report is that while recognizing the benefits for transsexual people in undergoing gender reassignment, they repeatedly state that transsexuals would be better off without it.

The report later states, "For some the surgery is undoubtedly a disastrous error."[18] The Evangelical Alliance repeatedly expresses concerns that some trans people will regret surgery and that long-term studies have not been done to determine the efficacy of the treatment. Yet this comment creates a conundrum since they advocate that gender reassignment surgeries should not be done; if that is the case, then no long-term studies could be completed. They also make the argument that gender reassignment surgery is not a "cure-all" because transsexuals usually need to take hormone treatments for the rest of our lives, and that unscrupulous medical doctors may be preying upon transsexuals by urging us to have surgery so that the doctor can achieve financial gain. I do not think that the use of hormones is particularly burdensome for transsexuals; no more so than living in a personally unacceptable gender. Many people take medications on a regular basis without it negatively impacting their quality of life. Nor

17. Ibid., 24.
18. Ibid., 25.

have I heard of anyone who felt that they were pushed into unnecessary surgery against their wishes, although some trans people do feel that surgeons and other medical care providers are making a good deal of money from our community. I think that the concerns in the report express the paternalism of the authors more than genuine concern for the well-being of trans people.

Despite the fact that gender reassignment can bring fulfillment to transsexuals, in their view such surgery is not appropriate:

> Christians believe that personal happiness and fulfillment are found through pleasing God and obedience to his revealed will. The adoption of a theological position that regards an individual's sex as a "given" from God implies that radical modern plastic surgery, notwithstanding that it may offer what many transsexual people desire, represents a distortion of God's creation. Of course, the problem with this line of argument concerns where we draw the line, and most Christians do happily accept many forms of cosmetic surgery.[19]

One of the strengths of this report is that it does express counterarguments to their thinking, such as the attitude of most Christians toward plastic surgery in general; however, its weakness is that they do not address their own counterarguments. As this quote highlights, they do stress strongly that gender reassignment attempts to alter what they perceive as a given from God, while not making any similar complaints about other forms of plastic surgery, such as rhinoplasty.

Over and over the Evangelical Alliance stresses that sex cannot be changed on a chromosomal level and that no amount of surgery or hormonal treatments can actually change a person's sex. Any differences in appearance then become factors that "disguise" the person's "actual" chromosomal sex. Clearly for the authors, this objection is one of their key stances on gender reassignment.

An underlying fear in this report exists that the general public, as well as the congregation, could be misled about the chromosomal reality of someone in their midst. Yet, exactly what harm does it do if someone is unaware of my chromosomes? Most people do not know their own chromosomal makeup.[20] I imagine a version of genetic Peeping Toms, desiring to know

---

19. Ibid.
20. In a number of conditions, people have recognizable male or female genitals, but have the chromosomes of the opposite gender or have additional X- or Y-chromosomes; most people in these

the "truth" about other people's bodies. Why would it be the business of a church community to know genetic information about one another? Why would this knowledge be important to the spiritual life of the members? The concern about the question of deception seems overrated to me. Rather than focusing primarily on the spiritual well-being of transsexuals or any other members of the congregation, the report emphasizes very strongly the point about deception.

Rev. Tom Lynch, a Catholic bioethicist, champions an idea that people cannot actually change sex. He states, "Our conclusion is that, as a matter of fact, you can't change your gender. You can alter your external appearance, but that doesn't make a woman a man or a man a woman. Each one of your millions of cells is male if you're male, or female if you're female, and they'll disagree with you."[21]

Despite these objections, the Evangelical Alliance's report does provide an exception to their condemnation of gender reassignment in the event of "pastoral emergency," in which the suicide of the patient seems very likely without it. This approach certainly hearkens back to the early days of the gender clinics where suicidality was one of the criterion that some clinicians used before being willing to approve a patient for treatment. But why must a patient be able to access treatment only when suicide is the option? How much unhappiness is enough misery to qualify a patient for treatment? The Evangelical Alliance states that they do not want to list reassignment surgery and treatment as a "last resort," lest too many people choose the last-resort option. This group seems willing to state that for the good of the Christian community and its need not to be "deceived," transsexuals should not receive medical treatment but should endure the hardships of gender dysphoria until they reach the point of killing themselves. This claim is easier to make about other people's happiness and satisfaction in life than making it about one's own life. I don't perceive the Christian community as so weak as to need protection from my life or the lives of others like me. Why must extreme unhappiness be the cost of participation in a Christian community?

---

positions are unaware of their chromosomal differences. The Olympic committee tests the chromosomes of Olympic athletes; the results are occasionally surprising to the athletes, and people have been barred from competition because of a chromosomal condition that was unknown to them before that point.

21. Bob Harvey and Joe Woodard, "Serving God After a Sex Change," *Calgary Herald*, March 3, 2001, Religion, p. OS10.

As an alternative, the Evangelical Alliance suggests a course of action where the individual learns to accept his or her birth gender. They acknowledge that, "The pathway of growth, sanctification and change can be expected to be slow and painful. Struggle and relapse can be anticipated."[22] I cannot concur that this slow and painful path is a better alternative than the path of transition.

The alliance makes two arguments that I think bear further discussion. The first is their argument that gender reassignment therapy does not address any underlying psychological problems that may have led to the gender dysphoria. Certainly, anecdotal evidence in the trans community indicates that some people approach transition assuming that it will solve all of their problems — only to discover that depression, unemployment, a history of sexual abuse, and other problems continue to plague them in the new gender as much as in their former gender. I have heard, in online discussions, where someone will say that they expect that their "real life" will begin once they begin hormones or have a particular surgery. Clearly, this step is not a panacea.

However, the treatment not being a cure-all is no reason to deny all people gender reassignment; rather, that fact speaks of the need to prepare each individual realistically for treatment. Certain people will always believe that their happiness depends solely on a new job, new spouse, new treatment, and so on, who subsequently discover that those things will not, by themselves, bring happiness to life. Nevertheless, serious attention should be given to any underlying psychological illnesses that a trans person faces.

The second issue is perhaps the most interesting part of the report; here the Evangelical Alliance argues that transsexuality is a version of Gnosticism. The transsexual, they state, is experiencing a sense of alienation between spirit and body. The answer then is to reconcile the spirit to the body, rather than altering the body to match the spirit. As the report says:

> Experience of sex/gender alienation of the self is undoubtedly a complex phenomenon, and "real," at least in the sense that many people *experience* some measure of such alienation. The Christian gospel is one of reconciliation and peace. It points towards the truth that human beings really *are*

---

22. Evangelical Alliance Policy Commission, *Transsexuality,* 82.

alienated! One form of that alienation is undoubtedly alienation from self, and one aspect of *that* alienation is sex/gender alienation.[23]

They argue that the place to start healing such a division between body and spirit is to acknowledge the primacy of the *truth* of sex, as an objective, physical reality, over the *belief* of gender, which is subjective and cultural. Gendered bodies have specific meanings in our society, and some are elevated while others are abused; clearly we learn to relate to those bodies in different ways. We do not want to separate the spirit from the body or ignore those experiences of the body. Yet, in my experience and in my conversations with transgendered people, I have seen a sense of anger, betrayal, and discomfort with bodies, but also a very real sense of being connected with the body. If we could so easily separate our bodies from our spirits, perhaps the sense of dysphoria would not be so intense. We examine this point more closely later as we look at body theology from a transgendered perspective.

The report does state, in a section on pastoral considerations, that churches should not require specific dress or behavioral expectations of transsexuals who attend church, nor should someone be pressured into returning to his/her birth gender. The alliance advocates working out a treatment plan, in consultation with experts, before pursuing this course of action, which should take place over a lengthy period of time. The alliance acknowledges, too, that the baptism of the eunuch in Acts 8 does provide a precedent for the baptism of transsexuals, yet they also state that repentance should be considered prior to baptism, although that step is certainly not mentioned in the Acts account.

In addressing the advent of a transsexual into the church, the Evangelical Alliance notes that different churches have different views. Some churches might allow a transsexual to attend worship; others might allow transsexuals to take communion, while membership could be denied until the person begins to change back to the gender assigned to them at birth. In speaking about a transsexual's participation in a congregation, the alliance report states the following:

> The fundamental pastoral challenge may be seen as the need to genuinely welcome transsexual people into a caring and compassionate Christian community in which all stand in need of the love, mercy and grace of God,

---

23. Ibid., 62.

and which recognises that the transsexual person is just as "human" as anybody else. It should nevertheless be understood that the presence of transsexual people within the body of Christ may unfortunately frequently provoke human reactions of hostility, together with a wide range of concerns which may especially include any perceived impact on the younger members of a church community, where attempts at explanation may be well nigh impossible, let alone offensive and unadvisable.[24]

The impact of the rejection or hostility of church members toward someone who enters their midst could also, of course, have a deeply negative impact on the spiritual development of children in the congregation. Nowhere do they advocate education or counseling for the community to become more accepting of people in their midst who are different in any way, nor does the alliance speak of the spiritual impact of discrimination.

In their recommendations, the Evangelical Alliance offers the following statement:

> We deeply regret any hurt caused to transsexual men and women by any unwelcoming or rejecting attitudes on the part of the church. We call upon evangelical congregations to genuinely welcome and accept transsexual people, whilst acknowledging the need for parallel teaching, wisdom and discernment, especially where children are concerned. Within the context of a loving Christian environment, we hope and anticipate that transsexual people will come in due course to accede to the need to reorient their lifestyle in accordance with biblical principles and orthodox church teaching. We urge gentleness and patience in this process, and ongoing care even following gender reorientation.[25]

This approach seems to me to be a spiritual Trojan horse. While welcoming transsexuals, they nonetheless expect that through participation in Christian community, a transperson will seek to return to the gender assigned to them at birth. A genuine welcome does not begin with a desire for another person to be different, but accepts the other as they are into the community of faith.

The concept of initially welcoming a transgendered person, in the gender in which they present themselves, and then later introducing the idea of a reversion to the earlier gender as the person grows in faith is not

---

24. Ibid., 79.
25. Ibid., 85.

unique to the Evangelical Alliance. A male-identified, female-bodied person active in the transgendered community in California several years ago is an Orthodox Jew. He spent considerable time studying with a rabbi and was accepted as part of a yeshiva, along with other young men. As he continued in his studies, however, the rabbi told him that he was now mature enough to realize that he was genuinely a woman, and not a man, and encouraged him to wear dresses and present himself as a woman, which s/he did. The most difficult part of the process was seeing someone who was energetic and enthusiastic when presenting as male appear depressed and hopeless in describing why she must now curtail her masculine behaviors and appearance and become a proper woman, giving up her religious studies.

Some faith communities proscribe particular roles for women and for men, reacting negatively to any blurring of those lines. As Kathy Rudy notes,

> For example, in the 1992 The Gay Agenda in Public Education, one conservative commentator complained that he could no longer "tell men from women." "Men are growing breasts [a reference to the visibility of transgendered people at a gay pride march], and women are taking their shirts off. You can't even tell they're women." What's at stake in this comment is the need of those conservative Christians to know who and what (gender) they are, especially in relation to God. Conservative men and women feel that their access to God is dependent on their gender and their sexual orientation; if the distinction between men and women or gay and straight is challenged or deteriorates, how will they know how to relate to God?[26]

The fear of trans people can arise out of the concern that God will somehow be absent if traditional ways of appearance and religious practice are threatened.

Mainstream Communities of Faith

The mainstream churches, most reeling from their fights over the ordination and marriages of gay, lesbian, and bisexual persons, seem to have even less of an articulated position than the conservative churches. Mary McClintock Fulkerson notes that a Presbyterian Church (USA) report

---

26. Kathy Rudy, *Sex and the Church: Gender, Homosexuality, and the Transformation of Christian Ethics* (Boston: Beacon Press, 1997), 65; brackets are Rudy's.

on issues of sexual orientation specifically excludes the question of cross-gendered behavior from its discussion.[27] The WOW-2000[28] conference had a very small number of transgendered participants and only two openly transgendered speakers. Sàra Herwig, a conference attendee, wrote in a review in *Transgender Tapestry* that even open-minded folks at the conference had difficulty understanding the difference of issues between sexual orientation and gender identity and that there were not enough transgendered speakers or participants.[29]

The most prominent instance of a mainline church dealing with transgendered issues is the Atlanta Presbytery's decision to uphold the ordination of Rev. Dr. Erin Swenson, a therapist and ordained minister, when she transitioned from male to female in 1995. According to an article in the November 4, 1996, issue of *Newsweek*, Swenson's case was the first instance in which a major Christian church had dealt with the issue of the ordination of a transsexual.[30]

Swenson had wrestled with the issues of gender identity for many years, since childhood. She had sought expert treatment and participated in many years of therapy in an attempt to alleviate a devastating level of depression that occurred frequently in her life. In the end, she found that only gender transition could provide the relief that she needed. In 1994, she began to take steps toward transition and, as part of that process, requested that the Presbytery of Greater Atlanta change her name. Her letter to the Presbytery began a process that took almost two years as the Church struggled with, and ultimately decided to uphold, her ordination.

The Committee on Ministry in the Presbytery requested a meeting with Swenson after receiving her request for a change of name and gender. After meeting with her, they recommended to the larger Presbytery that they approve her name change. She did not attend the Presbytery meeting in June 1995 when this issue was considered, in order to spare herself the

---

27. Mary McClintock Fulkerson, "Gender — Being It or Doing It? The Church, Homosexuality, and the Politics of Identity," in *Que(e)rying Religion: A Critical Anthology*, ed. Gary David Comstock and Susan E. Henking (New York: Continuum, 1997), 197.

28. WOW-2000 (Witness Our Welcome) was a conference that brought together mainline groups who advocate for the rights and full participation of all in the church, regardless of sexual orientation.

29. Sàra J. Herwig, "WOW-2K: LGBT People of Faith in Mainstream Christianity," *Transgender Tapestry* 92 (winter 2000): 38.

30. Daniel Pedersen, "Can a Transsexual Minister Retain Her Ordination?" *Newsweek*, November 4, 1996, 66.

"inevitable questions and stares,"[31] a decision that she later regretted. The Presbytery declined to approve the committee's recommendation and sent the issue back to the Committee on Ministry for further study.

Swenson heard nothing else from the Church until September when the Committee on Ministry faxed a list of over fifty questions to her and stated that they needed a response within five days. The questions are far-reaching and complex, dealing with every aspect of gender transition. The questions range from the ability of post-operative MTFs to achieve orgasm, the biblical basis for sex change surgery, her childhood experiences, her consideration for the unity of the Church, and the specifics of her personal finances. In reading the complete list of questions, you can perceive various levels of support, hostility, and fear on the part of the questioners; clearly an already divided committee wrote them.

The Committee on Ministry asked her about her consideration of the words of 1 Corinthians 8[32] and how her transition might be a stumbling block for others. Her response is as follows:

> Regarding 1 Corinthians 8 I anticipate that my gender change will be a stumbling block for many. Were this simply an expression of the freedom granted under the Gospel of Jesus Christ, as in the consumption of ritual meat, I would expect this passage to be a good reason to either not make the gender transition, or make it far from the sight of God's people. Such is not the case, however, for a gender change is not simply a casual expression of free will but a deeper movement toward wholeness and healing. If God's people are put off by an event of such profound healing, I would wonder if they are truly God's people.
>
> It seems to me that my change of gender is no more difficult to accept, no more of a "stumbling block" than the Gospel of Jesus Christ which calls us into radical acceptance of the self and other as we discover God's radical acceptance of us in Jesus Christ. A gospel that allows, no requires, us to become all we are created to be, whether that be male, female or transgendered.[33]

This exchange highlights a recurring theme in the dialogue between Swenson and the committee. They ask in a variety of ways how her transition will impact the unity and health of the Church; Swenson responds by

31. Erin Swenson in "Materials on the Ordination Case of Erin K. Swenson and the Presbytery of Greater Atlanta, Presbyterian Church, USA, 1995–1997," 8.

32. After discussing the eating of foods offered to idols, 1 Corinthians 8:9 says, "But take care that this liberty of yours does not somehow become a stumbling block for the weak."

33. Swenson, "Materials," 21.

challenging the Church to its full potential in living out the radical messages of Jesus and affirms the ability of the church to maintain unity even
while dealing with an issue such as transsexuality.

The committee later asked, "If you continue in Atlanta Presbytery it
will have a far reaching and devastating effect on Presbyterians. As a
minister of the Gospel do you feel it is worth the friction that will occur
and the loss of members which will come?" Her response:

> While I am aware that my continuing in the Atlanta Presbytery may well
> inspire some few disaffected church members to leave, I am also aware that
> there are many, perhaps now unchurched, who may consider the Presbyte-
> rian church a place where they may find an open and accepting fellowship
> as a result of this issue. I think that it is very important for the church
> to decide whether it will serve itself by "marketing" itself to the general
> populace and thereby diluting its message of radical reconciliation, or if
> the church can trust in God's call to be the church, fully committed to the
> words of Jesus that even "the least of these" can find a place in her bosom.[34]

Her insistence that the Church needs to consider the implications of a
decision not to support transsexuals as much as pondering the effects of
including transsexuals is important. Too often the Church has taken the
least controversial course, not examining the impact of that decision in
following the radically inclusive message of Jesus nor the ways in which
the Church has come to be seen as prejudiced and judgmental.

While Swenson kept the Church up-to-date on her transition, she did
not hear from them again until April 1996 when the Executive Presbyter
informed her that the Committee on Ministry was deeply divided on the
question of continuing her ordination and shared with her some of their
reactions. They asked her to again clarify her position on how her actions
would impact the unity of the Church and if she was acting in a way
that was self-centered without regard for her Church or her family. She
asked to meet with the committee but was not given an answer on that
question, so she arranged to meet one-on-one with as many committee
members as would agree to talk with her. Clearly those meetings were the
turning point in her relationship with the committee and in their decision
making. In September, the committee voted unanimously in her favor and
presented this information to the October Presbytery meeting.

---

34. Ibid., 37.

The debate at the Presbytery meeting lasted about an hour; the vote was close, 186–161, in favor of upholding her ordination. Objections and legal challenges to the decision were resolved in the next six months. The Presbytery asked two of its theologians, Shirley Guthrie and Ben Kline, to work with the Committee on Ministry to release a theological statement about this decision. The report cites three issues: "(1) the doctrine of human beings as the inseparable unity of body and soul; (2) the doctrine of providence; and (3) the doctrine of human beings in the image of God."[35] They also note that no Scriptures, Christian traditions, or doctrines give any explicit guidance on the subject of transsexuality.

The Atlanta Presbytery's report articulate the many ways in which modern people use medicine to solve a number of problems, ranging from poor eyesight to life-threatening conditions, without any debate about whether such actions are against the will of God or God's intention for that person. They go on to state:

> If we think as biblically faithful Christians, we cannot say that biological-bodily structure alone and in itself is determinative of who a transsexual person is and what God created him or her to be. That would be in a too materialistic or naturalistic way to deny the reality and importance of the psyche or soul. Nor can we condemn the desire of transsexual persons to express in their bodily (and therefore also sexual) life the "gender identity" that defines that they know themselves to be "on the inside." That would be to deny the fact that God created them too to live thankfully and obediently as embodied human beings. We have to remember the inseparable interrelatedness of body and soul that God wills for transsexuals as for all other human beings.
>
> If we do that, must we not welcome the wisdom and skill of modern science that understands the contradiction between body and soul in people who suffer from gender dysphoria, and seeks to restore to them the unity of body and soul that God wills also for them? Must we not be grateful to God that modern science has made it possible?[36]

In contrast to the view of the Evangelical Alliance, which sees a contrast between "bodily truth" and subjective (and, in their view, deceptive) self-understanding, the Presbytery makes a statement that both soul and body

35. Ibid., 77.
36. "Theological Reflection on the Affirmation of the Ordination of Erin Swenson by Greater Atlanta Presbytery, February 7, 1997," in Swenson, "Materials," 84.

contain truth and sees bringing these things into unity as a common goal shared by God and humanity. The body cannot live without the soul; the soul is not expressed (at least on earth) without the body. This distinction between the two reports is critical and shows a different theological underpinning for these two arguments. In my view, the Presbytery report is far more compatible with the ways in which we transgendered people see ourselves and provides a more holistic way of looking at human life and identity. The Presbytery clearly express that while the body is important, it is not the sole determinant of identity.

While acknowledging the ways in which people can experience alienation between body and spirit, they celebrate that paths for healing alienation involve both body and spirit. Rather than simply concluding that the soul must change or at least bend to the will of the body, the Presbytery notes that modern people have the capacity to heal bodies and bring them to greater wholeness, a fact for which Christians should rejoice. Jesus himself, they note, healed both bodies and spirits, not one without the other.

The report concludes with an acknowledgment of what the Presbytery has done by upholding Swenson's ordination. It ends with these words:

> First, the Presbytery acknowledged that the covenant promises of God are for her too; that in her present as in her earlier life God continues to include her as a member of God's covenant people; and that her present as well as her earlier life and ministry bears witness to God's steadfast faithfulness that does not take back God's promises.
>
> Second, following what the New Testament teaches us about what it means to be created in the image of God, the Presbytery refused to let sexual or gender issues alone define who Erin Swenson is, and asked about the larger dimensions of her life and ministry. Her personal life shows no indication of immorality in her relationships with men or women. She continues to care for her divorced spouse and to share care and responsibility for their children. Her ministry as a pastoral counselor, long recognized as legitimate by Greater Atlanta Presbytery, enables her in a way that reflects Jesus' own ministry to minister to people who are often despised and rejected in our society and church.
>
> None of us perfectly reflects the true humanity of God we see in Jesus Christ. But Presbytery's action regarding Erin Swenson was based on its decision that in her created relationship with the triune God, the relationship she confessed when she became a confirmed member of the church and again when she was ordained, and in her relationship with other people

in her personal life and ministry, she shows herself to be a faithful disciple of Jesus Christ and minister of the Gospel.[37]

This conclusion is important for several reasons. First, it affirms that the covenant of God, and God's love, guidance, and care, is for God's transgendered children as much as for anyone else. God does not remove God's promises to us but faithfully stands by us. Second, Swenson is viewed in the totality of her being, looking carefully at her gender and at more than her gender. We are not defined by our gender identities alone, and the decisions we make and the lives we lead come out of the complexities of our unique lives. Third, the Presbytery's report states that her relationship with the church and with God remain unchanged even while she herself undergoes a transformation of gender. That which she confessed earlier in her life remains true now. This last point in important spiritually to transgendered people and affirms that regardless of our external, and internal, changes, we are known and valued by God as we are and as we change.

In an article in *The Other Side* entitled "Body and Soul United," Swenson had this to say: "Questions about gender, and the deeply held myths that surround it, are certain to raise fear and anger within the church. We are accustomed to minding our bodies; we are much less comfortable embodying our minds. Transgender reality calls this into question, and may become the center of the struggle in years to come."[38] This contribution is, I think, the most important one that Swenson's case has had to the conversation about transgendered people and the church. Rather than letting the conversation be a simplistic discussion about "the truth of the body," this case has led us to consider the complexity and truth of both body and spirit, and has brought that conversation within the confines of a mainstream church. They, too, had to wrestle with the question face to face with a valuable member of their Presbytery, in the life of a colleague in ministry.

The Anglican Church has recently dealt with an issue similar to that of Swenson's case when the Rev. Peter Stone had gender reassignment and returned to serve her parish as the Rev. Carol Stone amidst widespread

---

37. Ibid., 86–87.
38. Erin Swenson, "Body and Soul United," *The Other Side* 37, no. 3 (May and June 2001): 31.

support within the congregation, with more than 90 percent of the con-gregation wishing for Stone to remain as vicar. In describing her letter to her bishop, letting him know of her transition, Stone wrote:

> I did feel sheer terror. Everything was on the line. I had no precedent to work on so when I wrote the letter I did so with hope, faith and trust. I really had to expect the worse. It has turned out that after a lifetime of personal anguish and secrecy I find it truly remarkable to be here. It was beyond my wildest imagination that this has been accepted and my people accepted me and I now look forward to new beginnings.[39]

The bishop, The Rt. Rev. Barry Rogerson, found no ecclesial or ethical reasons that would prevent Stone from serving and spent considerable time consulting with Stone and experts before affirming Stone's continued service.

The announcement of Stone's transition brought a negative response from the Evangelical Alliance, which is cited in the *Calgary Herald* as stating that "transsexuality is a 'fantasy' that is incompatible with being a Christian."[40] The article goes on to state that while the Unitarian Univer-salist Church, Metropolitan Community Church, and the Presbyterian Church (USA) had ordained transsexuals, many other denominations have not. They note that a Roman Catholic priest in New York had applied for laicization prior to proceeding with sex reassignment surgery. In addi-tion, "Other Catholic priests in Italy and Britain have left the priesthood after undergoing a sex change. There are also known cases in the U.S., Britain, and Australia involving Southern Baptist, United Methodist, East-ern Orthodox, evangelical, Anglican and Presbyterian clergy who resigned after sex changes."[41]

I am personally aware of one instance in which the United Methodist Church required an MTF clergyperson to resign, not because she was transgendered, but because she would not leave her relationship with her wife of many years. The Methodist Church alleged that that gave the appearance of lesbianism (and one could argue, the reality of a lesbian relationship) and therefore considered the clergyperson in violation of the Book of Discipline's prohibition of practicing homosexuals as clergy. I find it baffling that the church would prefer that a family be separated from

---

39. PlanetOut, 3/19/01.
40. Harvey and Woodard, *Calgary Herald*, March 3, 2001, Religion, OS10.
41. Ibid.

one another rather than appear to be made up of loving spouses of the same gender who care for their children and are faithful to their vows. Surely we need to be wary of such a position and condemn it for putting appearances before love and family bonds.

A recent series of articles in progressive magazines *The Other Side* and *The Witness* provides a great deal of information and may well be the first place that some Christians have considered the connection between transgendered people and the church. Here Mollenkott outlines her argument, presented more fully in *Omnigender,* calling for the church, and society as a whole, to move away from a bigendered perspective into a broader view of gender and human expression which she calls "omnigender."

In reviewing Mollenkott's book, Mary Hunt writes:

> [T]he entrance of trans people in their many forms — intersexual or hermaphrodite persons, transsexuals, transvestites or cross-dressers, drag kings and queens or performance artists, transgenderists or bigenderists and androgynes, to name only some of the newly emerging categories — effectively changes the panorama forever. No longer can we tell players with or without a scorecard. No longer can we assume anything about anyone, or so it seems, with gender categories as fluid as warm honey and sexual orientations multiplying like dot-coms in the Silicon Valley. The point is that all must be made welcome, just as they are, in communities that call themselves Christian.[42]

This view represents the most radical of the approaches that I encountered — that everyone should be welcomed regardless of their gender identity or any other characteristic. For some, this broad welcome is a prerequisite for a Christian community. Of course, this practice is far easier to accomplish in theory than within a worshiping community.

Gay and Lesbian Communities of Faith

Several years after I transitioned, I was a guest at a Metropolitan Community Church that described itself as a progressive congregation. One of the staff members was giving me a tour around the building on a break in our meetings. As we approached the rest rooms, he pointed at the

---

42. Mary E. Hunt, "GRACE — is a Transgender Person who Loves Women and Men," *The Witness* 84, no. 7/8 (July–August 2001): 28–29.

women's rest room, turned and said to me, "that's the one you should use." At this point in time, all of my identification was male and I was always seen as male in public. At the same time, I transitioned while working for the denomination, with the overwhelming support of many of our leaders and members. Other transgendered people within MCC have had similar experiences within congregations of sometimes being overtly told that they do not fit in and in other cases being warmly welcomed into the congregation.

Some congregations, like MCC New York, have developed support and prayer groups for transgendered people and actively do outreach into the transgendered community. For several years, the group Gender People has been meeting on Sunday afternoons providing support, encouragement, and prayer for its members. A number of participants have emerged from that group who are now providing leadership for other transgendered people within the denomination. MCC St. Louis conducts a Bible study for trans folk, called Transgender and the Bible. Similar to classes held for gay and lesbian people to explore homosexuality and the Bible, this study provides a way for participants to process the experience of being faithful and trans.

MCC of the Hudson Valley in Albany, New York, put out a brochure, "What is There for Transgendered Folk at MCC of the Hudson Valley? 8 reasons why you will feel at ease worshiping with us." The brochure states that MCC is "A place where you are accepted fully, just the way that you are. MCC believes that each person brings with them a wealth of innate uniqueness and talents. Participation in the worship life of the faith community is not based upon the clothing you wear but rather upon your desire to be active. People are not judged by society's expectations but welcomed by God's law of love." Several MCCs have also included heterosexual cross-dressers in their leadership and as active participants in their congregations.

Gatherings of transgendered people at MCC conferences have seen a fairly rapid increase in participation in recent years. Some people have, like me, transitioned while in places of visible leadership. One of our elders, the highest elected body in our denomination, transitioned during her term of office. Many congregations have the desire to be welcoming but may or may not fully understand what they need to do to express a genuine welcome.

Jeff S. described how he decided to attend a temple, Beth Chaddishim, after he transitioned. He did not feel comfortable participating in services until he had begun hormones, had chest surgery, and was seen as a man by the congregation. He began attending a primarily gay and lesbian synagogue, and began Hebrew studies as part of preparation for his bar mitzvah. He felt that it was important that he talk with the rabbi before the ceremony so that she knew his background as a transgendered person. This action was important to him because he did not want to compromise the rabbi's position or do anything that was misleading for her. As he reports their conversation:

> I told her my situation and...well, she's a rabbi, so its going to be a very rabbinic response. The first thing she asked me was did I feel my life was at stake. I said yes, I was suicidal, had I not done this I am absolutely positive that I would have committed suicide. And her response was then whatever you needed to do to maintain your life is what you should do and that is all there is to that and that's a very Jewish way of looking at things. And then she said if somebody converts to Judaism, it is wrong and insulting to refer to the person as an ex-Christian because they're not. They're a Jew now and that's all there is to it. She says by the same token, you're a man now and that's all there is to it and that was the last discussion we ever had on the matter.[43]

I asked Jeff what role his bar mitzvah played in affirming his transition. He responded, "You know the boy stands up at the *bema* and says, 'Today I am a man.' And I always said if my religion couldn't give me anything else, I would be able to stand up on the *bema* in front of an entire congregation and say, 'Today I am a man.' I didn't actually say that during my bar mitzvah, but you know that's why you are there."[44] Through this ritual, Jeff's faith tradition recognized his transition by allowing him to take part in a ritual that affirms him as a man, and is, itself, symbolic of a transition from childhood to adulthood.

One church that has distinguished itself in its ministry with the transgendered community is City of Refuge Community Church in San Francisco. City of Refuge is a primarily African American, Pentecostal, United Church of Christ congregation in the heart of San Francisco. I spoke with Ashley Moore, who directs at the church a transgendered

---

43. Interview with Jeff S., August 1, 2001.
44. Ibid.

choir called Transcendence Gospel Choir. She described how she came back to church at about the same time that she began her transition from male to female. As she began to consider her own transition, she noticed the spirituality that seemed present in the lives of other trans people, which led her back to reading the Bible that had been part of her faith as a younger person. In reading the Bible, she discovered a God of love not often preached about in Christian churches. When she found City of Refuge, she found a community where the God and Christ she saw in the Bible were known, preached, and worshiped. She told me in an interview, "I also found that it's a refuge. I mean, to me, I came back to Christianity very clearly at the beginning of my transition because this is... what I grew up with. But it also is what resonates with me. Not in the way that it had been presented to me in the past... once I began my intimate relationship with God it felt... right."[45]

ACCEPTANCE WITHIN A FAITH COMMUNITY is important for many transgendered people. Many of our faith traditions encourage us to worship and pray together in community, and yet we place many barriers on the participation of gender-variant people. Many of these conversations are taking place before congregations have the opportunity to connect the issues of transsexuality with issues of sexuality (although transgendered people are often included in name in the GLBT [gay, lesbian, bisexual, and transgendered] community) or with a church's general support for "traditional" values and rigid gender roles, and this timing is helpful. As this issue becomes more commonplace within communities of faith, I suspect that the types of responses will become less varied and more standardized within a particular tradition. As that is happening, we must continue to raise our voices and call for communities that affirm the diversity of God's creation and mirror the welcome that God extends to all.

Ann Thompson Cook raises the following questions in *Open Hands* magazine:

> As a community of faith, we are fond of saying that each of us is made in the image of God, yet I and countless others are sidetracked early in life trying to re-make ourselves to some other image, some human-designed image. Those who can't or won't play along are taunted, ostracized, often either

---

45. Interview with Ashley Moore, August 2001.

directly or indirectly killed off. As a community of faith, we go along with a system that re-makes people into our own image of male and female, rather than enjoying, appreciating, and nurturing what God has placed in front of us. Consider the possibility that what God wants more than anything is for each of us to be fully who we are, for each of us to develop our God-given talents full-out and have that be our contribution to the world. What if, as faith communities, we stopped assuming that we can design God's image better than God? What if we emptied ourselves of our sex/gender constructs and simply took in each child, each person, as they are, and looked for that of God in each of them. And what if we took on supporting and nurturing whatever love emerged in our communities and laid aside the question, "Is this kind of love okay?" Perhaps then all our labels would disappear — they would be of no further value, no longer needed.[46]

What powerful questions for communities of faith to consider. What if we laid aside any desire or need to regulate those who gather with us for worship and fellowship and instead simply opened the doors to welcome in those who seek solace, refuge, joy, and spirit within the community? Perhaps then we will begin to live the words of the prophet Isaiah, "My house shall be called a house of prayer for all people."

---

46. Ann Thompson Cook, "Made in God's Image: Re-Thinking Constructs of Gender and Orientation," *Open Hands* 14, no. 1 (summer 1998): 21.

Chapter Five

Creating a Genuine Welcome for Trans People in Communities of Faith

Trans people encounter a wide range of responses when entering a faith community. Many times, trans people choose not to attend worship in order to avoid what may be an uncomfortable experience and the judgment that they perceive will come from a community of faith. Many congregations, however, have either never considered the possibility of the presence of transgendered persons in their midst or have no idea how to extend a welcome to trans folks. A critical component to welcoming the transgendered is being intentional about attitudes, language, physical space, and programs. We first explore in detail what barriers prevent full participation of transgendered people within a community and then how a congregation might work to increase welcome and integration of trans people within the community.

Barriers to Participation

In a number of different ways, a congregation can explicitly or unconsciously create an atmosphere that conveys to transgendered people that we are not welcome there. Communities of faith also need to be aware that they need to extend a welcome that bridges the fear of rejection that a transgendered person may have that prevents them from seeking acceptance within the congregation. This one barrier is probably the single largest to the participation of transgendered people in communities of faith. People censor themselves before they even begin to seek a place to worship and fellowship. When I have asked trans people about their attendance in worship, particularly those early in transition, I have frequently received the answer, "Of course, I could not go to church/synagogue/temple." A number of people that I spoke with only

---

Barriers to Participation

- Fear and unfamiliarity on the part of the congregation and the transgendered
- Language issues
- Physical layout that separates people by gender
- Programs that exclude or separate by gender
- Pathologizing or designating trans issues as sinful
- Overt hostility

---

entered houses of worship when attending a funeral or wedding, and then many stated a fear that "the roof would cave in" or God's judgment would be seen in some other way. Congregations that seek to be welcoming must think carefully about this fear that trans people bring to the community of faith. When someone enters with this level of fear of judgment, that person will leave again as soon as something validates that fear. We need to respect the courage that it takes for an individual to overcome this fear and enter the congregation at all.

Religious leaders also need to take into account the fears and misconceptions that the congregation may have. We live in a society that discourages and punishes gender difference; our congregations are part of that society. Make no mistake about it: gender variance breaks the rules of our society, and some members of our congregations will be uncomfortable with that rule breaking. Most people are very unaccustomed to seeing societal rules being broken in a religious setting; more often, our communities of faith support, encourage, and enforce society's expectations and norms. Most of our society has very little information on the subject and what they do know they may have learned from sensationalist talk shows that, of course, do not represent the average transgendered person. The point of those programs is, after all, ratings and advertising revenue, not factual information. You need to replace the misinformation with accurate knowledge.

Gender difference, too, is a source of humor in our culture. From Monty Python to the local drag bar, gender variance is considered to be funny entertainment. Some members of the congregation may feel that gender variance in church is therefore mocking the community or mocking God, rather than an authentic expression of a person's selfhood. Gender variance can also be seen as a sign of disrespect for the traditions of the worshiping community rather than an affirmation that the gender-variant person feels safe enough to bring his/her whole self to worship.

Some people view gender difference with a sense of discomfort both because it breaks the rules of society and because it highlights for that person some sense of discomfort for their own gender identity. Very few of us fit neatly into the boxes of masculine male and feminine female that our society lifts up. A man who dislikes sports but happily identifies as male may be uncomfortable with a male-bodied person who chooses to wear a dress because that person raises the question of his own gender nonconformity. The same is true of a woman who was a tomboy as a child but feels uncomfortable with women who question their status as female. Issues of gender are prevalent in our society, and gender variance pushes our buttons. Some people may resent those who feel freer to break outside of the stereotypes and norms of gendered behavior, wishing that they too could express themselves in different ways. Obviously, stares and uncomfortable looks often quickly discourage a transgendered person from staying or returning to worship and can do terrible damage to that person's sense of self-worth and to their relationship with God and the community of faith.

Particular issues also face transgendered people within congregations comprising, or welcoming, gay and lesbian people. Some people fear that the presence of the gender-variant will erode gains made by lesbians and gay men, because transgendered people are just too shocking. In these congregations in particular, people may be sensitive to their own gender variance; gay and lesbian people are often identified by their gender differences and can be in danger because of them. Little boys are called "sissy" and "fag" because they may be feminine; lesbians are targeted on the streets because they are perceived as masculine. Patricia Groves, a lesbian parent and a member of a United Methodist Reconciling Congregation, wrote in an article for *Open Hands* entitled "Learning from Our Daughter," about the experience of an MTF attending their church. In the article, Groves wrote:

> When our daughter was about three years of age, there was a transgendered person who regularly attended our church. She worked in a blue-collar job, and would come to church dressed as a man if she was going to work. If

she had Sunday off, she would dress as a woman. Our daughter believed her to be two different people.

My uncertainty about addressing our own family issues led me to believe that I should not point out the fact that both the male and female presentations were manifestations of the same person. It seemed complicated enough that we were a family with two female parents, and it was incredibly complicated to imagine introducing the concept that gender could be anything other than dichotomous and clearly defined.

As we have all grown through the process of being the family which we are, it has occurred to me that my daughter has a better understanding of sexuality orientation and gender identity than I do. At age 11, she has an intense interest in understanding relationships and identity issues. She does not have to categorize people in relation to scientific definitions. She has not thought about the quest of biological determinism or social construction of identity. She is able, through her experience, to see people for who they are and by how they present themselves.[1]

Keeping children sheltered from the presence of gender-variant people is a theme that is prevalent both in this article and in many of the responses to transgendered people within the church. Parents and congregational leaders need to think carefully about why they are shielding the children and from what. What are we afraid that our children might learn from the presence of transgendered people? Perhaps the perceived link to sexuality is the reason; we feel that cross-dressing and transsexuality are manifestations of sexuality and therefore appropriate only for adults. However, this perception is not valid. Children are very much subject to the gender pressures of our society and also need affirmation that they can express themselves in ways that are right for them.

Children are often better at seeing the nuances within a person than adults ever believe. In the years that I was in denial about my gender identity, one of the things that bothered me the most was that children would ask me if I were a boy or a girl, even when I was wearing dresses. When I taught preschool, one little girl kept insisting I was a man and told me that I should grow a mustache. Not until years later did I perceive what it was that she saw and did I understand the source of my own discomfort with her comments. Children are well aware of gender differences even when we attempt to hide them. Groves concludes her article as follows,

---

1. Patricia A. Groves, "Learning from Our Daughter," *Open Hands* (winter 2001): 23.

Transgender persons should expect the same of me which I expect of heterosexuals. I want parents to tell their children that there are families in which two women or two men love each other as a man and a woman love each other. I should tell my children that gender is not fixed and biologically determined. There are people who were born female, who identify themselves as male and vice versa. There are also males who identify with a feminine role and vice versa. In my life, it is my daughter who has taught me these lessons.[2]

Gender variance is part of the natural order and God's plan for creation. If we believe this statement, then we have a responsibility as communities of faith to move beyond our fears and teach this to our children, letting them interact with a wide range of people, and encouraging them into their own authentic selfhood, however that is expressed.

In addition to the fears, discomfort, and lack of information that congregations bring to an encounter with transgendered people, a congregation's actions and choices put up barriers, even if the barrier is created inadvertently. Language is often a major issue. The most devastating aspect of this communication is calling transgendered persons by pronouns and names that do not represent their current gender presentation or identity. Such language can cause a great deal of pain and discomfort. I firmly believe, based on my own experiences and observation of other people, that a person can learn to use pronouns that are appropriate regardless of one's own ideas about the person's gender presentation or biological sex. The issue is one of respect for that individual to address them in the way in which that person wishes to be addressed, whether with male, female, or gender-neutral names and pronouns. Asking someone how she or he wishes to be addressed is better than making assumptions that may not be accurate. Not all gender-variant people wish to be addressed in the same way. An FTM wearing a suit to your worship service may adamantly want to be called by male pronouns and names while a butch lesbian in the same suit will be equally adamant about her status as a woman. The same may be true of an MTF in a dress and a gender bender wearing his dress with a goatee. Simple answers to these questions are not available, which is why we must approach them individually. Everyone needs to be welcomed into the house of God, and we should learn enough about all

---

2. Ibid., 23.

persons who enter our communities to know how they see themselves and with which pronouns to address them.

While many transgendered people do identify clearly as one gender or the other, some people are quite uncomfortable with this system. A binary approach can present a barrier to people's participation when worship includes an overemphasis on gendered language. If everyone is addressed as either "sister" or "brother," that language is problematic for people who do not feel that they fit into either of those categories or where they identify with the other category. MCC New York uses the term "sibling" to replace "sister" and "brother," which is certainly a good attempt to emphasize the meaning of the terms rather than focusing on gender. The point of using the terms "sister" and "brother" in worship is to identify a particular kind of relationship and not necessarily to place people into categories of a binary gender system. "Friend" might be a better term.

Another problem occurs when congregations state that they comprise or welcome the gay, lesbian, bisexual, transgendered, and intersexed communities (LGBTI or GLBTI, for short) and then provide no programming or mention of transgendered or intersexed persons. While including these additional terms is politically correct, my opinion is that they should not be used unless a congregation intends, and follows through, on specifically including intersexed and transgendered people. To include these titles in the name but not in the life of the congregation creates a false hope and expectation on the part of those who may wish to worship with that community. Honesty in advertising is important. If you feel neither called nor able to address the issues of transgendered or intersexed persons, do not include us in your press releases. At the same time, evaluate the reasons that you are unable to address the needs of such persons and explore ways that the community can be more fully embracing.

The physical layout of space can also provide a clear sense of welcome or exclusion to transgendered persons. In some orthodox communities, men and women sit in separate places during worship or prayer. For such a community to include transgendered persons requires careful thought about how and when a person should sit on which side of the aisle. More commonly, congregations do not separate people for worship, but still have separate rest room facilities and sometimes programs that are gender segregated. The bathroom issue is one of the most frequent questions that congregations ask me to address when they are seeking to be inclusive of transgendered persons. Some in the transgendered community have joked that our rallying cry should be, "Let my people pee." People who do not visibly fit the categories of male and female often have no place to go. People who have a gender identity that is different from their physical appearance can also find it very emotionally painful to have their sense of gender incongruity reinforced every time they need to use the rest room. While it may seem rather insignificant, this issue is a major barrier to participation.

Some congregations provide separate programming for women and for men. In a sexist society that treats men and women differently, some times and topics are certainly appropriate for men speaking with other men and women with other women. Be thoughtful and intentional, however, about how and when transgendered people are incorporated in such programs. Discuss these issues before they arise, before a transgendered person has attended the group. Planning and thinking ahead can prevent someone from experiencing the pain of exclusion and the awkwardness of letting someone know that s/he is not welcome at a particular event.

In some congregations, a transgendered person faces overt hostility. I have heard anecdotally of church ushers telling cross-dressers that they should not come in to worship. More commonly, transgendered persons are allowed to come to church and then hear a religious leader condemning them as either sinful or sick. Such condemnation can happen in both liberal and conservative congregations. An MCC colleague once told me very authoritatively, years before my own transition, that transgendered people were ashamed of being gay and changed gender to justify their choice of a sex partner. According to this colleague, more therapy and affirmation of being gay would solve the problem better than transition. This theory does not take into account, however, transgendered people who identify as gay or bisexual after transition, nor does it allow for the individual's expression of both gender identity and sexual orientation. Condemnations, however well meaning, are not helpful to a transgendered person and certainly do not make us feel welcome in communities of faith.

Signs of a Welcoming Community

A community can show its welcome and acceptance of transgendered persons in a number of ways. The first is being able to offer a simple,

---

A Welcoming Community

- Genuine hospitality
- Nondiscrimination policies and attitudes
- Appropriate and inclusive language
- The visible and audible presence of trans people and programs
- Provision of meaningful rituals to mark changes
- Outreach to trans groups and individuals
- Opportunities for the congregation to learn accurately about trans issues
- Rest rooms that the gender-variant can access

---

nondramatic, comfortable welcome when someone arrives at your services. Sometimes well-meaning people try too hard to let others know that they are welcome. Unfortunately, such as approach can serve to drive people away. What is helpful is an expression of genuine hospitality. Use greeters who can convey a warm sense of welcome to your community. Be sure that greeters have some training around trans issues. For example, if a person who appears female asks for a name tag that reads "Samuel," have greeters who are able to accommodate this situation in a friendly and relaxed manner. You want to convey to transgendered people that we are both expected and welcomed at your community.

Your congregation may be the one place, outside of a person's home, where she or he can be genuinely themselves. You may provide a very meaningful opportunity for self-expression to a cross-dresser by creating a safe and respectful environment in which that individual can dress as he or she wishes to dress. Perhaps your congregation can be the place where someone tests out a new name and new pronouns to see how they feel. A faith community can become literally a sanctuary in which a trans person is able to feel safe, whole, and dignified. That feeling alone is an incredibly valuable gift for someone, especially early in dealing with her or his trans feelings.

Another way to show that a community is prepared and able to deal with transgendered persons in your community is through trans-friendly policies. Include gender identity in your nondiscrimination policies and talk about this concept with the community's leadership. Clear, well-thought-through, and well-articulated policy should exist about gender-based programming. As stated earlier, having these discussions only when someone has arrived at the first women's or men's gathering is never helpful. Again, be as inclusive as you possibly can be. Discuss this issue thoroughly with program leadership and with transgendered people within the community. Where the group intends to include transgendered people, say so explicitly. Transgendered people are accustomed to being excluded; you need to make your inclusion as broad as possible and obvious to all participants. For example, you might say in a brochure for a men's group that it is open to all persons who identify as men or that a women's retreat welcomes all women, including transsexuals or transgendered women. The categories of pre- and post-operative are rarely helpful in these situations; a community is highly unlikely to be asking people to expose their genitals at a religious event. Gender is much more complex than genital config-uration, and a faith community is much more likely to be focused on emotional and spiritual issues than on physical ones (although exceptions certainly exist).

Congregations should consider several things about gender-based pro-gramming. First, let the decisions be based on the content of the programs. If the topic of the men's program is to examine how growing up as a boy has affected the men they've become, then a transsexual is unlikely be com-fortable or able to contribute much to the group, although listening to the discussion could be valuable. On the other hand, someone who identifies as a cross-dresser or transgendered might have important insights about approaching and broadening one's sense of what it means to be a man. No formulaic answers for these questions are available; you need to look at the specific situation.

Second, consider how the congregation can offer programming that is gender inclusive or focused specifically on transgendered individuals. Men's groups and women's groups should not be your only options. Provide a third option or programs to which everyone is welcome, remembering that some people no longer consider themselves transgendered after they transition. Finally, evaluate with gendered groups that wish to be limited to only "biological" (nontransgendered) men or women what is moti-vating that desire. Is it program based or a result of prejudices? Or is the transgendered person bringing a different gender socialization to the program? I have heard a number of women who lead women's groups state that MTFs bring "male energy" that is inappropriate to a women's group. Evaluate how much of that assessment is based on stereotypes (for example, being assertive is a male trait), how much is discomfort at someone crossing those barriers of gender, and how disruptive the behavior is to the group. The group may be very helpful in aiding an individual in forming a positive self-image in the gender of her/his choice and in guiding them to make choices that are liberating. In general, excluding people should be done as rarely as possible. Society already has too many places where we exclude people, particularly transgendered people.

Language is very important in conveying your sense of welcome to transgendered people. In brochures, during sermons and announcements, talk about people of many genders and include examples of transgendered people. As said before, simply including the word "transgender" does not necessarily do the job; people may assume that they are part of a laundry list rather than being specifically included. Be sure that you have a good grasp of current terminology that the transgendered community uses and be able to include terms in a way that conveys your knowledge. You may want to develop a specific brochure or outreach material that states explicitly the welcome and programs that you have that are open to transgendered people. Remember, too, that transgender is not a sexual orientation and does not belong in that category on any surveys or feedback forms that you develop. Ask about gender identity separate from sexual orientation. Doing so will show that you have a more sophisticated grasp of the issues.

Be able to address an individual with the name and pronouns of her/his choice. Learning to do this comfortably is absolutely vital to your ability to attract and include trans people. While everyone makes mistakes from time to time, focusing on getting pronouns right is easier than trying to rebuild trust with someone who has felt excluded. Addressing someone as they wish to be addressed is a matter of courtesy and respect. Make every effort to convey that respect to those who attend your community's events. This simple action becomes easier with practice.

Trans people should be heard and seen in your worship service and programming. An usher or greeter who is gender variant can immediately let a trans person who is entering the church know that s/he is welcome there. Of course, not all trans people are visibly obvious as trans; in fact, many of us are indistinguishable from other women and men in society. In addition to thinking about the balance of men and women leading worship, consider the level of gender variance of your participants. Include people who fall outside of the conventional range of looks.

Prepare your music program to accommodate people whose voices may be unusual for their appearance. While FTMs' voices fall with hormones, MTFs' voices do not move higher. MTFs learn to speak in higher ranges, but many return to their original voice range for singing. Is your choir prepared for a baritone who looks every bit a woman?

One important way to serve the trans community is to provide meaningful opportunities for people to ritually mark the changes that are occurring in their lives and to have the community's prayers and blessings. Having a service to celebrate and bless a change in name, which acts as a public pronouncement of the name and of the transition, adds considerable meaning to a person's transition. Such a service recognizes the event spiritually and allows the community to witness and bless this milestone. Depending on the community's understanding of baptism, this service may include a reaffirmation of the baptismal covenant or a rebaptism with the new name. The faith community needs to put the word out to trans folks that this option is available in your place of worship; people may not be aware that a church or synagogue will offer this type of ritual.

Consider, too, having specific programs for transgendered people. To welcome a small trans group, for example, conveys a sense of inclusion and focus on the specific needs of trans people and gives you an opportunity to meet those needs. The transgendered community is small, and we do not yet have many places where we can gather. Providing a safe haven and a place to learn and grow together is a valuable service. Remember, too, that gender is not the only issue in trans folks' lives. Invite trans people to participate in other ministries throughout the congregation. No one likes to be tokenized or pigeonholed into just one identity. In general, people early in transition are more interested in gender-focused events while people who have transitioned quite a while ago are often more interested in a broader range of topics. Find out what each person's interest is and steer him or her in that direction.

You can use other ways to convey a sense of honor and inclusion. Plan a worship service that features transgendered people and offers thanksgiving for our presence in the midst of the community. Consider explicit ways to form alliances with local trans groups and their leaders. When giving awards for community service, consider people who are leaders in the trans community as potential honorees. Invite a trans community leader as a guest speaker or preacher. You can select someone from within your own area or invite a nationally recognized author or activist and then publicize the event widely in the community.

Go to events in the trans community and do outreach for your group. Let people know in clear terms that they are welcome in your community of faith. You will need to overcome people's hesitations and fear with language that explicitly includes them. Hold a fund-raising event for a trans group or invite a group to use your space for a special event or cosponsor it. Because a great deal of trans community organizing is in its nascent stages, groups may not have a lot of money to spend on space for events or meetings. Donating space to groups can be a valuable investment in community relations. Bringing people into your building where they can see the efforts that you are making to include the transgendered can be a very positive part of your outreach.

Unfortunately, trans people are all too often the victims of hate crimes. If one occurs in your area, volunteer to help organize a vigil or memorial event. Advocate in the legislature or before your city council for nondiscrimination and anti–hate crime laws that include gender identity. Be public in your affirmation that trans lives are just as valuable as every other human life. Let the trans community and its leaders know that they can trust you to be present with them and to stand beside them as an activist.

In order to accomplish these tasks, you need to educate your faith community about the lives and needs of transgendered people. Provide educational events that give your members an opportunity to ask questions in a safe environment. Let them hear the life stories of some transgendered people from your area. Preparing your faith community to be a welcoming and affirming place is a vital step. All of your program and outreach efforts will not matter if the congregation itself is not accepting of transgendered people.

A transgendered person quickly feels looks of discomfort or awkward stares from members of the congregation. In order to be genuinely welcoming of transgendered people, the community needs to talk about these issues and become comfortable with some level of gender variation. In the long run, this approach also provides a space where all members can feel freer to express themselves in ways that may or may not fit with the gender paradigms of our society. The congregation also needs basic information about transgendered people. People in our congregations need to know that gender variance is natural and an important part of many cultures. They also need to learn that stereotypes of transgendered people are not true. Provide members of your church, temple, or synagogue with basic terminology and demographic information about transgendered people. You also need to counter stereotypes about the causes and manifestations of gender difference.

Finally, we return to the rest room question. Provide places where men, women, transgendered people, children, and anyone else can use the rest rooms in a way that is physically and emotionally safe. Some church growth literature stresses that the cleanliness of the women's rest room is one of the things on which the growth of that congregation depends. In the same way, your ability to provide rest room space may well dictate the ability of your congregation to do meaningful outreach in the trans community. This factor is so inconsequential in many ways to the life of faith that we should not let such a barrier interfere with connecting with God's transgendered people.

To address this issue, we have to look first at why we have separate rest room facilities for men and for women. Women's rest rooms often serve a sociological function of policing gender.[3] Masculine women often comment that they are asked to leave women's rest rooms and face comments from other women in the rest room about their gender presentation. This happened to me a number of times during the periods of my life when I had very short hair. If we want our congregations to move beyond the policing of gender, then having rest rooms that serve this purpose leads us further from our goals. The fear also exists that men may prey upon women in the rest rooms. Certainly we should be doing more to prevent violence and sexual assault against women than simply maintaining separate washrooms. Finally, women's rest rooms are notoriously cleaner than men's rest rooms; each rest room should be kept clean in the church in order to provide a comfortable atmosphere for all.

---

3. Judith Halberstein spoke at the 1997 Sex Panic Summit outlining some of these ideas, which I have then expanded upon.

Instead, congregations should look for ways in which they can have unisex rest rooms, particularly facilities for one person at a time, or provide multiple options. An increasing trend is toward the creation of multisex rest rooms (sometimes called "family rest rooms") where a daughter can comfortably escort her elderly father, a dad can take his young daughter or a mom her young son, etc. When a church creates a space for people who fit neither gender category and for people who have need for facilities for both genders in a rest room, it increases accessibility not only for the transgendered but for others as well. Some places, such as malls, academic settings, and hospitals, provide this space in addition to rest rooms for men and for women. Congregations should consider this possibility when building a new space or refurbishing existing space.

Providing a genuine welcome for transgendered people requires intentionality and planning. You can't just decide to "be more welcoming" after a single planning weekend. Because it is such a pervasive force in our society, gender becomes a dividing line within our congregations as well. In order to change that situation, you need to think carefully through everything that your congregation does that is gender-based or gender-specific. You will also be dealing with a community that is, at best, somewhat suspicious of your motives and fearful of condemnation. The transgendered community, though, is hungry for inclusion, is spiritually seeking, and has learned important things about God's presence in our lives.

Chapter Six

Transgendered People and God

Transgendered people are resourceful seekers, and many of us have found a powerful ally in the Divine. We do not accept as the last word the confused stance of our communities of faith, nor do we allow voices of condemnation to determine the course of our spiritual lives. Trans people call upon many sources that provide us spiritual strength and succor and enable us to deepen our lives and our understanding of our own purpose and meaning.

Encountering God

Of all the spiritual resources available to trans people, the most powerful are the times when God speaks directly to us of the freedom to be ourselves and to follow the path that God sets before us. In these moments, God connects with us to confirm the course that we are taking or cuts through the pain and fear that we experience with a new and life-affirming word that changes everything. God may shatter our feelings of inadequacy or calm our fears of sinfulness. Sometimes God speaks to us to turn us aside from the negative messages that we hear from others. At other times, God's voice of love and certainty comes to us in a time of transformation with little familiarity. The voice may call us to greater spiritual growth and depth. Experiencing the presence or the voice of God is a personal revelation — one that only that person can know. And God does speak to us as transgendered persons.

Many religious institutions stress far too often the judgment of God and fail many times to focus on the mercy and love that God has for us. As we have seen, transgendered people have faced this kind of condemnation from communities of faith and even from within our own hearts.

Too many people have grown up believing that they cannot know directly God's will for their lives or that God cannot speak to them without some intermediary from a religious institution. Some feel the need to try to hide from God the true nature of their lives. Yet throughout history, God has defied conventions and religious strictures to speak to God's children who are in need of a divine voice, comfort, and aid. While some people deny that God approves of transgendered people, many of us know differently based on our direct experiences of God and God's interventions in our lives.

I have heard a number of trans folks state that, for them, transition was primarily a spiritual process. This assessment is not true for all transgendered people, of course. For some of us, however, transitioning is a time of deepening spirituality and a journey to come home to ourselves in body, mind, and spirit. This time can include a sense of learning more about the divine as we learn more about ourselves, and may mean finally coming to terms with the idea of being a child of God, put on this earth for a purpose, or simply arriving at self-acceptance. While some people may view religious faith as contrary to the development of a transgendered identity, for many of us faith is a critical component of our transitions and the strength that we draw upon to live in this world as gender-variant people.

Jade Devlin, a cross-dresser who set up a website and e-mail list to reach out to other Christian transgendered people, says that her response when people ask her about how she deals with being both Christian and a cross-dresser is this: "Reconciled? I have never believed that God opposed crossdressing. Accept myself? Without Christ, I don't know how I would ever have had the strength. Guilt? God has always been my way out of guilt, not into it. I feel like a skydiver being asked how she reconciled her skydiving with her parachute."[1] What a great image for people of faith! God is not a force to be reconciled to, but the Great Reconciler. God is not the one from whom we must be saved, but the source of our strength. Rather than being a barrier to our freedom, God urges us to soar and explore all of the possibilities before us.

God may be the one who gives us the courage to continue on in our search for our transgendered selves. In her article, "The Spiritual Side of Gender Journeying," Petra Doan writes about a terribly low moment in

---

1. Quoted in Vanessa Sheridan, *Crossing Over: Liberating the Transgendered Christian* (Cleveland: Pilgrim Press, 2001), 82.

which she questioned whether she should kill herself rather than continue on her path of gender transition. It was a time of personal alienation and struggle on a family trip. She writes:

> After everyone else left, I went out and stared at the mountains and wondered whether I should take one of the cars parked nearby and find a cliff to put an end to my suffering. . . . Suddenly an image flashed into my head of Jesus on the Mount of Temptations with the devil tempting him by saying, "Throw yourself off this mountain. God won't let you fall." As I was contemplating this image, I suddenly felt a warm loving voice that said simply, "I am with you. I am always with you." With a huge sense of relief, I sat back in the summer sunshine and felt my death wishes fade away.
>
> I knew suddenly that God was with me on this path to authenticity. Indeed, in following this path in spite of my fears and tears, I was taking the first step in understanding the obedience part of integrity. I can't pretend to have reached a place of wholeness, but I can feel a presence within that stills the fear.[2]

God's presence in our lives has this power. Our holy writings give us the message that we are to trust that God is with us and not to be afraid. Whatever we are going through, God is present and is a part of the situation. Gender transition is not too great for God to deal with, regardless of what anyone may have told us. In this instance, God was not necessarily sought but reminded her of God's abiding presence.

We may need to feel a sense of permission or affirmation from the divine before we are able to move ahead with transition. Patrick Califia, an ordained minister in the Fellowship of the Spiral Path, notes: "My patron goddesses kept telling me that it didn't matter whether I lived as a man or a woman, that they didn't care. That I would always be part of both of those categories, with a large part of me belonging to neither one. And if I wanted to try living as a man, they thought that was trippy, and they'd go along for the ride. So far, they have kept their promise. I feel that getting more honest with myself and taking this risk has made me stronger spiritually."[3]

God can be a source of comfort for us during times of transition that feel awkward or overwhelming. Califia explained his understanding of the divine as follows:

2. Petra Doan, "The Spiritual Side of Gender Journeying," *Transgender Tapestry* 92 (winter 2000): 42.
3. Interview with Patrick Califia, July 26, 2001.

When you ask how I experience the divine, that's such a hard question to answer because god is in everything. We are the ones who are blind and deaf to that presence. If I am able to attune my perceptions and open my heart I can see divinity in a loaf of bread or some silly Top 10 song on the radio. Divinity appears in my heart when I clean and straighten up and make the world a more orderly place, because I am expressing care and mindfulness. It's easier to see the divine in a beautiful spectacle of nature, but it's also there in the bare bones of a dead rabbit or a burning piece of wood. We are upheld by an enormous ocean of love and understanding. I feel very fortunate to be alive in this amazing place, this earth.

When I asked him how he experienced the holy during his transition, he answered:

I prayed a lot more. I needed reassurance, and it was always there, even when other people in my life made me feel wrong. I got shelter and love, I got affirmation that I was valuable, that I was not a mistake. I was told again and again that there was a reason why I was made the way that I was made, and that it was important for me to be honest about it. I don't know how people who have no spiritual refuge can handle the stress of transition. They must be very brave people. I was often quite the coward, seeking refuge in divine skirts.[4]

I certainly do not see him as a coward for seeking refuge in the Holy One. I find his imagery beautiful and compelling. His image is of God/Goddess as a sanctuary and a source of affirmation and power, clearly a description of the kind of strength that we can draw from the Holy when we seek God intentionally through prayer.

God can also be a model for us as we look for faithful ways to move forward. Su Penn, a Quaker, spoke to a gathering of Friends for Lesbian and Gay Concerns in 1999. She described how, two years earlier, her lover Beth made the decision to transition to become a man, David. She spoke about the struggles that they as a couple went through:

David would frame it differently, but for me it was all about God. When my mother asked what my talk was going to be about today, I told her, "It's about how God saved my relationship." I was only half-joking. Not even half-joking. I literally could not have accepted David's transition before I became a Quaker: I would have said that my lesbian identity was too important to me, and left him. This is in fact what many of my friends, especially lesbian friends, expected and encouraged me to do....

4. Ibid.

But through the practice of silent worship I have learned to recognize the presence of God, at least sometimes, and I had felt the presence of God in my relationship with Beth. In fact, I had often thought that it was in my relationship with Beth that I felt the divine presence most forcefully. Last year, maybe eight weeks after David told me his decision, I was in Meeting for Worship at the FLGC Midwinter Gathering, and I got a message reminding me of that. I made a decision then to stay with David, because I could not imagine God making any other choice. How could I abandon a relationship that God had not abandoned? To walk away from my relationship with David would have been to walk away from God, to close myself off from one of the portals in my life through which I hear God speaking to me.[5]

Through her practice of faith, Su received a message to stay in the relationship; she was willing to follow God's example in her own life. She was able to see that same God at work in her partner's life and within their relationship and was able to trust what she saw and experienced there, even through a period of change and turmoil. Her image of God as one who would not abandon either her or her partner provided her with the spiritual guidance that she needed to make a crucial decision.

She titled the speech "A Lover's Leap of Faith" and said "a leap of faith as a sharp, punctuated movement into the unknown must be the sexiest and most exciting of our spiritual tools."[6] This way of looking at the situation is profoundly positive. She brings a sense of adventure and sexiness to her encounters with her own spirituality and with God, and that clearly made a difference in her ability to remain in relationship both with David and with God during this time. We also need to remember that we do have a choice about how we can view a time of gender transition; we can choose to affirm the sense of journeying toward that which is whole and healthy and to see it as an adventure in faith.

In my own journey, one of the wonderful aspects of transition was a strong sense of God's presence each and every moment. One of the things that I've learned through this process is that the more comfortable I become with my own presence on this earth, the more I am able to be aware of resting comfortably within God's embrace. God was no less there when I felt a sense of incongruity and discomfort within myself; in fact, I

---

5. Su Penn, "A Lover's Leap of Faith: Plenary Speech at the Friends (Quakers) for Lesbian and Gay Concerns Midwinter Gathering," February 1999, *http://my.voyager.net/supenn/flgc-speech.html*, 11/21/00.
6. Ibid., 1.

would suspect that the opposite was true. But the more whole I feel, the freer I am to look around me and discover the Holy in the world, or as Patrick Califia said, in a loaf of bread or a Top 10 song. The greater my sense of congruity within me, the more I am able to be in the world with a sense of God's abiding peace.

I had a strong and real sense of God as the one who knew me when everything else was changing, the one who kept track of the me that was my essence and carried me through the time of transition to arrive safely on the other side. I also had an experience of hearing God's affirmation. I was raised in a liberal Presbyterian church, and so audibly hearing the voice of God was not part of my spiritual upbringing; I knew that other people believed that they had heard God, and I respected their belief, but I never felt that direct communication from God was part of my spiritual makeup or journey. As I prepared to go into surgery, however, I was nervous, as people are before surgery. I was lying in the surgeon's office, waiting for them to call me back into the surgical suite. I was praying, trying to stay calm, when suddenly I felt God's presence palpably around me and I heard a voice within my head, saying, "You are my beloved child. I love you." Immediately, I felt a sense of peace and calm — not a certainty that the surgery would be fine necessarily, but a sense that I would be well because I was with God, whatever happened.

And that is the point. Whether or not God speaks audibly, the point is for us to know that we will be well, that God is present with us, through a journey of gender or whatever may come our way. People may have all kinds of ideas and theories about transgendered people, they may condemn or accept us, but they cannot prevent God from reaching out to us with a message of love and hope. The Christian Scripture tells us that nothing can separate us from the love of God, and I believe that.

The Image and Gender of God

Transgendered people also have a unique opportunity to witness to the gender of God. We who embody more than one gender within our lifetimes have learned something about our ability to hold both of those spaces within one body. If we, as human beings, can do it, surely God can do it. As several Christian writers point out, if the Divine has room for the trinity, there is room for at least two genders; if Jesus can be both human and divine, surely the Holy One can be broader than human categories of sex and gender. The patriarchal system in which we live, however, sets the gender of God as surely as it creates a bigendered social order.

How we view the gender of God, and how God's gender relates to our own gender, affects crucial areas of life, such as self-esteem. Jann Aldredge-Clanton, in her study on the effects of the perceived gender of God, writes as follows:

> [W]omen who conceive and speak of God as androgynous or transcendent of gender tend to embrace a wide variety of interests. Their high level of creativity often takes unconventional forms. They tend to associate ideas in unusual ways, and to be venturesome, aesthetically reactive, clever and quick to respond. Progressive and original, they value intellectual and cognitive matters. Opening their minds and spirits to the diversity and expansiveness of God, these women unlock the treasures of creativity deep within themselves. The way women conceive of God affects their level of self-confidence. The women in my research sample who see and speak of God as more than masculine scored higher in self-confidence than those whose God is masculine. Women with androgynous or gender-transcendent images of God are thus more likely to be initiators, confident of their ability to achieve goals. Feeling satisfied with themselves, they have social poise and presence. They have a high aspiration level and behave in an assertive manner. These women tend to be determined, confident, ambitious, assertive, energetic, enterprising, outgoing, outspoken, and talkative.[7]

She goes on to describe the ways in which a broader understanding of God's gender is beneficial to men as well and does not lead to any erosion of a man's sense of masculinity nor of his self-esteem, noting, "Men, as well as women, benefit from gender-inclusive images of God. Equality of male and female, in heaven and on earth, does not lower the self-esteem of men. In fact, males can feel new kinds of power through androgynous concepts of God and of humanity."[8] Thus we need to be able to recognize a connection between the gender of God and our own gender, as well as seeing God reflected in the genders in which we view humanity.

If a sense of God as encompassing or transcending gender is important to the sense of self-worth and power of both women and men, then surely transgendered people must see our genders as reflective of, and reflected

7. Jann Aldredge-Clanton, *In Whose Image? God and Gender* (New York: Crossroad, 2001), 82–83.
8. Ibid., 99.

in, the gender(s) of God. Aldredge-Clanton includes in her discussion an individual who identifies with both genders. While she does not specifically state that he is transgendered, he does fall within our broad definition of the term. Dr. Phil Compton identifies as 55 percent masculine and 45 percent feminine, according to Aldredge-Clanton. She quotes him as saying, "Thinking of God as male and female points out in a very forceful way that it's unhealthy to put God in a box. The idea of being both male and female is something that's very difficult to comprehend, and God should be something that's difficult to comprehend."[9]

One of the things that is spiritually important to Compton is this sense of God as transcending human categories and limitations to encompass both male and female as he himself does. If we are made in the image of God, as the Jewish and Christian traditions believe, and if some of us are both masculine and feminine, both female and male, then we would be viewing in those persons a reflection of God beyond the categorical limitations of gender. At the same time, understanding God as both male and female, or neither male nor female, can be liberating for someone who sees him/herself as becoming like God, who is both/neither, and should enhance a sense of self-worth in the ways that Aldredge-Clanton notes for women. Among the trans folk that I interviewed and interacted with in writing this book, all but one had developed an image of God that transcended gender.

Broadening our understandings beyond the entrenched notion of God-as-male allows us to consider more options for both the divine and for ourselves. This greater sense of freedom may allow us to reconceive our relationship with God. In her book *Sex and the Church*, Kathy Rudy writes, "When restrictive notions of gender are challenged, God can be understood not as a gendered person 'himself,' but rather as a loving creator and sustainer who transcends the socially organized gender systems developed on earth. When earthly gender codings no longer restrict us, we are free to negotiate different relationships with a loving, nongendered God."[10] When we are dealing with trans folk, the freedom from gender norms for ourselves and for God allows us to explore and appreciate different aspects of both God and humanity. We need both the liberation from the view

---

9. Ibid., 96.

10. Kathy Rudy, *Sex and the Church: Gender, Homosexuality, and the Transformation of Christian Ethics* (Boston: Beacon Press, 1997), 42.

of a highly gendered, masculine God as well as from the restrictive norms that prevent us from expressing and living our genders fully. We need to see both God in us and ourselves in God. This power and promise comes from seeing ourselves as made in the image of God, no more and certainly no less than any other being.

A transgendered image of God allows us to see God beyond binary categories. In fact, when gender is not emphasized first about God, it expands our ability to see other characteristics as more important than gender. After all, the gender of God does not make God divine. So much of human life is filtered through the lenses of "is it a boy or a girl?" that we consciously or unconsciously use these same filters for God. The level of passion evoked by discussions of inclusive language shows the level of fear that surrounds the very question of God's gender. The gendered nature of language that has shifted so dramatically in our broader culture in the last fifty years or so has barely begun to change in our religious communities. Even in denominations like Metropolitan Community Church that have an official policy about inclusive language, for some people inclusive language is at best controversial and at worst seen as a sign of denigrating the divine.

Yet an intersexed or transgendered image of God, one that embodies both male and female, is more biblically accurate than one that forces God into a single-gendered box. This image is also borne out by a study of other world religions in which the divine is seen in both feminine and masculine expressions. For transgendered and intersexed people then, we can look at God and see ourselves in the divine image — what is true about us is also true about God and, conversely, the nature of God is also our nature. This fact, the ability to embody both the masculine and feminine simultaneously, made some cultures view two-spirited people as sacred.

In light of this fact, consider the point made by Riki Ann Wilchins: "I am deeply uncomfortable when transpeople tell me glowing tales about how revered the Native American berdache was: transpeople as gifted shamans. I don't want to bear the burden of being especially good any more than I want to bear that of being especially bad. Both inscribe my identity in ways which take it out of my hands."[11] The point is not for us

---

11. Riki Ann Wilchins, *Read My Lips: Sexual Subversion and the End of Gender* (Ithaca, N.Y.: Firebrand Books, 1997), 67.

to engage in culture appropriation but rather to say that we are clearly made in the image of God. I am uncomfortable when we say that we are more sacred than others; at the same time, saying that we are less than any other part of the creation is blasphemous.

The point is rather that our sacred writings and faith traditions do tell us clearly that the divine embodies both genders, as do we, and so we are made in the image and likeness of God as surely as is every other person. The nature of God is to embody all genders, and thus it is natural for those of us who do as well. Rather than being outside of the divine order, intersexed and transgendered individuals are an integral part of creation, a creation that God declared was good.

We can also see how God's transgendered nature has, particularly in Judaism, Christianity, and Islam, been kept hidden by millennia of gender cloaking. People who speak of God as fully and wholly male ignore those parts of sacred texts that refer to God in feminine terms. The intersexed nature of God is thus hidden from view of worshipers and believers as certainly as we conceal the evidence of intersexed and transgendered humans. The time has come to tell the truth about God even as we tell our own truths. We also need to begin to focus more on what makes the divine holy rather than on delineating a limiting gender for God. Our time would be perhaps better spent focusing on the mercy of God rather than on God's masculinity, more on God's faithfulness and less on a discussion of femininity. For we have learned in our transgendered and intersexed lives that we are more than gender, that broader questions form our natures and humanity than whether we are female or male. The same is true of God.

And as it is true of God, so, again, is it true for us.

Trans Christology

Some transgendered and queer authors have raised the question of Jesus' gender and participation in gender roles in recent years in new ways. These questions apply both to the historical Jesus and to our understandings of Christ.

Clearly, Jesus broke through barriers of gender many times during the course of his ministry. He spoke with women, he washed the feet of his disciples (an act usually performed by women or slaves), and he included women among his followers. Danielle Webster writes, "... Christ boldly broke through many barriers, including gender barriers (e.g., His encounter with the Samaritan woman) in part to show He wants us to understand how much freedom we really have, if we are only willing to accept it."[12] One of the controversies of Jesus' life was his willingness to act in ways counter to societal convention in order to live out his spiritual truth. He defied gender norms in order to transform the lives of both women and men.

Some authors have argued for or considered the possibility of Jesus as a gender-variant person himself. In *Omnigender*, Virginia Mollenkott includes Edward L. Kessel's analysis that considers whether Jesus was the result of parthenogenesis (which would also explain the virgin birth) and intersexual. Kessel argues that virgin birth is most likely possible among humans as the result of parthenogenesis. If Mary became pregnant in this way, she would have only passed on XX chromosomes, and thus Jesus would have been born female. He then goes on to speculate that Jesus had undergone some type of sex reversal, which he states is a biological possibility for humans. Thus Jesus would be an intersexed person who went on to challenge the gender norms of his society. While I found this speculation interesting, I did not find it compelling as an argument, largely because there is no way for us to ever know the truth about this and the chances of this being the case are extremely, astronomically remote. I believe that a stronger case can be made for Jesus as a transgressor of society's gender boundaries than that he himself was intersexed.

Michelle Dee, on her web page, "Good News! Jesus Loves Us, T*oo!," speculates about how Jesus might have acted if he were transgendered:

> A question that often puzzled me is whether Jesus would have crossdressed, had he been transgendered. (Remember, this is a supposition, not a revision of history!) I believe he would have, only because Jesus' record on upholding the letter of The Law of Moses was clearly checkered. (Crossdressing was prohibited by the letter of the law [Deuteronomy 22:5]). However, Jesus consistently upheld the spirit of The Law.[13]

This perspective is an interesting take on the "what would Jesus do" speculation and provides some rationale for how a cross-dresser might be able to see him/herself in relationship with Jesus.

---

12. Danielle E. Webster, "Dealing with Deuteronomy," *Transgender Tapestry* 92 (winter 2000): 34.
13. Michelle Dee, "You're Transgendered: What Would Jesus Do?" *http://members.tripod.com/ ~michelledee/jesustg.html*, 11/22/00.

Dee sees a number of ways in which Jesus was similar to modern transgendered people. We face harassment not only on the streets, but in our
homes; Jesus talked about situations in which families were separate. Trans
people, particularly those who are visibly gender variant or are in a typically gender-segregated career, are very often unable to find meaningful
employment in our fields; Jesus said that even he had no place to lay his
head. Trans people are even killed because of who we are as Jesus was
killed. Being able to identify with Jesus in the midst of suffering and hard-
ship is one way that people through the centuries have found comfort
and hope.

Marcella Althaus-Reid, in *Indecent Theology*, points to Latin Americans'
devotion to *Santa Librada* to show how Jesus is embodied by more than
one gender:

> The *Santerias* of Buenos Aires display statues and stamps of a young woman
> who looks like the Virgin Mary, yet she is crucified and her body hangs from
> the cross, reminding us of Jesus. She is called *Santa Librada,* and her wor-
> ship is very popular amongst the poor urban people of Buenos Aires. As in
> the case of the Virgin Mary or Jesus, there are prayers and rituals associ-
> ated with her (Christian) worship, prayer cards, candles and the customary
> novenas with the "Our Father," "Hail Mary" and "Glorias" at the end of
> the prayer. *Santa Librada* means literally Saint "Liberated" and the origin of
> the worship goes back to a Roman Catholic saint (*Santa Liberata*), a virgin
> and martyr who as such has never been popular.... The issue of *Librada's*
> body is ambiguous: sometimes she has a well defined female body with full
> breasts and round hips (especially on prayer cards) but in statues she often
> looks elfin, like a Peter Pan who will never grow up, as Jesus will never be
> old. Her clothes are similar to the Virgin Mary's traditional attire, includ-
> ing sometimes a head cover.... And *Librada* is hanging from a cross but
> smilingly, as a Virgin Mary transgressing by her presence the traditional site
> of Jesus, the cross. *Librada* is neither Jesus nor Mary, but a dress, a cross
> and superficial gender challenges which present us with a pattern of divine
> transvestism.[14]

In Santa Librada, a Christ figure is depicted who blends both male and
female, and in doing so transcends both the categories of gender and the
delineation of Mary and Jesus.

---

14. Marcella Althaus-Reid, *Indecent Theology: Theological Perversions in Sex, Gender and Politics*
(London: Routledge, 2000), 79–80.

Robert Goss argues for the need to add the dimension of gender as performance to our understanding of the Christ. He notes Eleanor McLaughlin's analysis, which puts Jesus in the category of transvestite because of the ways in which he crosses gender lines in the course of his life. As Goss writes:

> Jesus the Christ is a liminal figure, and queer postmodern representational strategies reclaim the sexuality of Jesus/ Christ and play with fluid gender constructions intersected with diverse sexual attractions. The mixing and matching of signifiers of gender difference and sexual difference in representational strategies of the Christ provide alternative ways of envisioning the Christ as having liberating significance for the queer community. Our queer exploration cuts the Christ from the moorings of dominant, heterosexist and patriarchal theologies while rearticulating the Christ within diverse sexualities and diverse theologies that affirm sexual and gender alterities. The queer Christ is impelled by dogmatic constructions that refuse to recognize that all women, gender variant folks, and sexual minorities image the Christ. The silence has been a core construction that allows church violence to be directed against us and against many others.[15]

Just as we need to free ourselves from our rigid gender constructs, so too do we need to free Christ from our limited and limiting understanding of Christ. By rearticulating Christ, we are able to see ourselves in Christ and Christ within ourselves. This approach is a critical component of a movement for spiritual liberation. Christ becomes then the spiritual force behind liberation, rather than the right-wing vision of Jesus as the enforcer of social norms and limitations.

Jesus was undeniably queer within his own life, death, and ministry — queer in that he differed from that which was expected and sanctioned by his society and the religious leaders of his day. We can never know if Jesus himself was intersexed, but we do see the record of his ministry and the ways in which he challenged faithful people to a radically inclusive view of the world and of the holy. We see how queerly he interacted with religious authorities and ordinary people, in ways that shocked, challenged, and transformed them. Some left his presence scandalized while others followed filled with hope and a new vision of their lives and their world.

---

15. Robert E. Goss, *Queering Christ: Beyond Jesus Acted Up* (Cleveland: Pilgrim Press, 2002), 181–82.

The same is true today. The queer Christ is shocking to some and liberating to others, and, at our best, we can allow ourselves to be both shocked and freed, to be challenged and to be comforted, to be human and holy.

Jesus himself undergoes a remarkable process of transition through his death and resurrection. He is transformed in his life through his encounters with others, is transfigured upon the mountaintop, and finally is transformed through death from the living Jesus to the resurrected Christ, who is unrecognizable to those who knew him until he reveals himself. Within his body, he contains both finite life and eternal life, both death and resurrection, in the way that transgendered people embody both male and female. The holiness of Christ is that he is both/and, both human and divine, both mortal and eternal.

When we are baptized, we are baptized into this changing, transformational Christ, who rises above human limitations of gender, class, and nation, as Paul declares in Galatians 3:28. We are called beyond human limitations to be participants in the realm of God, a dominion of justice and mercy. Baptism is the external symbol of our participation in God's realm and, for adults, the sign of a willingness to declare ourselves to be Christ's people.

I have heard a number of transsexuals speak about experiencing a sense of resurrection as one part of them dies and another is reborn in their new gender. Karen Kroll writes, "Sexual reassignment surgery for me was a rebirth, because it gave me my life; I was finally in union with my world."[16] Transition is, in this sense, a way of participating in the resurrection and of being born again. This image is a powerful one. At the same time, I am wary of the imagery that requires us to kill off part of ourselves in order to become something new and of fairly violent language used by some in the trans community to describe ways in which they did away with that former sense of self and the "old" gender.

Jesus' example may guide us to a healthy way of looking at this transformation. Jesus' body was changed, both by becoming alive after death and in ways that made him appear different to those who knew him; at the same time, he was the same Jesus who had been among them, as Jesus' revelation to Thomas shows us. Here Jesus is careful to make the

---

16. Karen F. Kroll, "Transsexuality and Religion: A Personal Journey," in *Gender Blending*, ed. Bonnie Bullough, Vern L. Bullough, and James Elias (Amherst, N.Y.: Prometheus Books, 1997), 494.

point that he is both the same and different, which is true of us as well. Jesus did not die and return as a wholly different being but a transfigured and resurrected one. In this way, Jesus is a trans person, both through his personal transformations in body and spirit, and in the ways in which he embodies, transcends, and defies categorization.

God and the Natural

One of the primary arguments that people pose against the possibility of gender transition or variance is that it is contrary to the natural order. Both Oliver O'Donovan writing in the 1980s and the Evangelical Alliance report of 2001 state that transsexualism in particular runs contrary to the natural order and thus cannot be from God. They see clearly gendered bodies as the final word about the diversity of creation. But another way is available to look at creation and see the vast diversity that is present within the natural order as normative, rather than anomalous. As Virginia Mollenkott writes:

> I have certainly noticed that One Source likes variety and has chosen to be incarnated in millions of diverse ways. I therefore assume that the ultimate reason for "queerness" does not lie in concepts constructed by society, or some eternal essence like "male" or "female" or "bigendered," but rather in the fact that God has chosen to embody Himself/Herself/Itself in just this person's particularities at just this time and place.[17]

This planet teems with diverse forms of life. Vast differences exist between leaves, snowflakes, species, fur types, and an infinite number of other things. That people can look at creation and see limitations rather than an ever-expanding array of difference is perplexing to me. If the Creator's will is expressed in the creation, then that will surely includes a passion for variety and exultation in the beauty of differences. Intersexed and trans-gendered persons are, then, expressions of the natural order and should be upheld as part of the sacredness of the Creator's world.

Some people view gender variance as a sign of a "mistake" made by God or a birth defect. One of the people that I interviewed saw it as a sign of the fallen nature of humanity. I do not believe that God made a

---

17. Virginia Ramey Mollenkott, *Omnigender: A Trans-Religious Approach* (Cleveland: Pilgrim Press, 2001), 16.

mistake or intended us to be anything other than exactly what we are. Instead of looking to the created order for clues about what God might have intended for us, the tendency exists to view anomalies as a mistake. I see our differences as integral to the natural order and a part of God's plan for creation.

Many of our faith communities, although not all, have stressed the importance of following human standards and categories rather than looking to this jubilation of diversity, and many transgendered people have never had the opportunity to look beyond what they were taught. Crossdresser Jaye Reviere posted the following comments on her web page about this encounter with God:

> I hated being different. I hated the desires I had. I hated the scorn with which I was treated if I allowed someone to see me as I really was. I hated not being like "one of the guys." I hated being feminine. I hated being left out. I hated all these things and more. I hated all this because I hated myself. I hated myself because I was different. I lay in prayer. The prayer was in profound anguish. I was defiant. I was hostile to my God. I was demanding. I was a petulant child demanding to be how I wanted to be, not hoe [sic] God made me to be. I was demanding to be how humans said I had to be, not how Almighty God had chosen for me to be. My one way conversation with God was angry, demanding, and insistent. Then it was interrupted. I think God finally had enough for my being like a stubborn two year old kid who demands to have his way, even when a loving parent knows there is a far better way. An awesome voice, still, soft, a bit angry sounding, and yet infinitely loving and tender, spoke in my spirit. The words are burned in my soul forever: "How dare you not want to be as I have made you to be! How dare you, indeed!" My attention was commanded instantly. A peace settled over me and I began to experience comprehension...then I began to realize, God had indeed made me as I am. After all, my spirit bore witness to the awesome presence of the Holy Spirit who had spoken those awful words: "How dare you..." in my soul. With this realization there came a peacefulness about being different, a peacefulness I cannot describe. Suddenly, I began to understand God had made me different for God's purposes. I didn't know them then, and I don't know them know [sic]. It is enough for me to know they are.[18]

If God created us each uniquely, then to erase the differences between us is to cover up the work of the Creator. Yet surely God did have a

---

18. Jaye E. Reviere, "Ethics and Crossdressing," *http://members.aol.com/_ht_a/gnlnews/ethics.html*, 11/22/00.

reason and a purpose for creating variations among us, including gender variation. In the midst of that, God speaks to Reviere to say, "How dare you...," which raises the question of whether we even have the right to erase differences among us, much less whether we ought to in the name of faithfulness.

I propose that we must take seriously this question of diversity and our role within it. Trans people commonly view gender variance within themselves as something that they cannot control, is permanent, and has arisen within them through no external force.[19] In this sense, for individuals to be the transgendered or intersexed persons that they are is natural. *We are natural, just as we are.* What is unnatural is our attempts to codify the natural into categories with which society is more comfortable. But society is not the Creator; God is.

Suppressing our nature, as we have seen, causes great psychological and spiritual suffering. Acceptance of one's own nature is a truer and easier path to take. We, as spiritual people, need to take seriously the question of whether we are violating the will of the Creator when we attempt to defy the differences within us. The faithful path is one that honors the Creator by loving the creation, with all of its uniqueness, in both the larger world and within our own lives. We ourselves, all of us, are sacred because we are created in the image and likeness of God. Our sacred writings tell us that God knew us even before we were born and shaped us. God must have known of this transgendered being, because God was present when I was conceived and when I was born. God has been present through all that I have experienced. And Scripture tells us that the Holy One saw what s/he had created and pronounced it good.

As Ashley Moore put it, "the long and the short of it is...God made you to be an individual, unique in all times on this planet, and you have to do the hardest thing and that is stand up and be the person that God has made you to be, and separate from everybody else if that's what needs to be."[20]

---

19. Richard Elkins and Dave King, "Contributions to the Emerging Field of Transgender Studies," *International Journal of Transgenderism* 1, no. 1 (July–September 1997).

20. Interview with Ashley Moore, August 2001.

Chapter Seven

Gender as a Calling

When asked by reporters about her transition from male to female, Anglican priest Carol Stone replied, "I have had only two vocations in life. One was to be a priest, and one was to be a woman."[1] I, too, have had a sense of being called into a gender, called to live beyond the limitations of our society's view of gender or what others told me was true about my own gender. I believe that God called me out on this journey of gender to learn particular things and to experience the world in a broader way. I was called to trust God and step out into uncharted territory to learn about myself and about who and what God has called me to be. Calling is about what we are to *do* and about who we are to *be*, as well as who we will *become*.

We have been taught to see gender as immutable and that people are born either male or female and nothing else. Yet this idea, perpetuated in Western culture, has formed a lens through which we view the world and see only two genders. Other cultures have drawn other conclusions. The bodies, lives, and witness of intersexed people, and the diverse genders of the natural world, teach us that gender is not binary but broad. The bodies, lives, and witness of transgendered people teach us, too, that gender is broader than we once conceived and is, in fact, changeable.

Some people have theorized gender as a social construct, merely a contract between human beings about what constitutes male and female. Others view it as a biological reality. Queer theory points to the performativity of gender. To this mix, I add the concept that gender is a calling. Looking at it through the lens of the religious language of a calling gives gender the ability to be personal, and to integrate the diversity and journeys of gender that some of us make over the course of our lives.

---

1. Bob Harvey and Joe Woodard, "Serving God after a Sex Change," *Calgary Herald,* March 3, 2001, Religion, OS10.

Rather than seeing transgenderism as a medical problem to be corrected, a psychological incongruence between body and spirit, or even a quirk of societal organization, I look at my experiences of gender as the following of an invitation from God to participate in a new, whole, and healthy way of living in the world — a holy invitation to set out on a journey of transformation of body, mind, and spirit.

Gregg Levoy describes calling in this way, both the calls that gather the community for prayer and the callings in our lives:

> The purpose of calls is to summon adherents away from their daily lives to a new level of awareness, into a sacred frame of mind, into communion with that which is bigger than themselves.... In the primary creation myth of Western cosmology, the very first call came through the voice that said, 'Let there be light,' and there was light, the words then becoming flesh. Every call since then has also been a call to form, a call to each of us to materialize ourselves.[2]

Calling is about a way of being — a calling to awaken to, realize, and manifest who we are. For trans people, our calling is to a way of embodying the self that transcends the limitations placed up on us. We physically and literally materialize who we are on the inside and bring it to reflection on the outside.

Others have experienced this sense of calling as well. In *Looking for Normal*, Ruth (Roy) describes her understanding this way:

> Roy: I had an experience. Several nights ago. Irma had gone to bed and I was down in the den, fighting one of my headaches. I was down on my knees holding my head and praying for it all to end. The pain was so unbearable. I was thinking of getting my old shotgun out of the basement and killing myself. And just when I was convinced that there was no other way out, I felt a warmth over my head, as if someone was holding their hand over me, to soothe me. The pain started to go away and I felt a lightness inside me, as if a big rock that had been sitting inside my head had just dissolved. And I heard a voice — it wasn't an actual voice, it was something I felt. There were words, not spoken words but an answer. Do you know what I mean...?

> Reverend Muncie: Well, yes, that's very similar to what I experienced when I was in graduate school. In my case, I believe it was the Holy Spirit calling me to serve. And what, in your case, do you think was the message?

---

2. Gregg Levoy, *Callings: Finding and Following an Authentic Life* (New York: Three Rivers Press, 1997), 2.

Roy: I felt that God had given me his blessing to make myself complete.

Reverend Muncie: Complete. Meaning...?

Roy: To have the operation to change my sex.[3]

While this dialogue describes the experiences of a fictional character, it is not unfamiliar to us. Rev. Muncie immediately recognizes the voice that Ruth (Roy) hears as the same one that spoke to him in graduate school and called him to the ministry. Later he doubts how this voice could possibly have called Ruth (Roy) to change her sex, but I believe that his first impulse was correct. We do hear voices of affirmation that urge us to be complete, whole, and holy, which means for some of us that we move forward through a process of trans-formation.

Raven Kaldera, an intersexed FTM activist and minister, writes of his early experiences of coming to terms with who he was:

> I owe three people for my coming-out process. The first was someone whose real name I never knew; I walked into a workshop on sacred androgyny at a gathering and a large, heavyset, hairy woman with a body like mine (and a five o'clock shadow like mine, only mine was blond and didn't show) got up and told everyone that s/he was an intersexual, and how s/he'd found a spiritual calling in hir[4] condition. I sat stunned, my tongue frozen in my mouth. I'd always believed that it was something to hide; a shameful, annoying thing. The husband and lover who each flanked me didn't even know what I was, I'd hidden it that well. And here was something like me, someone saying that this was a gift from the gods? I walked out shaking all over. It took me a year to get the courage to tell anyone (and only after divesting myself of both my husband and my lover) but I owe it to that one brave mythical beast, my sister/brother. S/he called hirself Siren; I never saw hir again, but someday I'm going to find hir and buy hir dinner to thank hir for my freedom.[5]

Looking at gender as a spiritual calling radically shifted Kaldera's view of what and who he was. Rather than being something to hide, he came to understand the giftedness of who he was. This call to a new way of thinking liberated him.

---

3. Jane Anderson, *Looking for Normal*, 12–13.
4. "Hir" is a pronoun used by some transgendered and intersexed persons as a third-gender pronoun in place of him or her. See above, p. 13, n. 2.
5. Raven Kaldera, "Do It on the Dotted Line," *Fireweed* 69 (spring 2000): 48.

I believe for a number of reasons that the lens of calling is a useful and relevant way to look at gender. One of those reasons is that it does make us look at the divine role in our gender and brings it forward as a positive part of our gender identity. Rather than simply being a fluke, an oddity, or a source of shame, gender variance comes to be seen as part of our God-given identities. Even more than that, it becomes our spiritual responsibility to explore fully the nature that God has given to us. Like a calling, our sense of our own genders arises from within us and, at the same time, seems to come from a source that is beyond our control or volition. The sense of our own genders arises from within and without, from us and from beyond us. We know it in our innermost beings, and it comes from a source that is greater than we are alone.

The word "call" has a number of meanings, including to shout, to summon, to name, and the power to attract or allure. The two most important meanings for this discussion are the sense of being summoned or urged in a particular direction, inspired or led by the divine, and the act of naming. These meanings apply to the word "to call" in the Hebrew Scriptures as well. The very first chapter of Genesis describes God creating and calling each element of creation by name; God brings each animal to the first human, who is charged with naming each animal whatever it was to be called. In the same way, our callings encompass both our names (our identity) and our ongoing creation, from the moment of our birth through the unfolding of our lives, until our death and beyond.

The act of naming is important for transgendered people. What we are called affects how we see ourselves. Many people who cross-dress select a name that they use when they are dressed, one that matches the clothing that they are wearing. A male cross-dresser, for example, may select a female name to represent his/her female side that comes out when s/he is dressed. Transsexuals select new names as part of the gender transition process that signify the gender to which they are transitioning. People who identify as a third gender may select a gender-neutral name as a way of establishing an identity that is both/neither male and female. One of the fundamental signs of respect for us as transgendered persons is to call us by our right, chosen names.

The search for the right name is often a long and sacred process. Sometimes God comes to us in unexpected ways to help us on this quest. Darin Issac Blue writes of his search for a name:

Maybe I asked the great beyond to send me the name I would live with, and weeks later I woke with it heavy on my tongue, as though angels had rested their flaming swords in my mouth while I slept, breathed its syllables into my dreaming head. If I told you that I pulled this name out of my ass, would you understand how sacred that origin is to a faggot like me? . . . in this name I am conceived. The pause between names was pregnant with me. My blood is learning to pulse and flow. My body, raw and red and wet, is taking its shape.[6]

This image of the holy coming to him in the time that was pregnant with him is a powerful one. During that time, angels came and ministered to him in his dreams in a way that moved him along on his journey, making sacred the-between-time, but also providing a way to continue to transition into a new name and a new way of being. I see in this image of pregnancy and naming the presence of God calling him forward to be a new thing, a new creation, being born and named as part of his revealing of himself. God reveals to him a name so that he can continue on his search for his identity. He describes it as being reborn into his body as it learns to pulse and flow.

A calling is also a summons to be or do something that reflects our true selves. As Marsha Sinetar writes: "Are we called out by a hidden love to be who we are, in truth? To become faithful to our talents and unique disposition means to affirm our inner press for wholeness. That press involves a call, a longing, a quiet, patient invitation to be purely ourselves."[7] Trans people know well the sense of inner longing that calls us to consider setting out on this path. We respond to the inner knowledge that there is more to our lives than meets the eyes, that something different about us compels us forward to begin this process of transformation. Mollenkott explains as follows: "As Apache transman Gary Bowen puts it, 'Spirit gives each of us Visions of who we are which we must manifest in the material world to the best of our ability. Transgender people, combining elements of male and female, are at the interstice of the material and spiritual worlds, and are thus able to act as mediators for the benefit of our communities.' "[8] We bring into the physical those visions that we have been given about ourselves, and, in doing so, we fulfill a sacred purpose.

---

6. Darin Issac Blue, "Translations," *Fireweed* 69 (spring 2000): 11.
7. Marsha Sinetar, *Holy Work* (New York: Crossroad, 1998), 22.
8. Virginia Ramey Mollenkott, *Omnigender: A Trans-Religious Approach* (Cleveland: Pilgrim Press, 2001), 163.

Finding our calling requires us to give up the masks that we use to hide behind and to let go of that which is not truly us. Parker Palmer, in his excellent book on vocation, writes:

> "Faking it" in the service of high values is no virtue and has nothing to do with vocation. It is an ignorant, sometimes arrogant, attempt to override one's nature and it will always fail. Our deepest calling is to grow into our own authentic selfhood, whether or not it conforms to some image of who we *ought* to be. As we do so, we will not only find the joy that every human being seeks — we will also find our path of authentic service in the world.[9]

Our calling cannot just be about what we are not, but also about who we genuinely are. It is about authentic selfhood and about service in the world. We each have a unique role to play in the world, and discovering ourselves is part of the process of fulfilling our part in the pageant of life. Realizing our calling is a gradual unfolding of who we are.

Our callings, too, lead us away from that which is not helpful to us. As Erin Swenson writes:

> My entire life has been filled with the struggle, often with God, about the difference between what I looked like — how I was treated by others — and what I felt like on the inside. My own patriarchal feelings contributed to my sense that it was somehow shameful that I felt like a woman and wanted desperately to be one. I knew for certain that I would become a miserable outcast were I ever to reveal my terrible truth. But throughout history God has been calling people away from the ancient myth that men and women are somehow of different substance and therefore profoundly different from each other. God has continued to lead us away from the prejudice and ignorance to which we all are victim, toward the light of truth.[10]

We know in our bodies, in our experiences, that God calls us to something greater, something stronger than where we have been.

In her book on group spiritual direction, Rose Mary Dougherty describes how she came to understand that God's will is not an external force, to be feared or even obeyed, but rather an expression of God's prayer within us. She writes as follows:

> Just as we can trust God's loving prayer for us in our prayer, so too we can trust that prayer for us in all of life, including the decisions we must

---

9. Parker Palmer, *Let Your Life Speak: Listening for the Voice of Vocation* (San Francisco: Jossey-Bass, 2000), 16.

10. Erin Swenson, "Body and Soul United," *The Other Side* 37, no. 3 (May and June 2001): 30–31.

make. As we join the prayer of God within us, our defenses and our images of ourselves are gradually chipped away; we begin to know ourselves for who we are in God — beings who are loved very much, who are invited to become who we really are, beings in love. From that place of core identity we want to make decisions compatible with who we are.[11]

Our genders are not something external to ourselves that we are seeking, but rather arise out of God's prayer for us, a prayer that comes with great love. We seek to be what we really are, and for people of faith, that seeking brings us into loving cooperation with God.

This kind of loving prayer can be invaluable in our process of decision making as transgendered people. A connection exists between self-love and our gender transitions or expressions. Until I had developed a sense of love for myself, I was unable to even look at the question of gender. But once I began to love myself, the question was seemingly there every time I prayed, every place I looked, behind every thing I sought. As I was able to love myself, God called me on to explore more deeply my own calling and to express more authentically who I was. Other transgendered people have told me that once they began to see on the outside what they had known on the inside, they began to fall in love with themselves and build within their hearts a sense of self-love. Callings arise from our deepest passions, in the place where God dwells within us, which we access through love. As Dougherty points out, the call is not about searching for what God wants outside of ourselves but finding within ourselves what God is praying for us. She writes, "In the stance of trust we can wait for Love to unfold. We can ask of ourselves with God, 'What do I want? What do I really want?' and believe that in that answer Love will begin to show itself."[12]

Prayer can be a space for us in which we let down the barriers we have erected around ourselves and open our hearts to God as fully and authentically as we can. It can be the place where we can allow God to separate us from the societal pressures to conform and therefore see more clearly what is true for us. Prayer can help us gain perspective, focusing on and trusting in God, rather than on our fears and doubts. Spending intentional time in prayer can be the way in which we come to understand what our calling is and how we will live it out.

---

11. Rose Mary Dougherty, *Group Spiritual Direction: Community for Discernment* (New York: Paulist Press, 1995), 30.

12. Ibid., 31.

Seven characteristics of calls are important to look at specifically as we explore the relationship of a calling to transgendered people.

1. **Callings are individual and personal.** They are given to each person uniquely and are for that person alone. The calling that I experience is unlike that of anyone else and it speaks directly to me. In his *Journals*, Søren Kierkegaard wrote, "The thing is to understand myself, to see what God really wants *me* to do; the thing is to find a truth which is true *for me*, to find *the idea for which I can live and die.*"[13] A calling will not necessarily make sense to anyone else; the call is about what is true for me and for me alone — my unique destiny and an embodiment of the word that I can uniquely bring to the world.

Gender, too, is unique and individual. The actuality of human gender expression rarely lines up perfectly with the binary categories of masculine and feminine. Each of us comprises a blend of things that our society has labeled masculine and feminine. We have choices about engaging in behavior that is deemed appropriate for one gender or another, although we may suppress expressions of gender that we feel are shameful or inappropriate. We may not be aware that we have choices at all in how we express our gender. Each person is a unique mix of what we call "masculine" and "feminine." A man might choose to become good at auto mechanics and needlepoint; a woman might be both compassionate and a strong leader.

If we are open to gender as a calling, then we will make prayerful and faithful choices about how we express our gender. We can select the expressions of gender that are right for us uniquely. We can combine these attributes in an infinite number of ways, and our medley of them is ours alone. Using the language and lens of calling allows us to discern which path is ours and which combination of characteristics best represents our self. If we allow ourselves the freedom to discern our calling of gender, we will most likely end up with a blend of expression.

I, and only I, can know exactly what gender is true for me. God has written it on my heart of hearts, and only God and I can discover what is there. The way I am to be in the world is mine and mine alone. Yet...

---

13. Søren Kierkegaard, quoted in Os Guiness, *The Call: Finding and Fulfilling the Central Purpose of Your Life* (Nashville: Word, 1998), 3.

2. **Callings are usually affirmed by a community and sometimes come from the community.** Others look at us and are able to notice something about us that speaks to the ways in which we are called. They are external witnesses of an internal process. This witness can be the support of our loved ones as they see us come to a place of peace within us or the witness of our therapist or physician who affirms us on our path in keeping with the Harry Benjamin Standards of Care. But I mean something more important and more powerful than the process of seeking permission from those who staff the gates of gender transition. The witness of the community is not about regulation of gender but about a holistic recognition of the call and process of another person.

Our most important witnesses are those who tell us what they see, sometimes even before we ourselves may be aware of it. My drama teacher in high school almost always cast me in male or tomboy roles, as I mentioned earlier, saying that my energy was not right for the female ones. I always felt both delighted and ashamed, mortified and gratified because, up there on the stage playing a priest, spy, or some other male role, everyone could see externally what was happening to me internally. By acting out a role, I came closer to my own truth. By making that possible, my drama teacher witnessed to something that she saw going on inside me, whether or not either of us was consciously aware of it.

Some people say to us, "This seems right for you." They affirm what they see within us. They are also witnesses to the changes that take place within our bodies, and, as importantly, in our spirits. The testimony of my loved ones is part of what has clarified and validated the calling that I felt within myself to make this journey.

A spiritual director or another person who acts as a companion on our journeys can be invaluable in helping us to discern our callings.[14] Several

---

14. I am not aware of any literature on spiritual direction that mentions transgendered people. James Empereur has written *Spiritual Direction and the Gay Person* (New York: Continuum, 1998) about spiritual direction with gay and lesbian persons. As Empereur writes: "Homosexuality is one of God's most significant gifts to humanity. To be gay or lesbian is to have received a special blessing from God. All humans receive their own special graces from their creator, but God has chosen some to be gay and lesbian as a way of revealing something about Godself that heterosexuals do not. On the acceptance of this premise all authentic and successful spiritual direction with gays and lesbians stands or falls." This insight applies, too, to a spiritual director's willingness and ability to view transgendered people as gifted in a similar way. An appropriate spiritual director or companion on the journey of a transgendered person should affirm and seek that which God has specially revealed to and through transgendered persons. Other valuable works on spiritual direction, such as Margaret Guenther's *Holy Listening: The Art of Spiritual Direction* (Cambridge, Mass.: Cowley Publications, 1992), and Margaret

Quakers that I spoke with and read about talked about gathering together a Clearness Committee — a group of four people who come together to ask questions of the one seeking clearness in order to help the person come to their own truth — to help sort out the question of gender and the rightness of gender transition. Petra Doan describes how her Meeting assisted her: "I asked for a Clearness Committee from my Monthly Meeting to help me discern whether this was in fact a leading. The committee met with me for six months and explored the nature of my leading and the probable impacts of my following it on my family and on the meeting. At last the committee helped me to see my children were unlikely to stop loving me for being an authentic person, and that the Meeting community would welcome me no matter what."[15] The Clearness Committee was able to help her by creating a space in which she could explore the impact of her decision as well as seek divine guidance for it. From her testimony, the committee helped her sort out the difficulties that needed to be addressed from the fears that had little likelihood of coming to pass. Our spiritual companions can help us with the process of discerning our paths by providing realistic feedback and encouragement along the way. As we approach decisions about our trans selves, we need both challenging questions, to help us to hone our intentions and understanding of our needs, and encouragement, to give us the strength to continue through the challenges and to help us know that a light is present at the end of the tunnel.

Sometimes we can use a community as a space in which to try on a new identity or a new way of being in the world. I met monthly with a small group of friends in the year leading up to my transition. Long before I went public with the information that I was transgendered, this group knew about my feelings. With them, I was able to test out a new name and see if it felt right, and have them address me with male pronouns so that I could feel if they rang true for me. They made a place for me to be genuinely myself and championed my growth as I changed.

Our spiritual community can serve to hold us accountable to our values and our faith. When I interviewed Richard, he talked specifically about

Ruthing's *Spiritual Direction: Beyond the Beginning* (Mahwah, N.J.: Paulist Press, 2000) could be utilized with adaptations for work with a transgendered person.

15. Petra L. Doan, "The Spiritual Side of Gender Journeying," *Transgender Tapestry* 92 (winter 2000): 42.

disclosing his transsexual status to others in his prayer group for account-ability and feedback from them. Seeking external affirmation of our inward callings can be something that happens spontaneously or because we seek the advice and wisdom of others within our faith communities. The witness of the community is an invaluable part of our journeys.

3. **Callings manifest themselves to people of varying ages.** Another reason that the concept of calling is useful to us in looking at gender is that a calling, like the urge to transform or surpass gender, is recognized and realized by people at a variety of ages and points in their lives. For some, the awareness of gender dysphoria is something that has been present with them for as long as they can remember. When they were aware of some sense of self, that self felt uncomfortable in the gender with which s/he was identified. Yet for others, that awareness does not come until much later in life. We are each different and are able, at different points in our lives, to explore our own selves. In addition to our awareness of gender, we are willing and able to look at what that might mean and to do something about it at varying segments of life.

4. **Callings may last for a season of time or a whole lifetime.** A given calling may differ from one season of life to another. A more powerful approach for me is to understand that I had a season of my life to be female and a season of my life to be male, rather than seeing one of those seasons as a "mistake" or "wasted time," as I have heard others sometimes describe their life before transition. When a person speaks of their life just beginning at the point of transition, or at some point within that process, does this not erase the accumulation of experiences that created that person as s/he is today? The concept of gender as a calling allows me to be called to live one way yesterday, another way today, and even yet another tomorrow.

5. **Gender, like any other calling, is also an ongoing revelation.** In living a life open to the voice of calling, we recognize that we never truly have the answer. One is not done receiving callings in one's life, but rather they unfold before us as we move along. Gender is the same way. While systems are in place to try to prevent transgendered people, particularly transsexuals accessing medical technology, from making a "mistake," the fact is that none of us can predict what we will be called to do and be in the future. While that assessment of the situation may not be popular with people who control the access to medical transition, the reality is present

in the lives of people who transition. I have met people who decided after a number of years that they needed to transition back. Viewing gender as a calling allows us room to see it as an ongoing revelation.

The International Bill of Gender Rights says, "All human beings carry within themselves an ever-unfolding idea of who they are and what they are capable of achieving. . . . [I]t is fundamental that individuals have the right to define, and to redefine as their lives unfold, their own gender identities."[16] No single answer applies for our whole lives. Knowing that I am a man does not tell me what kind of man to be, nor does it finalize the question of my gender expression. We will continue to see our genders unfold and develop even as we unfold and develop as human beings, just as our callings continue to unfold in our lives. Our genders and our callings are both processes not set in stone for eternity, but dynamic, evolving, and growing — as we are.

Our calling also gives us room to see how the experiences of our lives change and transform us as we follow it. Being read in this world as a man now, and not as a woman, has lead to vastly different experiences than I had before. These experiences have shaped my mind and spirit even as the hormones and surgery have transformed my body. Seeing a different face in the mirror changes the being inside who is looking through those eyes at that reflection. Moving in the world as a different gender than the one I was born with has transformed the way I move in that world and live my life. Each change begets a new change, and in changing, reveals yet another new piece of this journey of transformation. I do not know what the end of this journey will be like; I only know that I continue to seek the path before me as God reveals a call to me.

6. **To be fully realized, individuals must develop their callings and act upon them; that is true of gender transformation as well.** When someone is called, s/he often needs to develop the skills, tools, and perspective necessary to effectively fulfill that calling. The person must also act. This is not a passive activity but an active one. What that action may be, however, varies with the individual. If a person is called to be an Olympic athlete, yet never trains, s/he will not make it to the Games at all. In the same way, an examination of our own gender requires a response from us. Every person need not transition, but we do need to look at things

---

16. International Bill of Gender Rights, International Conference on Transgender Law, 1995.

from a different perspective, to say yes or no to what we feel called to be, and to learn what we need to know in order to live out the calling.

To follow our callings as transgendered people means that we need to make a shift in our lives. This shift may or may not mean action in terms of how we access medical technology to change our bodies, but it does mean taking ourselves and our genders seriously and acting to identify ourselves with who we are and who we are becoming. I do not believe that we can remain passive and still genuinely answer a calling. God calls us to move beyond our fears, beyond our doubts, and beyond the pressures of society and family to say "yes" to true selves. That declaration is an act of faithful response to our calling.

7. **Callings move us toward wholeness and purpose.** If it comes from God, then the calling moves us toward wholeness and a sense of our own life's purpose. We are not called to do things that take us away from well-being and wholeness but rather that move us toward them. I felt within me for many years a restless sense of needing to be and do something that was altogether different than the way I had been living up to that point. I sought a sense of wholeness and healing that had eluded me for as long as I can remember. But when I began to be aware of my own sense of gender dysphoria, I found that each step I took in the direction of changing my life brought a greater feeling of wholeness. Each step felt right and even holy, even if it was difficult.

One part of that journey is removing the barriers that stand between us and the successful fulfillment of our callings. In her article on transgendered theology, Starchild concludes:

> If God calls us to be farmers, shop-keepers, house-wives, lawyers, craftsmen, pastors, laborers, or whatever, God expects us to find fulfillment in that calling. If something stands in the way of that inner fulfillment and satisfaction, it stands in the way of our ability to serve God and God's world well in our calling. A sense of Vocation would drive us to remove whatever barriers make it difficult for us to fulfill our calling. If Gender Dysphoria keeps one from being who they truly are and fitting into the reality around them, then it keeps them from serving God to the best of their ability. Vocation then demands that the individual do whatever they can to change this Gender Dysphoria. We now know that the body's gender can be changed to fit the mind's gender, but the opposite cannot be done.
>
> So these two Reformed doctrines, Creation and Vocation, not only support people with unusual gender conditions having a freedom within the

Church to change their outward gender, but in a sense they teach us that such folk are actually engaged in a sacred and holy task when they undertake such a difficult passage. Rather than attempt to see this passage as something shameful and guilty, we must see it as children of God taking seriously God's creation of them as creatures who are made in the image of God being therefore co-creators with God and see it as children of God taking seriously God's calling of them to ruthlessly remove any hindrances to their being whom God desires them to be so they may serve God to their fullest.[17]

Thus we have a responsibility to become fully who God wants us to be so that we might live freely and so that we can serve God.

I believe that transgendered people are called by God to transcend the boundaries of male and female to which our society has limited us. We are also called to transform our bodies, whether through our adornment of them or through medical means; our minds, whether through new perspectives or hormonally induced differences in thought; and our spirits, whether freeing our sense of being "trapped in the wrong body" or embracing the wholeness of the self. We are called to be transformers, of both ourselves and the world around us.

By answering the calling of our gender, we may find clarity about other vocations as well. As Patrick Califia noted: "You ask how I knew this was the right thing to do. Well, I'm not sure that's why I took T [testosterone]. It was more because I had run out of every other damn thing I could think of to try to feel better. It was my last option. But I got permission to take it from higher up, and today I feel that being able to stand between genders (which is where I will always be no matter how male I look) gives me a unique perspective on the lives of men and women, and increases my ability to empathize with or serve the spiritual needs of others. It makes me a better priest."[18]

Once we find a sense of affirmation and blessing on our transitions, we begin to discover what is blessed about them. I too have a sense that I am a more skilled pastor because of my transition. I was speaking with a woman pastor about what it meant to be a woman pastor at that particular church as opposed to being a male pastor because I knew what both of those things meant. More broadly, as Patrick states, it increases our ability

17. Starchild, "A Transsexual Theology," *www.whosoever.org/v2Issue2/starchild.html*, 5/14/01.
18. Interview with Patrick Califia, July 26, 2001.

to empathize and understand experiences from both perspectives. That skill is valuable in fulfilling any vocation in our highly gender-segregated society. The more spiritually authentic we are and the more whole we become, the more we have to offer others through our service. When we are busy maintaining a mask or avoiding God's calling within us, we may be busy distracting ourselves with service, but of a different kind. To genuinely fulfill our vocations in the world, we must be true to ourselves and to the still small voice of God calling us home.

Chapter Eight

Transgendered Body Theology

Bodies are critical to a discussion of a transgendered theology. Bodies are, after all, the way in which we express our gender-varied selves and the ground on which many of the theological battles over transgenderism are fought. Transgendered bodies are the source of our pleasure and our pain, a sign of our incongruity and our internal unity. We may struggle with our bodies, rejoice in our bodies, weep over the parts present or the parts absent, see our bodies as a prison and live to view them as our source of liberation. Trans bodies are often changing bodies, bodies that hold more than one essence, transitional bodies and transformational bodies. What we do to and with our bodies fascinates people and leads to questions about our sanity all in the same moment.

A common conception of transgendered people is that we are "women trapped in men's bodies" or "men trapped in women's bodies." Theorists and activists rarely use that terminology today, although some individuals still feel that it is an accurate description of their experiences. In my opinion, this way of looking at our bodies necessarily sets up dualisms: not only the split between female and male but also the division between body and spirit. In this view, these pairs become essentialist and oppositional and no collaboration can exist between them. In a certain sense, another being which inhabits the body must be liberated from it, rather than coming to a place of unity between body and spirit. The "trapped" terminology also establishes a paradigm of victimhood by saying that we are trapped and must be freed from our own bodies, which are, after all, ourselves.

This question of being trapped in the wrong body is controversial among trans folk. As Riki Ann Wilchins comments:

> The problem with transsexual women is not that we are trapped in the wrong bodies. The truth is that that is a fairly trivial affair corrected by doctors and sharp scalpels. The problem is that we are trapped in a society

which alternates between hating and ignoring, or tolerating and exploiting us and our experience.

More importantly, we are trapped in the wrong minds. We have, too many of us for too long, been trapped in too much self-hate: the hate reflected back at us by others who, unwilling to look at the complexity of our lives, dismiss our femaleness, our femininity, and our sense of gender and erotic choices as merely imitative or simply derivative.[1]

We must remember that the struggle around trans bodies is not with those bodies per se, but with the meaning attached to them by society, by medical science, by our lovers, and by our families. As Wilchins reminds us, we need to take a holistic look at trans lives and shake off the self-hate that traps too many of us in ways more complex and nefarious than simply being in the "wrong" body.

At the same time, one of the characteristics that identifies us as transgendered people is a sense of incongruity between the gender assigned to us (to our bodies) at birth and our own sense of ourselves. Our bodies can be a source of pain and discomfort when we feel alienated from them because they do not match what we feel they should be (a feeling not limited to trans folk, of course). Our bodies can also be a source of pleasure, joy, and affirmation both as they are and when we have altered them through clothing, hormones, exercise, or surgery.

One of the challenges that comes from people and groups who oppose our right to such modifications is the view that trans people promote a kind of modern Gnostic alienation from the body. Oliver O'Donovan writes, "If I claim to have a 'real sex,' which may be at war with the sex of my body and is at least in a rather uncertain relationship to it, I am shrinking from the glad acceptance of my self as a physical as well as spiritual being, and seeking self-knowledge in a kind of Gnostic withdrawal from material creation."[2] He then goes on: "Transsexuals do not retreat from their bodies into a Gnostic spirituality; if anything, they are preoccupied with them. Their very insistence on pursuing the hope of surgical intervention shows with what anguish they experience the dividedness of physical sexuality from gender identity."[3] Thus, he concludes that the answer is to heal this

---

1. Riki Ann Wilchins, *Read My Lips: Sexual Subversion and the End of Gender* (Ithaca, N.Y.: Firebrand Books, 1997), 47.
2. Oliver O'Donovan, "Transsexualism and Christian Marriage," *Journal of Religious Ethics* 11 (spring 1983): 147.
3. Ibid.

division, rather than encourage or affirm it by providing medical treatment. Victoria Kolakowski writes in response to O'Donovan: "There is no evidence suggesting that transsexuals can adapt their self images to conform to their bodies. Most recent studies demonstrate that transsexuals who have sex reassignment surgery adjust better than those who do not have surgery, and almost all post-operative transsexuals surveyed would decide to have the surgery if they had to choose again."[4] While we can say that pitting the body against the spirit is undesirable, that assessment does not help us address people who genuinely and profoundly experience differences between our bodies and our spirits. Kolakowski correctly chides O'Donovan by saying that, "dismissing the stated experience of many people about their own identity in support of a theoretical position should not be undertaken so casually."[5]

Promoting a sense of disconnection from the body is neither healthy nor desirable, although many people experience this disconnection — particularly, but not exclusively, trans people. My own experiences and those described by others point to the fact that transgendered persons pay very close attention to our bodies. Rather than simply acting as if the body were not important, we find our bodies and the meanings they convey deeply important — important enough, in fact, that we feel strongly that they must express the right meanings for who we are. Our bodies are important enough, too, that we are willing to invest our time, money, and lives to change them. We also discover that our bodies are more malleable than our spirits and that congruity can come through loving the body enough to change it and mold it.

Because of the particular nature of the body in the experience of those who are transgendered, we must look closely at what the body means to us theologically. As James Nelson writes in *Body Theology*:

> The task of body theology is critical reflection on our bodily experience as a fundamental realm of the experience of God. It is not, in the first instance, a theological description of bodily life from a supra-bodily vantage point (as if that were possible, which in actuality it is not). Nor is it primarily concerned with articulating norms for the proper "use" of the body. Body theology necessarily begins with the concreteness of our bodily experience,

---

4. Victoria S. Kolakowski, "Towards a Christian Ethical Response to Transsexual Persons," *Theology and Sexuality* 6 (March 1997): 22.
5. Ibid., 21.

even while it recognizes that this very concreteness is filtered through the interpretive web of meanings that we have come to attach to our bodily life.[6]

First and foremost, the aim of body theology is to examine our bodily experiences as the way in which we experience God. The only way that we know God is as embodied people. Through our bodies' capacities for sight, sound, emotion, thought, intuition, and other senses, we are able to experience the divine. The sacred comes to us through our bodies and within our bodies.

The image and likeness of God permeates our being. Scripture does not tell us that only our spirits were made in the image and likeness of God, but our whole being, including our body. The Hebrew people did not distinguish between the creation of body and soul, but saw only embodied spirits.[7] As J. Philip Newell writes: "A nineteenth-century teacher in the Celtic tradition used the analogy of royal garments woven through with gold. If the golden thread were to be ripped out of the clothing the whole garment would unravel. So it is with the image of God woven into the mystery of our being. If somehow it were to be extracted we would cease to exist. The image of God is not simply a characteristic of our humanity. It is the essence of our being."[8] We are inseparable from our bodies and inseparable from the image of God contained within us. We cannot have one without the other.

Our bodies are made in the image and likeness of God and are the only ways in which we experience the divine. We have no way of knowing God except as we are — embodied beings. The concreteness of the specific body creates a unique experience and manifestation of God, and the experience of a transgendered body is necessarily different from one that is not transgendered. This statement is true for each unique individual. We who are transgendered know God through our trans bodies. Through different bodies, God speaks different words to that individual and to the world. Because we are unique, we can know unique aspects of God's being and speak a distinct word of God to the world. Theologian Mary Timothy Prokes says, "[F]rom within the totality of the individual, the living body

---

6. James Nelson, *Body Theology* (Louisville: Westminster/John Knox Press, 1992), 43.

7. Mary Timothy Prokes, *Toward a Theology of the Body* (Grand Rapids, Mich.: William B. Eerdmans, 1996), 59.

8. J. Philip Newell, *Echo of the Soul: The Sacredness of the Human Body* (Harrisburg, Pa.: Morehouse, 2000), xi.

(Real Symbol) manifests the whole person.... [E]ach person is spoken into being by God; each is called to be an effective word or message of love in the world.... Every person is uniquely flesh made word, communicating a message that is written bodily into a people, a place, and a moment in history."[9]

This idea is echoed in Nelson's work and in other texts on body theology. Then what is the message of trans bodies?

Three distinct issues are critical to an understanding of a trans body theology and need to be examined in detail: revelation, unity of self and body, and the right of bodily self-determination.

Revelation

Prokes argues that one of the fundamental aspects of a theology of the body is the revelation of God. The fact that we are created in the image and likeness of God, she says, shows our participation in the divine act of revelation from the moment we came into being. The Divine continues to be revealed by and to various persons. As Prokes explains:

> In faith understanding, *Revelation* means primarily divine Personal Self-disclosure of God's inner life, made known in a consummate manner in the Incarnate Word.... Revelation in this fundamental sense cannot be conjured, earned or forced. It is a gift to be recognized and received. The Scriptures indicated that primordial Revelation was given unexpectedly, in ways transcending human calculations, often overcoming seeming impossibilities. God's Self-manifestation exceeds human control and evokes (in Rudolph Otto's well-known terminology) both *fascination* and *awe*.[10]

She then goes on as follows:

> More than a conveying of information, Revelation is Self-manifestation of a divine communion of Persons, inviting response from those who receive it. The multiple accounts of those who were recipients of Revelation (whether in Old or New Covenants) shows how their lives were changed by it. They came to recognize that it was not for their personal consolation or aggrandizement. Rather, it incorporated a mission to be fulfilled for the sake of the whole people. There was fear, even terror, in those who recognized that they were being visited by a Self-disclosing God. *They found that in receiving*

---

9. Prokes, *Toward a Theology of the Body*, 82.
10. Ibid., 75.

divine Self-manifestation, they, too, were disclosed, known to the depths of their being.[11]

Revelation in this sense is about God's self-revelation to us *and* about being revealed and known in ways beyond human understanding. As she says, the process is terrifying and wonderful. Revelation also includes our process of being revealed to ourselves.

Through trans and intersexed bodies, God reveals Godself to be a Creator who loves diversity and variation, a Creator who improvises and varies the melodies that call each person into being. Through such bodies, we see the intricate differences that make an individual a unique creation and a fluid transition from one being to another. Trans bodies show us that the dichotomous ways in which we have viewed bodies are not God's ways, because our bodies make it difficult to divide human beings into two ways of being with nothing in between. We are the in-between, created in the image and likeness of God.

Trans bodies reveal an inner conviction and faithfulness to a sense of truth beyond what seems obvious and expected. The strength to maintain our convictions of what we know to be true about ourselves, even when our physical form is deemed to say otherwise and even through society's discouragement and punishment of variation, is a divine strength that we know in our bodies. Trans bodies are tenacious.

Trans bodies also speak of a collaboration between God and humanity in co-creating what our bodies are and what they become. This concept is true for all of us; while God set in motion the process that led to our evolution, conception, and birth, we who are these bodies make choices about what we will eat, how we will treat our bodies, how we move our bodies — and all of these actions play a role in shaping our bodies, literally and figuratively. As Carol Ochs says in *Song of the Self: Biblical Spirituality and Human Holiness*: "In opening up to Creation we must also be open to examining our own creativity. We are not simply created, we seem to be co-creators in forming and transforming our self."[12]

With trans bodies, the collaboration may be even more explicit as we make specific choices to reshape those bodies to look and be the ways that are right for us. Our bodies speak of the changing and changeable

---

11. Ibid. Italics are from the original work.
12. Carol Ochs, *Song of the Self: Biblical Spirituality and Human Holiness* (Valley Forge, Pa.: Trinity Press International, 1994), 5.

nature of human bodies. All of us are continually changing as our cells transform, our bodies age, our weight varies. Trans people are perhaps more active participants in that process, changing our bodies in more explicit, intentional, and external ways.

Holly Boswell, in a web article entitled "The Spirit of Transgender," writes, "[W]e, as divine agents, have the freedom to shape the material world we inhabit. Transgendered people are exercising this freedom when we reshape our bodies, via cosmetics or hormonal therapy or surgery, to suit Spirit. We take responsibility for our own manifestation."[13] Kate Bornstein speaks in her performances about the fact that all of the cells in the human body are replaced every seven years. Thus she asks, seven years after her transition, are all of her cells now girl cells? And what does it mean, she wonders, that we have a whole new body every seven years?[14] God created us as part of the ongoing cycle of change that exists in our universe, and God's word of adaptation, change, and transformation speaks through our bodies. Our bodies are both new and old, both changed and the same.

Our own processes of self-discovery mirror this process of Divine self-revelation. We set out on journeys of self-exploration, seeking to discover our identities within our bodies. As Boswell states: "Our gender transitions, the very process of gender-shift can be viewed as a kind of Vision Quest, addressing that age-old question: *who are we?* To transcend gender stereotyping is to dare to be fully oneself, fully human, as Spirit intended. . . . Once Spirit and Flesh are consciously joined, there is grounding, there is exaltation . . . there is balance."[15] The very actions of transition are themselves a part of a quest for self-revelation and a search to know ourselves better. God's self-revelation and our own are sacred moments.

The process of gender transition contains a number of revelations that continue throughout our lifetimes: the discovery within ourselves, the sharing of that knowledge with others, the revelation of the body as it appears in new clothes or with medical modifications, the telling of our stories, and the intimate knowing of our bodies by ourselves and with others. We reveal who we are becoming as we transform our bodies. The

---

13. Holly Boswell, "The Spirit of Transgender," *www.homestead.com/transpirits/files/SpiritOfTG.html.*

14. Kate Bornstein's performance was at California State Polytechnic University, Pomona, 1999, viewed by the author.

15. Boswell, "The Spirit of Transgender."

process of gender transition for transsexuals is an ongoing process of revelation. I have learned many things about my body that I did not know before I transitioned, like the fact that my beard grew in red, like the Irish ancestors that are part of my genetic heritage, or that my muscles and fat can regroup themselves to make my hips, my face, my waist all look different than they were before. I have learned that my muscles have considerably more strength in them when they are fed by testosterone than by estrogen, and that my moods depended more on my hormones than I was ever willing to admit.

I have also had to reveal my body and the new ways that it looks to those who know me: to my partner, to my family, to old friends who did not recognize me, and even to an ex-lover from many years ago who knew I looked extremely familiar but could not figure out if we had ever met. I have observed that people from some countries who knew me before transition have an easier time recognizing my changing body than people from some other countries; I think these observations must reveal some way in which we are culturally conditioned to recognize people by different cues and that my eyes must be more recognizable than my jaw line, for example.

Our trans bodies are fascinating to us as they change. We look eagerly for signs of differences in our bodies — for that little shift in hair growth or the beginnings of breast or genital development. Going through gender transition is very much like a second adolescence, including all of those awkward moments of not knowing quite what to do with these new body parts and staring at our newly revealed selves in the mirror.

The revelation of God to us and us to God, as well as our search to reveal us to our own selves, are all features of a trans body theology. The revelation of God to us is sacred, as is the process of our own revelations to ourselves, to others, and to God. Revelation is the moment of truth, realness, and integrity in which we come to know ourselves better than we did before, at depths greater than we had anticipated. We experience the affirmation that we are fully revealed and known to God.

Unity of Self and Body

A critical component of a movement toward a holistic understanding of ourselves as transgendered people is discovering that we are more than just a body or just a spirit but a whole being. As Lisa Sowle Cahill writes in *Sex, Gender and Christian Ethics,* "Fundamental to our embodiment is the fact that each person in his or her individuality is both body and the 'more' which selfhood entails (intellect, will, emotions, 'spirit,' and relationality, especially to other embodied individuals)."[16] One of the greatest challenges for us as transgendered people is to see a balance, as Boswell stated, between spirit and flesh, between the body and the "more." Ochs goes on to say:

> While we know that things cannot be absolutely other and still share the same universe, emotionally we tend to remain dualistic. Perhaps we are mind-body dualists because our bodies make us ill at ease, or we affirm the absolute distinction between good and evil because we are judgmental. And surely life is opposed to death, or else why bury the dead? But over time we see these dualisms break down. We come to know that the body is the physical expression of the mind. We come to see how closely good and evil resemble one another (which is why morality poses such difficult questions).[17]

One aspect of our maturity as spiritual people is learning to see beyond the dualisms, including the splits between life and death, female and male, spirit and body.

Achieving a sense of congruity between body and spirit is, for many, the goal of exploring gender transition or various gender expressions.[18] The sense of discomfort with our bodies drives our need to explore a reality beyond simply the basic anatomy of our bodies. As Becky Allison writes:

> It is almost the rule, rather than the exception. Someone has spent years in a church which gives easy answers to every hard question. Turn your burdens over to the Lord ... leave them at the foot of the cross. Ask in faith and you shall receive it. You have not, because you ask not. It sounds wonderful and we want to believe it. We do believe it! We live our lives believing it, for years praying for healing, for deliverance, for change. And change does not come. Finally we have to look at another perspective: perhaps change does not come because God wants us to deal with our questions in another

---

16. Lisa Sowle Cahill, *Sex, Gender and Christian Ethics* (Cambridge: Cambridge University Press, 1998), 76.

17. Ochs, *Song of the Self,* 9.

18. I am indebted to Guy Baldwin, who was my therapist when I transitioned, who gave me language and helped me gain this insight.

way. The spirit does not change.... [C]an the body change to match the spirit? To our amazement, we find that it can, and therein lies peace.[19]

In looking at our bodies in a new way, we then embark upon the process of reconciling the inner and the outer parts of our nature. As Allison says so clearly, we have long tried to make the spirit match the body. Now we discover a new way to approach this question. Ironically, I found that accepting my body as it was became much easier once I realized that my body would not always be that way.

We may also discover that this desire for body congruity extends beyond what anyone else may see or perceive about us. For many years I felt that if sexism were ended in our world, then I would feel comfortable as a woman. But not only did that answer feel utopian, it also felt incomplete. After transitioning, I realized that if I were going to spend the rest of my life on a deserted island, with no one else, I would still want a male reflection to look back at me from the water rather than a female one. Even if I could see no reflections, I would need to look out at the world with eyes from a man's body. I needed a connection between my body and my spirit that always felt lacking until I transitioned. I cannot explain the need for this connection exactly but I do know that the more years that pass in this body that now appears male in most ways, the more I come to love it and feel connected with it. I am becoming one with my body in ways that I could not possibly have conceived of earlier in my life.

We do need that sense of connection because we are not separate from our bodies. As Karen Kroll notes:

> In the Book of Genesis, for example, there are two creation accounts. In one of the accounts a human being is created in the image of God, and it is good. In the other account a human being is created from the dust of the earth and God breathes life into that human being. The interesting part of these different accounts is that God did not divide a person into two parts, one part soul and the other part body. A person is a whole being, composed of both body and soul, and created by God.[20]

Being one with our bodies is a spiritual task, given to us by God through the act of creation itself.

---

19. Becky Allison, "Life in the Leper Colony," *http://members.aol.com/_ht_a/gnlnews/lepers.html*, 11/22/00.

20. Karen F. Kroll, "Transsexuality and Religion: A Personal Journey," in *Gender Blending*, ed. Bonnie Bullough, Vern L. Bullough, and James Elias (Amherst, N.Y.: Prometheus Books, 1997), 492.

Learning to love our bodies is part of extending the love of God to our selves and achieving a healthy level of self-esteem. In James Nelson's words:

> Dominant Christian interpretations all too frequently have understood self-love as equivalent to egocentrism, selfishness, and narcissism, and hence incompatible with the religious life.... The good news is that self-love is not a deadly sin. Both Hebrew and Christian scriptures bid us to love our neighbors as ourselves, not instead of ourselves. Both religious traditions at their best know that love is indivisible and nonquantifiable. It is not true that the more love we save for ourselves the less we have for others. Authentic self-love is not a grasping selfishness — which actually betrays the lack of self-love. Rather, it is a deep self-acceptance, which comes through the affirmation of one's own graciously given worth and creaturely fineness, our "warts and all." Furthermore, genuine self-love personalizes the experience of one's own body. "My body *is* me, and I am worthful."[21]

Learning to see our trans bodies as worthy is so important to us as individuals and as a community. We must protect ourselves and one another from the violence that is aimed at our bodies and our spirits. This sense of being "worthful" is so important to developing our understanding of ourselves as worthy of human rights, worthy of being loved, worthy of feeling beautiful and handsome and happy in this world. We, our embodied selves, are worthy just as we are and as we are becoming. We are worthy of respect, of love, and of life itself. Knowing these facts is essential for our survival as a community.

Interestingly, Nelson also cites studies that demonstrate that a sense of being intimately connected to one's own body increases the ability to tolerate ambiguity in the world. He says, "The more connected and comfortable I am with my bodily reality, the more I am able to accept the confusing mix of things in the world I experience."[22] He then goes on to say that the opposite is also true: the more disconnected we feel, the more we see the world in binary ways. This observation has important implications for trans people and our ability to accept ourselves as nonbinary people. Anecdotally, I have seen this connection at play in trans people near the beginning of transition, who feel a strong sense of bodily incongruity and express a deep conviction for the binary nature of gender. An FTM

---

21. Nelson, *Body Theology,* 34–35.
22. Ibid., 43.

approaching the start of hormones may say, for example, that nothing about him in any way is feminine and that he never experienced a sense of himself as female. As the years pass and he becomes more at home in a male body, the urgency of defining himself as separate from any female identity may fade. I feel much more comfortable today recognizing the feminine and masculine within me than I did early in transition when I struggled so hard to express my long-buried masculinity.

Some of us also long for reconciliation between our transgendered selves and the body of Christ. As Rowen Williams writes about body theology: "The whole story of creation, incarnation, and our incorporation into the fellowship of Christ's body tells us that God desires us, as if we were God, as if we were that unconditional response to God's giving that God's self makes in the life of the Trinity. We are created so that we may be caught up in this, so that we may grow into the wholehearted love of God by learning that God loves us as God loves God."[23] God who loves us infinitely, in our bodies and in our whole personhood, desires us body and soul.

The Right of Self-Determination

Trans activist Leslie Feinberg says it simply: "I support the right of all people to self-determination of their own bodies."[24] We are our bodies, and I believe that we have a right to make choices about how we care for ourselves, shape ourselves, craft our bodies and our lives, dress ourselves, and move through the world.

Trans folk, like gay, lesbian, and bisexual people, can spend a good deal of energy speculating about why we are the way we are. Some in the community articulate a strong desire to find some kind of hormonal or genetic reason that explains why a given person is transgendered. If such a reason were found, it is argued, then our families and society would accept us because it would not be our fault for being different. I have seen flame wars erupt on a number of trans-oriented e-mail lists with people attacked and defending the essentialist argument about gender. But why must there be an external cause? Could the reason not simply be that we

---

23. Rowen Williams, "The Body's Grace," in *Ourselves, Our Souls and Bodies,* ed. Charles Hefling (Cambridge, Mass.: Cowley Publications, 1996), 59.

24. Leslie Feinberg, *TransLiberation: Beyond Pink or Blue* (Boston: Beacon Press, 1998), 19.

are this way because God wanted to create human beings who are different from one another?

The tendency exists within both the medical/psychological industry and the trans community itself to try to determine who are the "true trans-sexuals." This tendency stems from a fear that someone might transition who will later have regrets (with the attendant threat of lawsuits) or that some people will discredit the trans community and by their actions make it more difficult for others. Because we are such a small community, there is a sense that what one person does will directly affect how others are viewed. Another reaction in the community is against people who are obviously gender variant, who might be perceived as making life more difficult for those who want to pass unnoticed in society. When an FTM became pregnant three years ago, for example, some people predicted that his actions would directly lead to the death of other community members, who feared that they would be bashed by people who would view us all as "freaks."

Rather than policing one another or searching for a causal factor, I believe that our community will become stronger when we argue for each person's right to self-determination of his/her own body. Our bodies are our own terrain, part and parcel of our being. We have a right to transform our bodies in ways that make it possible for us to live fully as embodied, whole human beings, and we have a right to put the clothes on our bodies that make us feel comfortable and alive. We should be able to do this because it is right for us, not because we have been able to convince a doctor that we have sufficient self-hatred that this path is the only one for us if we are to avoid suicide, but because it honestly reflects the totality of ourselves. This is a spiritual issue because it is the way in which we physically embody the spiritual truths within us. That we reflect outwardly that which is inwardly true for us is a matter of integrity. The Spirit calls us away from self-hatred into an appreciation of the wonderful creation that we are.

Our physical transformation must come from a position of self-love, not out of a sense of shame or because we despise ourselves. We have to teach each other this lesson; we are not going to learn it from society or from most of our doctors and therapists. As intersexual Raven Kaldera writes of the guys in his FTM support group: "I learned from them that one didn't have to be squarely on the opposite side of the gender paradigm in order to change one's body; that you didn't have to live with the discomfort. Change was possible, and reasonable, and didn't have to be justified (to the people that count, anyway) except to say, 'This is right for me now.' "[25] We can learn from one another what the full range of options is, and from that broadened sense of choices, we can make the one that is right for us alone. I refused to consider surgery until I had worked through my discomfort with my own breasts. I wanted to love them into another form, not hate them off of my body. I felt it important that this process was about love and care, not about dysphoria and revulsion. I was subjecting my body — me — to surgery; the transformation was about healing, not illness; about hope, not despair; and about joy, not dysphoria.

Some of our therapists and doctors help with this approach. I was blessed to have a therapist who had seen a number of FTMs and was fully committed to exploring with me the whole range of what it meant to be a man and who allowed me to have my doubts and fears while still moving forward to a place of wholeness. I chose the surgeon that I did because he did not require letters from a therapist for me to have a mastectomy because, he said, it was my body and I could make that choice myself as long as I was willing to take responsibility for my actions. After all, nontranssexual women can choose to have their breasts enhanced and people elect to have their bodies changed by plastic surgeons all the time; surely we should have the same right.

Honoring our bodies means listening closely to them and making choices that bring out the best in us. We must choose with care and take responsibility for our actions. Honoring our bodies means learning to love our embodied selves so much that we dress ourselves as we long to dress, we shape our bodies as we want them to be shaped, and we do it from a sense of well-being. We need to proclaim the message widely in our community that you do not have to hate yourself any longer, that path to wholeness is open to every one of us. The first steps on that path are when we claim the right to our own bodies and the right to determine our own fate.

I believe that the question of altering our bodies through surgery is an individual decision that we must make, in consultation with our physicians and our loved ones, but ultimately our decision. As Riki Ann Wilchins writes: "You know, with transpeople, as opposed to any other medical

---

25. Raven Kaldera, "Do It on the Dotted Line," *Fireweed* 69 (spring 2000): 49.

intervention, we're forced to construct this entire narrative of legitimacy. To get surgery, you have to mount what I call an Insanity Defense: *I can't help myself, it's something deep inside me, I can't control it.* It's degrading. Getting medical intervention shouldn't require that; it should be a decision between a doctor and her patient."[26] The double bind of proving that we are sane enough to have surgery but crazy enough to need it is demeaning and ultimately unhelpful, placing gender transition squarely in the category of pathology rather than as a process of wholeness and transformation. Frankly, the necessity of this approach siphons energy needed for transition to a process of appeasing authority figures too much of the time. The authority and responsibility for transforming our bodies rests with us.

I knew that when I changed my body, I would feel more at home within myself. I had no idea, however, just how true that would be. I had not realized how difficult looking in a mirror had been until I became captivated by my own image. I did not know how truly uncomfortable I had been until I felt at ease within my body. I did not know the extent of the burden that I was carrying until I felt it lifted with a sense of joy and peace. That is the point of it all, is it not? We live our transgendered lives in many ways and seek a sense of congruity and peace to come from our lives, within our selves. Peace is possible; wholeness is what God wants for us and with us. Come home to yourself.

---

26. Wilchins, *Read My Lips*, 191–92.

Chapter Nine

Transgendered Theological Thought

The very existence of transgendered and intersexed people brings into question the binary categories that our society has created with such fervor. If transgendered persons, by our presence, break down binary thinking by inhabiting a middle place, then this disintegration of polemic categories affects the way we do theology as well. Theology is different if we apply to it a transgendered way of thinking. If we recognize and insist on the presence of things that transcend, encompass, or fail to fit the categories at all, then we approach seemingly opposite-looking things for that which binds them together or goes beyond them altogether. This process requires the thinker not to accept seemingly divergent points at face value and calls for a deeper and broader look at them.

When we begin to move away from oppositional categories, we see how two things that were once thought to be opposites can exist at the same time in a positive tension. For example, children need to have limits in their lives in order to grow into healthy, considerate people. At the same time, children also need the freedom to explore the world around them in order to learn and develop. Limits and freedom may appear to be opposites, but when we consider the case of a child (or an adult, for that matter), we realize that both, in balance, are critical for holistic maturation. In a number of categories, which I explore in this chapter, spiritual health is furthered by a view that embraces seeming opposites rather than claiming only one over another.

Unfortunately, religious groups can be all too hasty to present an either/or view of the world. Things are either good or evil, we hear Christian clerics proclaim. People will go to either heaven or hell. There is Jesus' way and the wrong way. In reality, however, good and evil, right and wrong are not always so easy to distinguish. We all face choices at times in our lives where the only options available to us call into question a principle that we may have. Some of Jesus' parables make it difficult to tell who was right and who was wrong. Was the persistent widow who wore down the judge right or wrong? Was the judge capitulating or merciful when he gave into her? What about the prodigal son's older brother, or the workers who worked all day for the same wage as those who came later? I believe that Jesus calls us to a more complex way of examining the world, a way that requires us to see things in a broader context. Jesus' faith and teaching was not about easy answers but about just ways of moving and living within a complicated world. The Jewish commentaries on the law and the prophets function in the same way. The point is not to know the only way of looking a text, but to tease out all of its possible meanings so that the reader has the richest available knowledge of how God spoke, and speaks, through that passage. Looking beyond binary thinking is a faithful way of viewing the world.

We understand, too, that a spectrum of being in the world fills in the space between the extremes. A middle ground can exist between seemingly oppositional ideas. Mediators work to help all involved parties find a solution that honors all sides. Although often difficult, discovering faithful positions between the poles and honoring the beliefs of different people is possible.

I want to conclude this book by exploring some of the polarities and middle spaces that open up when we are willing to see beyond binary thinking and see things in a trans-theological way. Sacred ground lies in the middle. Kim Lee Brown writes about an experience of the divine that came to her, as she sat in the time between night and day:

> Unexpectedly, that which I sought came to me. God spoke. Not in an audible voice, but powerful just the same. There is a place for darkness and a place for light, the mere existence of one does not destroy the other. Each complements the other and if you can look you can find beauty in both. However, it was the twilight which spoke so powerfully to me. It is this place in time when the birds can be heard singing, and it's the twilight where the resting flowers open their faces to greet the day. Suddenly, I realized that we are like the twilight, neither night nor day. We are that perfect mixture of each where the birds can sing and the flowers can open. This revelation is important to me because I have always tried to find my place in the world. I read all the writings about gender people in history and I felt better. But something was still missing. I am more than just a part of the gender community. I am part of the dawn. Without the dawn

there can be no morning. It takes all parts to make the day complete and it takes us, just as we are, to make humanity complete. We are indisputably a part of the greater humanity. And humanity has always sought its place and purpose in the universe. I now know that I am not accident. I have a place and a purpose. My problem is that I have always been in conflict with that purpose. I wanted to be the day and when I could not, I wanted to become the night. I was never content until I accepted myself as what God made me, a transsexual, neither night nor day, but a part of the dawn when the birds sing and the flowers open.[1]

The perspective of transgendered theology is necessary to move us toward completeness. This perspective offers an ongoing revelation that must be ever-expanding as we learn about God and the universe which God created. To know only day and night, without the dawn and dusk, is to miss the beauty of the ever-flowing cycles of time and movement.

Beyond Male and Female

Certainly the most obvious way that transgendered people break down categories is to call into question the essentialist understanding of what being male and female means. These humanly created boxes do not adequately describe the range of human physiology and behavior. Even transgendered people who believe strongly in a bigendered system show that we can at least cross the gender threshold that many people would call immutable, from one kind of body to another and from one social category to another. We can trace the journey from being identified as one gender to being seen as another. This act calls into question the absolute oppositional nature of masculinity and femininity.

This process is not limited to transgendered people; the dividing line between men and women is very different today than during my parents' and grandparents' childhoods. Lauren René Hotchkiss comments on this point, quoting from *A Course in Miracles* at the end:

We are now entering a changing age, a time when long venerated sex roles are being challenged. For the first time in recorded history we are afforded the rare opportunity to integrate our hitherto separate halves into a cohesive oneness; to explore, man and woman, the balancing of our male and female energy and to experience what has, up to now, been considered

---

1. Kim Lee Brown, "On Being Yourself," *http://members.aol.com/_ht_a/gnlnews/beingyourself.html*.

the exclusive domain of the "opposite" sex. Perhaps, for those of us who live a transgendered or androgynous existence, there is a reason why we were born as we were: to explore gender integration on both an outer and inner manifestational level. In the process of doing this, we learn to become true to who we are, more at peace with ourselves, and more able to be of service to others. "To heal or to make joyous is therefore the same as to integrate and to make one" (T 66/72).[2]

While some cultures have offered an avenue for people to integrate their masculine and feminine sides, this possibility has not been true until recently for our own culture and still is not comfortably accepted by all.

As transgendered people, we both face and give the challenge to integrate both female and male energies and selves into a coherent whole. Thinking of ourselves as the gender we want to be and rejecting all aspects of the gender we were assigned at birth can be easy. Seeing both within us is challenging and difficult, especially early in the process. But this perception can also be deeply rewarding as we expand our ways of thinking and being in the world. Rather than exchanging one category for another, we have the option of crafting another way — a way that truly reflects who and what we are. This individual path is one that God calls us to walk. To discern our true callings, we must look beyond the simple categories of male and female and see what our life is telling us about how we should live. We need to listen to our bodies, minds, and spirits. Integrating a masculine spirit with a female body or a feminine heart with a male body requires patience, imagination, love, and guts. Transgendered people do it all the time.

We know, too, what it means to have the opportunity to look at life through both male and female eyes. We have lived more than one way in the world. Experiencing life as both female and male gives us insight into our lives and into our world that we would not otherwise have had. Transgendered people can know this richness of experience. Even though I had paid close attention to gender issues all my life, I never really realized how many things were governed by gender in the world — who goes into elevators first, whose orders are taken first in restaurants, who gets help first from a sales clerk, who cedes the sidewalk space when there is only room for one — until I experienced all of these things from another

---

2. Lauren René Hotchkiss, "Is Transgenderism Wrong?" *http://members.tgforum.com/bobbyg/istranwrong.html*, 11/22/00.

vantage point. Learning these things helped me to see what is "me" and what is my gender in how I interact with the world and how others interact with me. I now have the option of making choices about how I live and move in the world that other people do not even consider because the information is so deeply ingrained in us that we do not even realize its full extent.

In the course of our lives, we can participate in communities of faith in more than one way, which is valuable because our religious practices and outlooks are often predicated on gender. We learn differently how to pray, what religious practices are acceptable, and what we are allowed to do within a religious service. The varied nature of our experience can increase our spiritual repertoire and allows us to learn more about our spiritual practices and about God because we are looking at these things from more than one vantage point. Given that we can only know the smallest fraction of the divine in the course of a human lifetime, increasing our knowledge of God by using all of the ways available to us may allow us to expand our access.

The Center and the Margins

Another binary category that falls apart is the concept of the center and the margins. A safe and obvious conclusion is that transgendered people, particularly those who are obviously or loudly trannies, live on the margins of our society. Transgendered people face rampant (and, in most places, legal) discrimination. A very small number of municipalities in the United States protect people based on their gender identities. Too many transwomen and transmen have been murdered for their differences. Gwendolyn Smith has put an entire web page, "Remembering Our Dead," on the Internet devoted entirely to those who were killed because of their different gender presentation.[3] Visibly gender-variant people are unwelcome in most places of worship and are a source of ridicule in the media. Many trans people have been thrown out of their own families and left to fend for themselves on the streets. As Riki Ann Wilchins writes:

> I hope . . . that there are those of us who remember that if that often absent
> and most unmentioned of queers — God herself — meant for us to learn

3. *www.gender.org/remember.*

anything from the journey through this particular kind of life, it is the experience of outsiderdom, and how the suppression of difference has the power to kill hearts and minds and even life.[4]

We know the experience of "outsiderdom" very well, as does our God. Throughout the sacred writings of the Jewish and Christian traditions, outsiders speak of God: the prophets who were maligned and threatened because of the words they spoke, Job the afflicted one, Mary who proclaimed that God would bring the mighty from their thrones and lift up the lowly, John the Baptist in the wilderness drawing the ire of the political establishment, Jesus hanging out with prostitutes and arousing the anger of the religious authorities and others.

We who live on the margins have learned that we can find the Holy One there. A sacred beauty is present at the margins, a kind of spiritual honesty that is not found in places of comfort and power. I see God at work in the transwoman who gets up in the morning and has the courage to go to work, gracefully ignoring the stares of co-workers. I see God in the lives of transmen and transwomen who pass and choose to speak out for our collective liberation, rather than simply melting into the crowd. I see the divine presence in every one who questions their gender and knows in their heart of hearts that they are different. I know that God was present with Brandon Teena and Tyra Hunter and all of the other martyrs. God is present with each tearful, defiant, proud, frightened, and hopeful one of us.

Too many religious institutions support the status quo and preach that the holy is found in the socially acceptable. Faith communities take social norms and conventions and declare that they are the gospel when that simply is not so. When churches, synagogues, and other groups take this approach, they substitute human standards for God's standards and thus lose part of the picture that God calls us to see. Discerning the divine pattern and plan for the universe becomes more difficult if it is obscured by the human desire for categories and neat, comfortable delineations. God does not follow our paths; rather, God exists in the places where the human heart strives for integrity and seeks God.

---

4 Riki Ann Wilchins, *Read My Lips: Sexual Subversion and the End of Gender* (Ithaca, N.Y.: Firebrand Books, 1997), 70.

In seeing God at the margins, we discover something else. We learn that wherever we are, we are at the center of the heart of God. God's center is where God's people are, particularly when we are in need of God, wherever that may be. When those of us at the margins seek God, then the margins are the place where the center can be found, and we are at the center of God's heart, and thus the world comes full circle. Margins and center occupy the same space, the same lives, the same hearts. The center of the universe of faith is wherever God is present, and God is at the margins.

Created and Creating

The Scriptures tell us that God was intimately and actively involved in our creation; Psalm 139 says God affirms that before we were formed in our mother's wombs, God knew us. God set the stars in orbit and evolution in motion, and we are a part of that same creative process. God formed us, body and spirit. At the same time, we learn that we have a responsibility for our own creation. Abraham Joshua Heschel was asked shortly before his death what word he would leave for youth. His reply, "Let them remember that there is a meaning beyond absurdity. Let them be sure that every deed counts, that every word has power, and that we all can do our share to redeem the world in spite of all absurdities and all frustrations and all disappointments. And, above all, remember . . . to build a life as if it were a work of art."[5]

We are called to be artisans of our own lives and bodies. We should take responsibility for our own continued creation, both the development of our inner selves and our outer bodies. As trans people, we should take seriously the task of creating for ourselves the lives to which we feel called and compelled. We are shape shifters, finding ways to move from one way of being to another; some of us do this over and over again while others change once. When we see this process as sacred, we can claim our places as artists cooperating with God in creating the developing, changing person that we are and that we are becoming.

Precisely this tension between being created and being a co-creator is expressed when we think about why and how we were created as we are.

---

5. Samuel H. Dresner, ed., *I Asked for Wonder: A Spiritual Anthology, Abraham Joshua Heschel* (New York: Crossroad, 1998), 63.

On one hand, the question is a mystery to me. I do not know precisely how or why I came to be a transgendered person. It feels to me like something that arose, unbidden, in my life. At the same time, my choice is to seek answers to this dilemma and not to back away from exploring fully the possibilities presented to me. The dilemma can be given to me by God, and still my responsibility is to bring it to fruition.

Dynamic and Constant Nature of God and Universe

One of the things we learn is that we remain the same person while changing and that the changes transform us into someone different. An essence in me is the same person that I was as a child, as a woman, and as a transman, yet I have changed in an infinite number of ways throughout that process. The changes that I have gone through — both through the processes of maturing, learning, and growing and changing gender — have continued to make me into something new. I am the same and I am different.

We can also see God through this lens. If the creation is made in the image of God, then the constantly changing nature of the universe, with its swirling atoms and continually dying and resurrecting forms, reflects God's changing nature. Yet, we know that God is constant and enduring, like the millions of eons that have passed since the creation of the universe. In an article in *Take Back the Word*,[6] I presented a view of Jesus as a changed and changing being who can therefore be a role model for me as I go through the changes of my life. This dynamic God is with me through the changes in my life and is the constant in the midst of them. At the same time, God is present in the stagnant parts of my life, calling me to change and grow.

Body and Spirit

As trans people, we learn that both body and spirit are integral to our identities. We are bodies, and we are not only bodies. We discover that our bodies do not completely define us. The information that our bodies

---

6. Justin Edward Tanis, "Eating the Crumbs That Fall from the Table: Trusting the Abundance of God," in *Take Back the Word: A Queer Reading of the Bible*, ed. Robert E. Goss and Mona West (Cleveland: Pilgrim Press, 2000).

convey about us is relevant, but it is not the only perspective. This information is not all there is to know. We learn, too, how important it is that our bodies tell the truth about who we are and that we need our bodies to be congruent with our identities. Precisely because we value our bodies, we need them to express — through our clothes or our physical form — what we know about ourselves. We love our bodies into new forms and new ways of moving in the world.

At the same time, we are spirits but more than spirits. Our spirits speak to us, often from a very early age, of a reality that is in defiance of what we are told about ourselves. Those spirits define how we see ourselves. The self that develops within us is independent of the body and simultaneously longs to be one with it. We cannot have one without the other and be whole, healthy, human beings. Being united in body and spirit is our goal and our strength.

Eternal and Finite

This life is the only life that we know, the only opportunity that we have to be happy and fulfilled on this earth, at least as far as we know. As people of faith, we know that we are part of something greater and that we will continue beyond this life. Both things are true simultaneously. As finite beings, we should take every advantage we can of the chances that we have to be happy and craft our lives in ways that are satisfying and whole for us. Deferring or ignoring the things that we need to have a fulfilling life wastes the precious time that we have on this earth.

Yet we are also part of a larger whole, part of a wider destiny. Our lives are bigger than just we ourselves, both because of the relationships which bind us to one another and to God and because we are part of a living earth. We have to live not just for ourselves but for those we love. What we know in this lifetime is not all that we will know. Our actions must take seriously the shortness and beauty of our lives and our part in the web of relationships that make up our world. That is our responsibility and our calling — to take action that honors all that we are, finite and infinite, body and soul, female and male. We will not, of course, always do so perfectly, but we do so humanly, seriously and joyfully, as transgendered people of faith.

Conclusion

An urgent need exists for our trans sisters and brothers to know of their spiritual worth. We need to know, deep inside ourselves at the core of our being, that we are holy and loved by God. We need to see that we were created this way by a loving Creator, who fashioned us carefully and joyfully, and called us out to discover the unique and wonderful gifts that the Creator placed within us. We need to leap into the unknown, confident that a loving God leaps with us.

Too many of our brothers and sisters spend sleepless nights worrying that they are going to hell for fulfilling the greatest dreams in their hearts. Too many have been told that God condemns and rejects them. Too many have felt that they must make a decision between their spirituality and their need to transition, and have walked away from either their religious practice or their dream of living as a fulfilled transgendered person. The time has come for us to stand up and put a stop to that. We know differently and our lives bear witness to that fact.

We need to do this for transgendered people so that we might live freely and fully, but we also need to take this stand for nontransgendered people. They need freedom from the strict gender policing of our society. They need to feel able to make radical changes in their lives simply because such change is the right thing for them to do. I am convinced that one reason that people become enraged by and frightened of us is because we have had the courage to change something fundamental about ourselves in order to become more fully realized human beings, more joyful people. That freedom and courage scares people, and push buttons for many, but that path is the road to liberation.

We need to speak our truth for the good of the religious and spiritual communities of which we are, or were, or wish to be, a part. Too many of them have become unquestioning supporters of the gender status quo and they need to be freed from those limitations. All of us need a place where we can go before God and before our community as our whole, authentic selves, worried about not whether we measure up to the folks in the pews beside us, but how we can bring about the promises of God in the world. The question of whether or not transgendered people are welcome in our communities of faith is not most important to me. We need to ask ourselves instead: How we can build lives that contribute to justice flowing down like the waters and mercy rolling over us like the waves of the sea? How can we change ourselves and our world so that people can make the best choices that they can in their lives as they feel called by God to make them? How do we become peaceful in our innermost selves so that we can help bring peace to our troubled planet?

These questions are important ones — not whether we can be transgendered and religious, not whether we are condemned or not, but how we can cooperate with God in our own hearts and in our world. We who have a unique perspective on the world can help everyone move past our gender fundamentalism, past the two restricting boxes of male and female, to see the beauty of diversity that God has created. I do not necessarily want a world in which there is no male or female; I am very happy as a man. But I do want a world in which I can make this choice without fear of rejection and violence. I want a world in which we are free to craft lives as holy and whole as we are capable of making them. And I want a faith community in which diversity is seen as a hallmark of God and fundamental to our understanding of God.

What I have learned about transgendered people, through my life experiences and through my research, is that we are a gritty, determined, lively, holy bunch. We who have changed our own lives and fulfilled our own dreams have much to offer a world in need of both transformation and greater dreams of its own.

Appendix

Liturgical Resources

Baptism

Reading and Response: Acts 8:25–39

Now after Peter and John had testified and spoken the word of the Sovereign, they returned to Jerusalem, proclaiming the good news to many villages of the Samaritans.

Then an angel of God said to Philip, "Get up and go toward the south to the road that goes down from Jerusalem to Gaza." (This is a wilderness road.) So he got up and went. Now there was an Ethiopian eunuch, a court official of the Candace, queen of the Ethiopians, in charge of her entire treasury. He had come to Jerusalem to worship and was returning home; seated in his chariot, he was reading the prophet Isaiah. Then the Spirit said to Philip, "Go over to this chariot and join it." So Philip ran up to it and heard him reading the prophet Isaiah. He asked, "Do you understand what you are reading?" He replied, "How can I, unless someone guides me?" And he invited Philip to get in and sit beside him. Now the passage of the scripture that he was reading was this:

> "Like a sheep he was led to the slaughter,
>   and like a lamb silent before its shearer,
>   so he does not open his mouth.
> In his humiliation justice was denied him.
>   Who can describe his generation?
>   For his life is taken away from the earth."

The eunuch asked Philip, "About whom, may I ask, does the prophet say this? About himself or about someone else?" Then Philip began to speak, and starting with this scripture, he proclaimed to him the good news about Jesus. As they were going along the road, they came to some water; and the eunuch said, "Look, here is water! What is to prevent me from being baptized?" He commanded the chariot to stop, and both of them, Philip and the eunuch, went down into the water, and Philip baptized him. When they came up out of the water, the Spirit of God snatched Philip away; the eunuch saw him no more, and went on his way rejoicing.

Minister:	How will you respond to the good news?
Candidate:	I hear God's call and ask for baptism.
Minister:	Baptism is a sign of the grace of God, given to those who desire to be unified with Christ and to participate in Christ's ministry of reconciliation. It is an outward and visible sign of the inner workings of the Spirit in the life of _____ . Jesus himself was baptized and calls us to baptize others.

Questions

Minister:	Do you renounce evil and all that calls you away from wholeness and life?
Candidate:	I do.
Minister:	Do you honor God, our Creator, who gives to you the gift of life and made you as you are?
Candidate:	I do.
Minister:	Do you trust in Christ who sets you free so that you may live abundantly?
Candidate:	I do.
Minister:	Do you seek the Spirit, our comforter and sustainer?
Candidate:	I do.
Minister:	Do all who witness this sacrament pledge to do all in your power to uphold and sustain _____ on her/his walk of faith?
People:	We do.

Blessing of the Water

In the beginning of time, O God, your Creating Spirit hovered over the waters, bringing forth every living thing. You declared that all the world and everything within it is good.

When your people were fleeing oppression and tyranny, you parted the waters that they might travel to a land of abundance and freedom. You called us to live faithfully.

You were born among us, from the waters of the womb, holy and human. You offer us the living water of your love and send us out to baptize others into your eternal life.

Bless this water, Loving God.
From it, may abundant and eternal life
Flow in _____
So that s/he may live in you.

Act of Baptism

_____ (name)
I baptize you
In the name of the Creator,
The Christ,
And the Holy Spirit.
Amen.
God is with you,

_____

Child of God,
Disciple of Christ.

Service of Renaming

Reading: Isaiah 56:1–5

Minister: Hear the promises and commandments of God:

Thus says our God: Maintain justice, and do what is right,
For soon my salvation will come,
and my deliverance be revealed.
Happy is the mortal who does this,
the one who holds it fast,
Who keeps the Sabbath, not profaning it,
And refrains from doing any evil.
Do not let the foreigner joined to God say,
"God will surely separate me from the people";
and do not let the eunuch say, "I am just a dry tree."
For thus says God:
To the eunuchs who keep my Sabbaths,

Who choose the things that please me
and hold fast my covenant,
I will give, in my house and within my walls,
A monument and a name better than sons and daughters;
I will give them an everlasting name that shall not be
cut off.

Minister: How do you respond to God's calling?

Candidate: I will seek God's presence in all things.

Declaration of Intent

Minister: We are here to affirm the name of _____.
This name symbolizes all that _____
Is and all that s/he is becoming, through the grace of God.

We honor the name given to her/him
By her/his parents
And acknowledge that the time has come to
Declare a new name.
This name is the culmination of a journey of discovery
And, at the same time, its beginning.

(to the congregation)
Will you do all in your power to assist _____
To maintain justice, to do what is right,
to honor God and hold fast to God's covenant?

Congregation: We will.

Minister: Will you honor _____
In name and in spirit as s/he continues on her/his path?

Congregation: We will.

Prayer of Blessing

Minister: Dynamic and holy God,
We remember how you changed the names of
Abraham and Sarah, as they set out to follow you.
We know that you changed the name of Jacob,
After a long night of wrestling with you.

> We now declare publicly and affirm
> the name you have bestowed upon _____:
>
> (*laying hands upon the head*)
>
> _____, receive the blessings of God,
> Creator, Christ, and Holy Spirit. Amen.
>
> Walk in the Spirit, this day and always,
> Knowing that God has made
> an everlasting covenant with you,
> That shall never be cut off.

Minister: Jesus said, "Rejoice that your names are written in heaven."

Congregation: Alleluia! Amen.

If this service is part of an order of worship, the following texts may be useful for a sermon or homily:

Texts

Genesis 32:24–30

Jacob was left alone; and a man wrestled with him until daybreak. When the man saw that he did not prevail against Jacob, he struck him on the hip socket; and Jacob's hip was put out of joint as he wrestled with him. Then he said, "Let me go, for the day is breaking." But Jacob said, "I will not let you go unless you bless me." So he said to Jacob, "What is your name?" And he said, "Jacob." Then the man said, "You shall no longer be called Jacob, but Israel, for you have striven with God and with humans, and have prevailed." Then Jacob asked him, "Please tell me your name." But he said, "Why is it that you ask my name?" And there he blessed him. So Jacob called the place Peniel, saying "For I have seen God face to face and yet my life is preserved."

Song of Solomon 1:2b–3

Your love is better than wine, your anointing oils are fragrant,
Your name is perfume poured out; therefore the maidens love you.

Isaiah 45:3–4

I will give you the treasures of darkness
And riches hidden in secret places,
So that you may know that it is I, the Sovereign,

The God of Israel, who call you by your name.
For the sake of my servant Jacob,
And Israel my chosen,
I call you by name,
I surname you.

Luke 10:20b

Rejoice that your names are written in heaven.

Becoming Joseph[1]

If there had been a ritual,
you would have had a right.
You could have pointed to the Bible page
hand-writing family history
and joining it to scripture. Here
the date when I was born, and christened:
1829. The preacher wrote the names
Father Son and Holy
Ghost and Lucy Ann in water
on my forehead, but only Lucy Ann
in black ink in the Bible. Honoring
the old names with new bodies:
further up the page the previous Lucy,
there from another branch the earlier Ann.
The biblical begats list strange half-lineages,
sometimes a man, sometimes
a woman, never the complete life
story in the verses. One name
seeds one name, not growing in a script
flowering of family tree but in the holy wandering
vine that explodes modestly into sweet
close fruit. Joseph dreams his way awake
and out of slavery, feeds others
by saving himself. Midway
down the blank page of the new book you are writing
is black ink, your hand
writing Joseph back into history, honoring
old body with new name, re-baptizing: So,
here is the date when, self-begotten,
Lucy Ann is become Joseph, emerging

---

1. Thomas Kelson Lewis, "Becoming Joseph," *Open Hands* 16, no. 1 (summer 2000).

into new air, taking the breath
that remembers all life before
as nearly drowning.

Nancy Nageroni speaking at 1994 Boston Pride[2]

Someone once asked me, "Are you really queer?" And I said, "Honey, I'm a transsexual. If that isn't queer, I don't know what is." And they asked me, "Are you REALLY proud to be Transgendered?" And I said, "Am I proud? You mean, am I proud to be uncovering the truth about gender? Am I proud to be exposing beliefs that are not true? Am I proud to have made peace with myself, and to be sharing it with others? Am I proud to be pursuing a life that keeps me growing? Am I proud to have found the courage to show my true nature? And am I proud to be associated with others like myself? You're damned right I'm proud." So to all those who still hide their true beauty, to those who care about where our society is heading, and especially those who fear for the welfare of their families, hear us today and take heart. Whatever your color, size, ability, beliefs, origin, language, income, gender, sexual orientation, or your special interest, join with us in cultivating pride and freedom of expression for everyone.

Prayer

Blesser of all things,
You created us in your likeness and in your image
And then pronounced us good.
We give you thanks for the gift of life itself
And for our uniqueness.
God of transformations,
You set us free
To change and grow,
You hold us close
In love and grace.
We rejoice in our transgendered lives,
Different, strong, dynamic and loved.
Amen.

---

2. Nancy Nageroni, "Price," *www.gendertalk.com/comment/pride.htm*, 3/19/01.

Bibliography

Albright, W. F., and C. S. Mann. *Matthew.* Anchor Bible. New York: Doubleday, 1971.

Aldredge-Clanton, Jann. *In Whose Image? God and Gender.* New York: Crossroad, 2001.

Allison, Becky. "Life in the Leper Colony." *http://members.aol.com/_ht_a/gnlnews/lepers.html,* 11/22/00.

Althaus-Reid, Marcella. *Indecent Theology: Theological Perversions in Sex, Gender and Politics.* London: Routledge, 2000.

Anderson, Jane. *Looking for Normal.* New York: Dramatists Play Service, 2002.

Beeler, Monique. "Transgendered and Ordained." *CLGS Outlook* 1, no. 2 (spring 2001).

Belenky, Mary Field, Blythe McVicker Clinchy, Nancy Rule Goldberger, and Jill Mattuck Tarule. *Women's Ways of Knowing: The Development of Self, Voice, and Mind.* New York: Basic Books, 1986.

"Beliefs That Can Kill." *http://transsexual.org/belief.html.*

Bishop, Clifford. *Sex and Spirit.* London: Duncan Baird Publishers, 1996.

Blue, Darin Issac. "Translations." *Fireweed* 69 (spring 2000): 9–15.

Bornstein, Kate. *My Gender Workbook: How to Become a Real Man, a Real Woman, the Real You or Something Else Entirely.* New York: Routledge, 1998.

Boswell, Holly. "The Spirit of Transgender." *www.homestead.com/transpirits/files/SpiritOfTG.html.*

———. "The Transgender Paradigm Shift Toward Free Expression." In *Current Concepts in Transgender Identity,* ed. Dallas Denny. New York: Garland, 1998.

Brown, Kim Lee. "On Being Yourself." *http://members.aol.com/_ht_a/gnlnews/beingyourself.html.*

Brown, Mildred L., and Chloe Ann Rounsley. *True Selves: Understanding Transsexualism — For Families, Friends, Coworkers, and Helping Professionals.* San Francisco: Jossey-Bass, 1996.

Bullough, Bonnie, Vern L. Bullough, and James Elias, eds. *Gender Blending.* Amherst, N.Y.: Prometheus Books, 1997.

Bullough, Vern L. "Transgenderism and the Concept of Gender." *International Journal of Transgenderism* 4, no. 3 (July–September 2000).

Burke, Phyllis. *Gender Shock: Exploding the Myths of Male and Female.* New York: Anchor Books, 1996.

Butler, Judith. *Bodies That Matter: On the Discursive Limits of "Sex."* New York: Routledge, 1993.

Cahill, Lisa Sowle. *Sex, Gender and Christian Ethics.* Cambridge: Cambridge University Press, 1998.

Cairns, Ian. *Deuteronomy: Word and Presence.* Grand Rapids, Mich.: William B. Eerdmans, 1992.

Califia, Patrick. *Sex Changes: The Politics of Transgenderism.* San Francisco: Cleis Press, 1997.

Cameron, Lorin. *Body Alchemy: Transsexual Portraits.* San Francisco: Cleis Press, 1996.

————."Can You Be Transgendered and Christian?" In Whosoever — An Online Magazine for GLBT Christians. *www.whosoever.org/v2issue2/index.html.*

Carbado, Devon W. *Black Men on Race, Gender and Sexuality.* New York: New York University Press, 1999.

Carmichael, Calum M. *The Laws of Deuteronomy.* Ithaca, N.Y.: Cornell University Press, 1974.

Comstock, Gary David. *A Whosoever Church: Welcoming Lesbians and Gay Men into African American Congregations.* Louisville: Westminster John Knox Press, 2001.

Conrad, Edgar W. *Reading Isaiah.* Minneapolis: Fortress Press, 1991.

Cook, Ann Thompson. "Made in God's Image: Re-Thinking Constructs of Gender and Orientation." *Open Hands* 14, no. 1 (summer 1998).

————. "Welcoming Transgendered Children." *Open Hands* (winter 2001).

Cousar, Charles B. *Galatians: Interpretation: A Bible Commentary for Teaching and Preaching.* Atlanta: John Knox Press, 1982.

Coventry, Martha. "Making the Cut." *Ms.* 10, no. 6 (October–November 2000).

Craigie, Peter C. *The Book of Deuteronomy.* Grand Rapids, Mich.: William B. Eerdmans, 1976.

Currah, Paisley, Shannon Mintner, and Jamison Green. *Transgender Equality: A Handbook for Activists and Policymakers.* San Francisco: National Center for Lesbian Rights and the Policy Institute of the National Gay and Lesbian Task Force, 2000.

Cymbala, Jim, with Dean Merrill. *Fresh Wind, Fresh Fire: What Happens When God's Spirit Invades the Heart of His People.* Grand Rapids, Mich.: Zondervan, 1997.

Darr, Katheryn Pfisterer. *Isaiah and the Family of God.* Louisville: Westminster John Knox Press, 1994.

Dee, Michelle. "Good News! Jesus Loves Us, T*oo!" *http://members.tripod.com/~ michelledee/jesustg.html*, 11/22/00.

———. "Jesus and Male and Female," *http://members.tripod.com/~michelledee/ jesustg.html*, 11/20/00.

Doan, Petra L. "The Spiritual Side of Gender Journeying." *Transgender Tapestry* 92 (winter 2000): 40–43.

Dougherty, Rose Mary. *Group Spiritual Direction: Community for Discernment.* New York: Paulist Press, 1995.

Dresner, Samuel H., ed. *I Asked for Wonder: A Spiritual Anthology, Abraham Joshua Heschel.* New York: Crossroad, 1998.

Driver, Samuel Rolles. *The International Critical Commentary on the Holy Scriptures of the Old and New Testaments.* New York: Charles Scribner's Sons, 1895.

Early, Tracy. "Greater Atlanta Presbytery Retains Member after Sex Change." *Ecumenical News International* (November 11, 1996).

Elkins, Richard, and Dave King. "Contributions to the Emerging Field of Transgender Studies." *International Journal of Transgenderism* 1, no. 1 (July– September 1997).

Evangelical Alliance Policy Commission. *Transsexuality.* Carlisle, Cumbria, U.K.: Paternoster, 2000.

Faith, Fellowship, and Order Commission (FFO), Metropolitan Community Church. *Report on Transgendered Persons and the Church,* 1990.

Fausto-Sterling, Anne. *Sexing the Body: Gender Politics and the Construction of Sexuality.* New York: Basic Books, 2000.

Feinberg, Leslie. *Transgender Warriors: Making History from Joan of Arc to Dennis Rodman.* Boston: Beacon Press, 1996.

———. *TransLiberation: Beyond Pink or Blue.* Boston: Beacon Press, 1998.

Fewell, Danna Nolan, and David M. Gunn. *Gender, Promise, and Power: The Subject of the Bible's First Story.* Nashville: Abingdon Press, 1993.

"First Trans Vicar," *www.moss-fritch.com/First_TransVicar.htm* 3/19/01.

Fitzmyer, Joseph A. *The Acts of the Apostles.* Anchor Bible. New York: Doubleday, 1998.

Fox, Everett. *In the Beginning: A New English Rendition of the Book of Genesis.* New York: Schocken Books, 1983.

Fulkerson, Mary McClintock. "Contesting the Gendered Subject: A Feminist Account of the Imago Dei." In *Horizons in Feminist Theology: Identity, Tradition and Norms,* ed. Rebecca S. Chopp and Sheila Greeve Davaney. Minneapolis: Fortress Press, 1997.

———. "Gender — Being It or Doing It? The Church, Homosexuality, and the Politics of Identity." In *Que(e)rying Religion: A Critical Anthology,* ed. Gary David Comstock and Susan E. Henking. New York: Continuum, 1997.

Gainor, Kathy A. "Including Transgender Issues in Lesbian, Gay, and Bisexual Psychology: Implications for Clinical Practice and Training." In *Education, Research and Practice in Lesbian, Gay, Bisexual, and Transgendered Psychology: A Resource Manual,* ed. Beverly Greene and Gladys L. Croom. Thousand Oaks, Calif.: Sage, 2000.

Goss, Robert E. *Queering Christ: Beyond Jesus Acted Up.* Cleveland: Pilgrim Press, 2002.

Goss, Robert E., and Amy Adams Squire Strongheart, eds. *Our Families, Our Values: Snapshots of Queer Kinship.* New York: Harrington Park Press, 1997.

Goss, Robert E., and Mona West, eds. *Take Back the Word: A Queer Reading of the Bible.* Cleveland: Pilgrim Press, 2000.

Gowan, Donald E. *Genesis 1–11: From Eden to Babel.* Grand Rapids, Mich.: William B. Eerdmans, 1988.

Graff, E. J. "Transpotting." *The American Prospect. www.prospect.org/print/V12/15/graff-e.html,* 8/17/01.

Gross, Sally. "Intersexuality and Scripture." *www.sonic.net/~cisae/IS_and_scripture.html,* 11/22/00.

Groves, Patricia A. "Learning from Our Daughter." *Open Hands* (winter 2001).

Guiness, Os. *The Call: Finding and Fulfilling the Central Purpose of Your Life.* Nashville: Word, 1998.

Hanson, Paul D. *Isaiah 40–66: Interpretation: A Bible Commentary for Teaching and Preaching.* Louisville: John Knox Press, 1995.

Harvey, Bob, and Joe Woodard. "Serving God After a Sex Change." *Calgary Herald,* March 3, 2001, Religion, p. OS10.

Hausman, Bernice. *Changing Sex: Transsexualism, Technology, and the Idea of Gender.* Durham: Duke University Press, 1995.

Heller, Lee Frances. "Grace and Lace." *http://members.aol.com/_ht_a/gnlnews/gracelace.html.*

Henkin, William. "Multiple Personality Order: An Alternate Paradigm for Understanding Cross-Gender Experience." In *Current Concepts in Transgender Identity,* ed. Dallas Denny. New York: Garland, 1998.

Herwig, Sàra J. "WOW-2K: LGBT People of Faith in Mainstream Christianity." *Transgender Tapestry* 92 (winter 2000): 37–39.

Horton, David. *Changing Channels? A Christian Response to the Transvestite and Transsexual.* Nottingham: Grove Books Limited, 1994.

Hotchkiss, Lauren René. "Is Transgenderism Wrong?" *http://members.tgforum.com/ bobbyg/istranwrong.html*, 11/22/00.

Hunt, Mary E. "GRACE — is a Transgender Person who Loves Women and Men." *The Witness* 84, no. 7/8 (July–August 2001).

International Bill of Gender Rights, International Conference on Transgender Law, 1995.

Israel, Gianna E., and Donald E. Tarver II, M.D., eds. *Transgender Care: Recommended Guidelines, Practical Information, and Personal Accounts.* Philadelphia: Temple University Press, 1997.

Jacobs, Sue-Ellen, Wesley Thomas, and Sabine Lang, eds. *Two-Spirit People: Native American Gender Identity, Sexuality and Spirituality.* Urbana: University of Illinois Press, 1997.

Johnson, Toby. *Gay Spirituality: The Role of Gay Identity in the Transformation of Human Consciousness.* Los Angeles: Alyson Books, 2000.

Johnston, Sal. "My TG Self." *Fireweed* 69 (spring 2000): 63–69.

Kaldera, Raven. "Do It on the Dotted Line." *Fireweed* 69 (spring 2000): 46–50.

Kellogg, Elisabeth Anne. "Transsexualism from the Perspective of the Biblical Eunuch and the Barren Woman." *http://members.tgforum.com/bobbyg/eunuch .html.*

Kessler, Suzanne, and Wendy McKenna. *Gender: An Ethnomethodological Approach.* Chicago: University of Chicago Press, 1978.

———. "Who Put the 'Trans' in Transgender: Gender Theory and Everyday Life." *The International Journal of Transgenderism* 4, no. 3 (July–September 2000).

Kolakowski, Victoria S. "Towards a Christian Ethical Response to Transsexual Persons." *Theology and Sexuality* 6 (March 1997): 10–31.

Kolodny, Debra R. *Blessed Bi Spirit: Bisexual People of Faith.* New York: Continuum, 2000.

Lake, Catherine. *ReCreations: Religion and Spirituality in the Lives of Queer People.* Toronto: Queer Press, 1999.

Levoy, Gregg. *Callings: Finding and Following an Authentic Life.* New York: Three Rivers Press, 1997.

Lewis, Thomas Kelson. "Becoming Joseph." *Open Hands* 16, no. 1 (summer 2000).

Licata, Salvatore J., and Robert P. Peterson, eds. *The Gay Past: A Collection of Historical Essays.* New York: Harrington Park Press, 1985.

Lombardi, Emilia L., and Gwen van Servellen. "Building Culturally Sensitive Substance Abuse Prevention and Treatment Programs for Transgendered Populations." UCLA Drug Abuse Research Center.

MacDonald, Diane L. Prosser. *Transgressive Corporeality: The Body, Poststructuralism and the Theological Imagination.* New York: State University of New York Press, 1995.

Main, Terri Lynn. "Gender Dysphoria and the Bible." *http://members.tripod.com/~terrim/BIBLE/htm,* 11/00.

Mallon, Gerald P. *Social Services with Transgendered Youth.* New York: Harrington Park Press, 1999.

Mann, C. S. *Mark.* Anchor Bible. New York: Doubleday, 1986.

Martyn, J. Louis. *Galatians.* Anchor Bible. New York: Doubleday, 1997.

McRae, Marie. "There Isn't a Term for Me Yet: Partner of FtM Discusses Identity Issues." *Sojourners: The Women's Forum* 26, no. 3 (November 2000).

Methany, Rachel. "That They May Be One: Rejecting Binary Categories to Be Whole and Holy." *Open Hands* 15, no. 2 (fall 1999).

Miller, Patrick D. *Deuteronomy: Interpretation: A Bible Commentary for Teaching and Preaching.* Louisville: John Knox Press, 1990.

Mollenkott, Virginia Ramey. "Gender Diversity and Christian Community." *The Other Side* 37, no. 3 (May and June 2001).

———. *Omnigender: A Trans-Religious Approach.* Cleveland: Pilgrim Press, 2001.

Monroe, Irene. "Remembering Rita Hester: The 'T' in LGBT." *Open Hands* 15, no. 2 (fall 1999).

Namaste, Viviane K. *Invisible Lives: The Erasure of Transsexual and Transgendered People.* Chicago: University of Chicago Press, 2000.

Nangeroni, Nancy. "Pride." *www.gendertalk.com/comment/pride.htm,* 3/19/01.

National Gay Pentecostal Alliance. *www.ameritech.net/users/lighthse84/ngpa_4k .html,* 3/5/01.

Nelson, James B. *Body Theology.* Louisville: Westminster/John Knox Press, 1992.

Newell, J. Philip. *Echo of the Soul: The Sacredness of the Human Body.* Harrisburg, Pa.: Morehouse, 2000.

Neyrey, Jerome H. *Honor and Shame in the Gospel of Matthew.* Louisville: Westminster John Knox Press, 1998.

Ochs, Carol. *Song of the Self: Biblical Spirituality and Human Holiness.* Valley Forge, Pa.: Trinity Press International, 1994.

O'Donovan, Oliver. *Begotten or Made?* Oxford: Clarendon Press, 1984.

———. "Transsexualism and Christian Marriage." *Journal of Religious Ethics* 11 (spring 1983): 135–62.

Paige, Chris. "OtherWise." *The Other Side* 37, no. 3 (May and June 2001).

Palmer, Parker. *Let Your Life Speak: Listening for the Voice of Vocation.* San Francisco: Jossey-Bass, 2000.

Patterson, Stephen J. *The Gospel of Thomas and Jesus.* Sonoma, Calif.: Polebridge Press, 1993.

Pedersen, Daniel. "Can a Transsexual Minister Retain Her Ordination?" *Newsweek,* November 4, 1996, 66.

Penn, Su. "A Lover's Leap of Faith: Plenary Speech at the Friends (Quakers) for Lesbian and Gay Concerns Midwinter Gathering, February 1999." *http://my .voyager.net/supenn/flgc-speech.html,* 11/21/00.

PlanetOut. *www.moss-fritch.com/First_TransVicar.htm,* 3/19/01.

Prokes, Mary Timothy. *Toward a Theology of the Body.* Grand Rapids, Mich.: William B. Eerdmans, 1996.

Queen, Carol, and Lawrence Schimel, eds. *PoMoSexuals: Challenging Assumptions About Gender and Sexuality.* San Francisco: Cleis Press, 1997.

"Religion and Transsexuals." *www.moss-fritch.com/religion.htm.*

Reviere, Jayc E. "Ethics and Crossdressing." *http://members.aol.com/_ht_a/gnlnews/ ethics.html,* 11/22/00.

Reyburn, William D., and Euan McG. Fry. *A Handbook on Genesis.* New York: United Bible Societies, 1997.

Riley, Gregory J. *Resurrection Reconsidered: Thomas and John in Controversy.* Minneapolis: Fortress Press, 1995.

Robertson, Pat. Transcript from the *700 Club* broadcast, October 5, 1999.

Rolles, Samuel. *The International Critical Commentary on the Holy Scriptures of the Old and New Testaments.* New York: Charles Scribner's Sons, 1895.

Roscoe, Will, ed. *Changing Ones: Third and Fourth Genders in Native North America.* New York: St. Martin's Press, 1998.

———. *The Zuni Man-Woman.* Albuquerque: University of New Mexico Press, 1991.

Rottnek, Matthew, ed. *Sissies and Tomboys: Gender Nonconformity and Homosexual Childhood.* New York: New York University Press, 1999.

Rudy, Kathy. *Sex and the Church: Gender, Homosexuality, and the Transformation of Christian Ethics.* Boston: Beacon Press, 1997.

"Ruling on Sex Change and Ordination." *Christian Century* 113 (November 20–27, 1996): 1140.

Salah, Trish. "Ghazals for Sharon Cohen (Dana International)." *Fireweed* 69 (spring 2000): 70–71.

Sarda, Alejandra. "Trans Sexual Lessons." *Anything That Moves* 17 (summer 1998).

Sarna, Nahum M. *The JPS Torah Commentary: Genesis.* Philadelphia: Jewish Publication Society, 1989.

Schauer, Galen M. "On Becoming the Man I Am." *Fireweed* 69 (spring 2000): 72.

Shanor, Robyn. "Finding Common Ground." *The Other Side* 37, no. 3 (May and June 2001).

Sheridan, Vanessa. *Crossing Over: Liberating the Transgendered Christian.* Cleveland: Pilgrim Press, 2001.

———. "Happily Christian, Openly Transgendered and — A Seminary Student???" *www.whosoever.org/v2issue2/Sheridan.html,* 8/25/99.

———. "Transgendered Christians, Gays, and Our Common Bond." Available online at *www.whosoever.org/v2Issue2/Shanor.html.*

Sinetar, Marsha. *Holy Work.* New York: Crossroad, 1998.

Spargo, Tamsin. *Foucault and Queer Theory.* Duxford, New York: Totem Books, 1999.

Speiser, E. A. *Genesis.* Anchor Bible. New York: Doubleday, 1964.

Spencer, F. Scott. *Acts.* Sheffield: Sheffield Academic Press, 1997.

Stabel, Carol. "From a Chapter on the ELCA Today — Transdenomination to Transgender." *www.whosoever.org/v2Issue2/elca.html,* 9/25/99.

Starchild. "A Transsexual Theology." *www.whosoever.org/v2Issue2/starchild.html,* 5/14/01.

Stephens, Christiann. "Love, Not Gender." *http://members.aol.com/_ht_a/gnlnews/lovenotgender.html,* 11/22/00.

Swenson, Erin. "Body and Soul United." *The Other Side* 37, no. 3 (May and June 2001).

———. "Christianity and Transgender" *www.erinswen.com/spiritua.htm,* 4/26/01.

———, ed. "Materials on the Ordination Case of Erin K. Swenson and the Presbytery of Greater Atlanta, Presbyterian Church, USA. 1995–1997."

Taste This (Anna Camilleri, Ivan E. Coyote, Zoë Eakle, and Lyndell Montgomery). *Boys Like Her: Transfictions,* with a foreword by Kate Bornstein. Vancouver: Press Gang Publishers, 1998.

Thatcher, Adrian, and Elizabeth Stuart, eds. *Christian Perspectives on Sexuality and Gender.* Grand Rapids, Mich.: William B. Eerdmans, 1996.

Thurman, Howard. *Jesus and the Disinherited.* Boston: Beacon Press, 1976.

Tigay, Jeffrey H. *The JPS Torah Commentary: Deuteronomy.* Philadelphia: Jewish Publication Society, 1996.

Tigert, Leanne McCall, and Timothy J. Brown. *Coming Out Young and Faithful.* Cleveland: Pilgrim Press, 2001.

Transgender Network of Parents, Families and Friends of Lesbians and Gays (PFLAG). *Our Trans Children.* 3d ed. February 2001.

Trilling, Wolfgang. *The Gospel According to St. Matthew.* New York: Herder and Herder, 1969.

United Church of Christ. *Human Sexuality: A Preliminary Study.* New York: United Church Press, 1977.

Valantasis, Richard. *The Gospel of Thomas.* London: Routledge, 1997.

Valerio, Max Wolf. "The Joker Is Wild: Changing Sex and Other Crimes of Passion." *Anything That Moves* 17 (summer 1998).

Viefhues, Ludger H. "Troubling the Waters of Gender Expectations: Religious and Queer Vocations." *Open Hands* (summer 1999).

Villón, Kyrsia Lycette. "Something Like a Bisexual." *Fireweed* 69 (spring 2000): 29–32.

Walaskay, Paul W. *Acts.* Louisville: Westminster John Knox Press, 1998.

Webster, Danielle E. "Dealing with Deuteronomy." *Transgender Tapestry* 92 (winter 2000): 30–36.

Weeks, Jeffrey. *Sexuality and Its Discontents: Meanings, Myths and Modern Sexualities.* London: Routledge & Kegan Paul, 1985.

Weinstein, Natalie. "A Jewish Dress Code." *http://members.tgforum.com/bobbyg/code.html.*

Wilchins, Riki Ann. *Read My Lips: Sexual Subversion and the End of Gender.* Ithaca, N.Y.: Firebrand Books, 1997.

Wiley, Cody. "I'm a Tomboy Who Grew into a Transman." *Sojourner: The Women's Forum* 26, no. 3 (November 2000).

Williams, Michael E. *Storyteller's Companion to the Bible,* vol. 1, *Genesis.* Nashville: Abingdon Press, 1991.

———. *Storyteller's Companion to the Bible,* vol. 7, *Prophets II.* Nashville: Abingdon Press, 1991.

Williams, Rowen. "The Body's Grace." In *Ourselves, Our Souls and Bodies,* ed. Charles Hefling. Cambridge, Mass.: Cowley Publications, 1996.

Williams, Sam K. *Galatians.* Nashville: Abingdon Press, 1997.

Index

Communities of Faith, 66, 73, 79, 80,
    84–128, 141, 144, 156, 158, 180,
    181, 185, 186
Compton, Phil, 136
Congruity, 47, 133–34, 163, 169, 170,
    175
Counseling, 20
Course in Miracles, 49, 178–79
Coventry, Marsha, 10
Coyote, Ivan E., 30–32
Creation, 53, 55–62, 65, 80, 105, 138,
    143, 149, 150, 158, 159, 164, 166,
    167, 170, 172, 173, 182
Cromwell, Jason, 14
Cross-dressers, 17, 22, 38, 46, 63–66,
    74, 84, 86, 89, 110, 111, 118,
    121–23, 130, 139, 144, 149
*Crossing Over: Liberating the Trans-
    gendered Christian* (Sheridan),
    11
Cults, 64
Culture, 13, 146

Daddy, 23
Dakota (Native American), 15
Death, 68, 142, 143, 149, 169, 173,
    184
Deception, 48, 98. *See also* Truth
Dee, Michelle, 50, 74, 139–40
Denial, 24, 37–44, 49, 53
Depression, 32, 34, 39–41, 99, 103
Deuteronomy, 62–69, 74, 77, 84,
    94–96, 139
Devlin, Jade, 130
Dinno, Alexis Belinda, 35
Discrimination, 44, 180, 186
Doan, Petra, 49, 130
Drag, 22, 116
    drag king, 22, 110
    drag queen, 22, 75, 89, 110
Drug Abuse. *See* Substance abuse

Effeminate boys, 23, 33, 36, 39, 117
Elkins, Richard, 17
E-mail. *See* Internet

Employment, 9, 35, 38, 40, 44, 51, 99,
    117, 140, 181
Eunuchs, 69–70, 72–79, 84, 93, 96,
    100
Evangelical Alliance of Great Britain,
    95–102, 105, 109, 143
Eve, 55, 57
Ex-Gay movement, 89
Exodus, 32

Families, 26–30, 33, 34, 38, 41–42, 44,
    62, 105, 109–10, 118, 128, 131,
    155, 158, 168, 172, 180
Fausto-Sterling, Anne, 13
Feinberg, Leslie, 13, 14, 172
Fellowship of the Spiral Path, 131
Female-to-male (FTM), 14, 20, 21,
    38, 40, 42, 52, 90, 119, 125, 171,
    173, 174
Female impersonator, 22
Femininity, 13, 49, 66, 81, 117, 136,
    138, 144, 153, 162, 172, 178, 179
Feminist theology, 80
First Corinthians, 81, 104
Fulkerson, Mary McClintock, 81–82,
    102

Gainor, Kathy, 14, 20, 41
Galatians, 80–83, 142
Gay, lesbian, bisexual, and transgender
    (GLBT) communities, 8, 23, 38,
    112, 113, 120
Gay men, 9, 14, 22–24, 68, 70, 87, 89,
    102, 111, 112, 117, 121, 172
Gay Pride, 48, 102, 193
Gender bender, 22, 119
Gender blenders, 17
Gender dysphoria, 19, 20, 24, 27, 35,
    38, 41, 45, 96, 99, 105, 156, 158,
    174
Gender identity, 23, 35, 45, 87, 103,
    105, 107, 117–19, 121, 124, 149,
    157, 162
Gender outlaws, 17
Gender-queer, 16